Safety Symbols

These symbols appear in laboratory activities. They warn of possible dangers in the laboratory and remind you to work carefully.

 Safety Goggles Wear safety goggles to protect your eyes in any activity involving chemicals, flames or heating, or glassware.

 Lab Apron Wear a laboratory apron to protect your skin and clothing from damage.

 Breakage Handle breakable materials, such as glassware, with care. Do not touch broken glassware.

 Heat-Resistant Gloves Use an oven mitt or other hand protection when handling hot materials such as hot plates or hot glassware.

 Plastic Gloves Wear disposable plastic gloves when working with harmful chemicals and organisms. Keep your hands away from your face, and dispose of the gloves according to your teacher's instructions.

 Heating Use a clamp or tongs to pick up hot glassware. Do not touch hot objects with your bare hands.

 Flames Before you work with flames, tie back loose hair and clothing. Follow instructions from your teacher about lighting and extinguishing flames.

 No Flames When using flammable materials, make sure there are no flames, sparks, or other exposed heat sources present.

 Corrosive Chemical Avoid getting acid or other corrosive chemicals on your skin or clothing or in your eyes. Do not inhale the vapors. Wash your hands after the activity.

 Poison Do not let any poisonous chemical come into contact with your skin, and do not inhale its vapors. Wash your hands when you are finished with the activity.

 Fumes Work in a ventilated area when harmful vapors may be involved. Avoid inhaling vapors directly. Only test an odor when directed to do so by your teacher, and use a wafting motion to direct the vapor toward your nose.

 Sharp Object Scissors, scalpels, knives, needles, pins, and tacks can cut your skin. Always direct a sharp edge or point away from yourself and others.

 Animal Safety Treat live or preserved animals or animal parts with care to avoid harming the animals or yourself. Wash your hands when you are finished with the activity.

 Plant Safety Handle plants only as directed by your teacher. If you are allergic to certain plants, tell your teacher; do not do an activity involving those plants. Avoid touching harmful plants such as poison ivy. Wash your hands when you are finished with the activity.

 Electric Shock To avoid electric shock, never use electrical equipment around water, or when the equipment is wet or your hands are wet. Be sure cords are untangled and cannot trip anyone. Unplug equipment not in use.

 Physical Safety When an experiment involves physical activity, avoid injuring yourself or others. Alert your teacher if there is any reason you should not participate.

 Disposal Dispose of chemicals and other laboratory materials safely. Follow the instructions from your teacher.

 Hand Washing Wash your hands thoroughly when finished with the activity. Use soap and warm water. Rinse well.

 General Safety Awareness When this symbol appears, follow the instructions provided. When you are asked to develop your own procedure in a lab, have your teacher approve your plan before you go further.

Animals

PRENTICE HALL Science Explorer

Taken from:

Prentice Hall Science Explorer:
Animals
by Michael J. Padilla, Ph.D.,
Ioannis Miaoulis, Ph.D., and Martha Cyr, Ph.D.

CALVERT
EDUCATION

Animals

Book-Specific Resources

Student Edition
StudentExpress™ with Interactive Textbook
Teacher's Edition
All-in-One Teaching Resources
Color Transparencies
Guided Reading and Study Workbook
Student Edition on Audio CD
Discovery Channel School® Video
Lab Activity Video
Consumable and Nonconsumable Materials Kits

Program Print Resources

Integrated Science Laboratory Manual
Computer Microscope Lab Manual
Inquiry Skills Activity Books
Progress Monitoring Assessments
Test Preparation Workbook
Test-Taking Tips With Transparencies
Teacher's ELL Handbook
Reading Strategies for Science Content

Differentiated Instruction Resources

Adapted Reading and Study Workbook
Adapted Tests
Differentiated Instruction Guide for Labs and Activities

Program Technology Resources

TeacherExpress™ CD-ROM
Interactive Textbooks Online
PresentationExpress™ CD-ROM
ExamView®, Computer Test Bank CD-ROM
Lab zone™ Easy Planner CD-ROM
Probeware Lab Manual With CD-ROM
Computer Microscope and Lab Manual
Materials Ordering CD-ROM
Discovery Channel School® DVD Library
Lab Activity DVD Library
Web Site at PHSchool.com

Spanish Print Resources

Spanish Student Edition
Spanish Guided Reading and Study Workbook
Spanish Teaching Guide With Tests

Acknowledgments appear on page 214, which constitutes an extension of this copyright page.

Cover Art: Top image courtesy of Art Wolfe/Getty Images; bottom image courtesy of Dale Wilson/Masterfile.

Taken from:

Prentice Hall Science Explorer: Animals
by Michael J. Padilla, Ph.D., Ioannis Miaoulis, Ph.D., and Martha Cyr, Ph.D.
Copyright © 2007 by Pearson Education, Inc.
Published by Prentice Hall
Upper Saddle River, New Jersey 07458

Pearson Learning Solutions, 501 Boylston Street, Suite 900, Boston, MA 02116
A Pearson Education Company
www.pearsoned.com

Printed in the United States of America

5 6 7 8 9 10 V0ZN 15 14

000200010270598625

CP

Kenya, Africa (top) and mother and calf (bottom)

ISBN 10: 0-558-86807-X
ISBN 13: 978-0-558-86807-9

Program Authors

Michael J. Padilla, Ph.D.
Professor of Science Education
University of Georgia
Athens, Georgia

Michael Padilla is a leader in middle school science education. He has served as an author and elected officer for the National Science Teachers Association and as a writer of the National Science Education Standards. As lead author of Science Explorer, Mike has inspired the team in developing a program that meets the needs of middle grades students, promotes science inquiry, and is aligned with the National Science Education Standards.

Ioannis Miaoulis, Ph.D.
President
Museum of Science
Boston, Massachusetts

Originally trained as a mechanical engineer, Ioannis Miaoulis is in the forefront of the national movement to increase technological literacy. As dean of the Tufts University School of Engineering, Dr. Miaoulis spearheaded the introduction of engineering into the Massachusetts curriculum. Currently he is working with school systems across the country to engage students in engineering activities and to foster discussions on the impact of science and technology on society.

Martha Cyr, Ph.D.
Director of K–12 Outreach
Worcester Polytechnic Institute
Worcester, Massachusetts

Martha Cyr is a noted expert in engineering outreach. She has over nine years of experience with programs and activities that emphasize the use of engineering principles, through hands-on projects, to excite and motivate students and teachers of mathematics and science in grades K–12. Her goal is to stimulate a continued interest in science and mathematics through engineering.

Book Author

Jan Jenner, Ph.D.
Science Writer
Talladega, Alabama

Contributing Writers

Fred Holtzclaw
Science Instructor
Oak Ridge High School
Oak Ridge, Tennessee

Theresa K. Holtzclaw
Former Science Instructor
Clinton, Tennessee

Evan P. Silberstein
Science Instructor
The Frisch School
Paramus, New Jersey

Consultants

Reading Consultant

Nancy Romance, Ph.D.
Professor of Science
Education
Florida Atlantic University
Fort Lauderdale, Florida

Mathematics Consultant

William Tate, Ph.D.
Professor of Education and
Applied Statistics and
Computation
Washington University
St. Louis, Missouri

Reviewers

Teacher Reviewers

David R. Blakely
Arlington High School
Arlington, Massachusetts

Jane E. Callery
Two Rivers Magnet Middle
School
East Hartford, Connecticut

Melissa Lynn Cook
Oakland Mills High School
Columbia, Maryland

James Fattic
Southside Middle School
Anderson, Indiana

Dan Gabel
Hoover Middle School
Rockville, Maryland

Wayne Goates
Eisenhower Middle School
Goddard, Kansas

Katherine Bobay Graser
Mint Hill Middle School
Charlotte, North Carolina

Darcy Hampton
Deal Junior High School
Washington, D.C.

Karen Kelly
Pierce Middle School
Waterford, Michigan

David Kelso
Manchester High School Central
Manchester, New Hampshire

Benigno Lopez, Jr.
Sleepy Hill Middle School
Lakeland, Florida

Angie L. Matamoros, Ph.D.
ALM Consulting, INC.
Weston, Florida

Tim McCollum
Charleston Middle School
Charleston, Illinois

Bruce A. Mellin
Brooks School
North Andover, Massachusetts

Ella Jay Parfitt
Southeast Middle School
Baltimore, Maryland

Evelyn A. Pizzarello
Louis M. Klein Middle School
Harrison, New York

Kathleen M. Poe
Fletcher Middle School
Jacksonville, Florida

Shirley Rose
Lewis and Clark Middle School
Tulsa, Oklahoma

Linda Sandersen
Greenfield Middle School
Greenfield, Wisconsin

Mary E. Solan
Southwest Middle School
Charlotte, North Carolina

Mary Stewart
University of Tulsa
Tulsa, Oklahoma

Paul Swenson
Billings West High School
Billings, Montana

Thomas Vaughn
Arlington High School
Arlington, Massachusetts

Susan C. Zibell
Central Elementary
Simsbury, Connecticut

Safety Reviewers

W. H. Breazeale, Ph.D.
Department of Chemistry
College of Charleston
Charleston, South Carolina

Ruth Hathaway, Ph.D.
Hathaway Consulting
Cape Girardeau, Missouri

Douglas Mandt, M.S.
Science Education Consultant
Edgewood, Washington

Activity Field Testers

Nicki Bibbo
Witchcraft Heights School
Salem, Massachusetts

Rose-Marie Botting
Broward County Schools
Fort Lauderdale, Florida

Colleen Campos
Laredo Middle School
Aurora, Colorado

Elizabeth Chait
W. L. Chenery Middle School
Belmont, Massachusetts

Holly Estes
Hale Middle School
Stow, Massachusetts

Laura Hapgood
Plymouth Community
Intermediate School
Plymouth, Massachusetts

Mary F. Lavin
Plymouth Community
Intermediate School
Plymouth, Massachusetts

James MacNeil, Ph.D.
Cambridge, Massachusetts

Lauren Magruder
St. Michael's Country
Day School
Newport, Rhode Island

Jeanne Maurand
Austin Preparatory School
Reading, Massachusetts

Joanne Jackson-Pelletier
Winman Junior High School
Warwick, Rhode Island

Warren Phillips
Plymouth Public Schools
Plymouth, Massachusetts

Carol Pirtle
Hale Middle School
Stow, Massachusetts

Kathleen M. Poe
Fletcher Middle School
Jacksonville, Florida

Cynthia B. Pope
Norfolk Public Schools
Norfolk, Virginia

Anne Scammell
Geneva Middle School
Geneva, New York

Karen Riley Sievers
Callanan Middle School
Des Moines, Iowa

David M. Smith
Eyer Middle School
Allentown, Pennsylvania

Gene Vitale
Parkland School
McHenry, Illinois

Contents

Animals

Discovery
CHANNEL
SCHOOL
VIDEO
Sponges,
Cnidarians,
and Worms

Discovery
CHANNEL
SCHOOL
VIDEO
Mollusks,
Arthropods, and
Echinoderms

Discovery
CHANNEL
SCHOOL
VIDEO
Fishes,
Amphibians,
and Reptiles

Discovery
CHANNEL
SCHOOL
VIDEO
Birds and
Mammals

Discovery
CHANNEL
SCHOOL
VIDEO
Animal
Behavior

Reference Section

Enhance understanding through dynamic video.

Preview Get motivated with this introduction to the chapter content.

Field Trip Explore a real-world story related to the chapter content.

Assessment Review content and take an assessment.

Get connected to exciting Web resources in every lesson.

SCiLINKS™ Find Web links on topics relating to every section.

Active Art Interact with selected visuals from every chapter online.

Planet Diary® Explore news and natural phenomena through weekly reports.

Science News® Keep up to date with the latest science discoveries.

Experience the complete textbook online and on CD-ROM.

Activities Practice skills and learn content.

Videos Explore content and learn important lab skills.

Audio Support Hear key terms spoken and defined.

Self-Assessment Use instant feedback to help you track your progress.

Activities

Labs — In-depth practice of inquiry skills and science concepts

At-Home Activity — Quick, engaging activities for home and family

Tech & Design — Design, build, test, and communicate

Math — Point-of-use math practice

active art — Illustrations come alive online

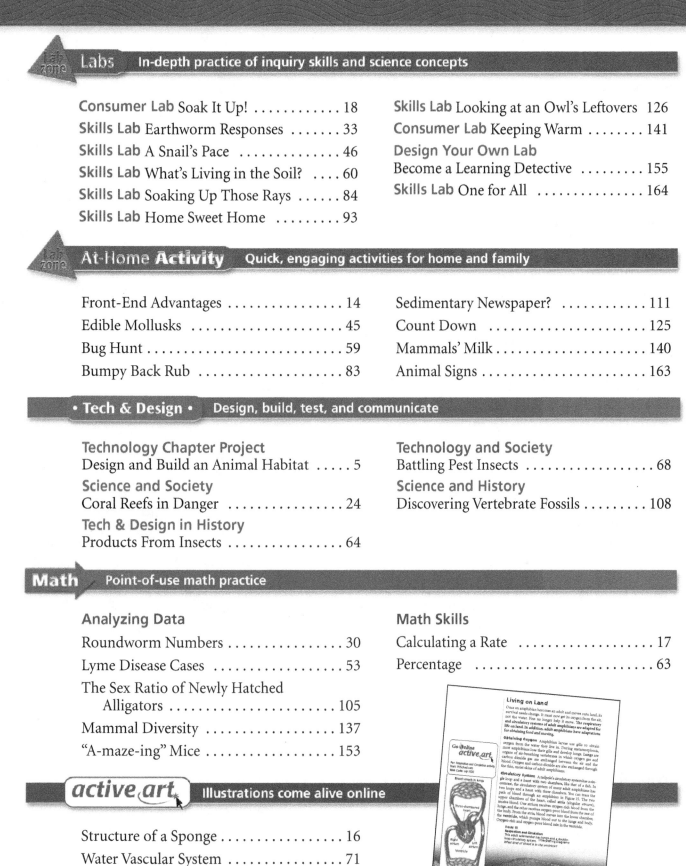

An Alligator's Sensitive Side

The first time biologist Daphne Soares got really close to an adult alligator was in a Louisiana swamp. She was bouncing around in the back of a pickup truck, helping to hold down an eight-foot American alligator. She was with a team of scientists doing fieldwork to learn how to protect alligators and their habitat. At the time, she was more curious than frightened.

"I was so interested in how alligators interact with the world around them," she remembers. "Why do these animals float half in and half out of the water? When I stick a branch in the water, why do they come toward it?" she wondered.

Daphne studies how the structure of an animal's nervous system influences its behavior and helps it survive. "When I got very close to the alligator in the back of that truck, I saw that its face was covered with little black dots. I thought, 'I wonder what those dots are.'" That simple question led her to make a surprising new discovery about why alligators are such good hunters.

Daphne in her lab

Career Path

Daphne Soares was born in Brazil. She received a Ph.D. in biology from the University of Maryland. Her investigation of the sensory dots of alligators began while she was still a university student. Currently, she holds a research position at the University of Maryland. Her plans for the future include becoming a university professor and doing more research on crocodilians.

Talking With
Dr. Daphne Soares

Daphne's study of the brains of barn owls led to her study of crocodilians, the closest living relatives of owls and other birds.

? How did you get interested in science?

I grew up on a horse farm in Brazil. Living on the farm made me curious about how animals interact with their environment. Later, while attending university in the United States, I became interested in the nervous systems of animals. One of the first animals I studied was the barn owl. These birds can hear so well they can locate a mouse in the dark, just by listening. I wanted to know how barn owls developed such a fine sense of hearing.

? What led you to study alligators?

I wanted to compare the brains of owls and other birds to the brains of their closest living relatives, a group of reptiles called crocodilians. The crocodilians include alligators and crocodiles. By comparing the nervous systems of birds and crocodilians, you can look for things they have in common. This can tell you what is most important in the development of sensory systems like hearing, vision, or touch.

? How did you begin your study of alligator dots?

I went to the library. By reading books and scientific journals, I learned that people had noticed the dots before and thought they were probably some kind of sense organ. They could have been smell detectors or taste buds. But no one knew for certain what the dots did for the alligator.

Alligators float partly above and partly below the waterline.

What was your first alligator experiment?

It was designed to find out whether the dots were connected to nerve cells. I put some red tracer dye on all the dots on the faces of a few baby alligators. This type of dye is picked up by nerve cells. If the dots were connected to nerves, then the dye would travel along the nerves to the brain. To my surprise, a lot of dye moved into the brain. The experiment proved that the dots are part of the alligator's nervous system. But it didn't tell me what kind of information is transmitted to the alligator's brain.

How did you discover what the dots are for?

I conducted another series of lab experiments. For each experiment, I put the small alligator to sleep, just as a veterinarian puts a dog or cat to sleep during surgery. Then I placed electrodes on nerves coming from some of the sensory dots. Whenever the nerves fired—sent a message to the brain—they created a tiny electric current. When this happened, I would hear a buzzing sound over an audio speaker I had hooked up.

I used this experimental setup with the electrodes in place to see what would cause those nerves to fire. I brought food near the spots, to see if the dots were like taste buds. I tried light to see if the spots acted like eyes. I even tried heat, to see if they were temperature sensors. Nothing worked!

One day I accidentally dropped a tool into the alligator's tank. The alligator was resting half in and half out of the water, as usual. When I stuck my hand in to get the tool out, I made ripples in the water. When the ripples reached the alligator's face, I heard a buzz on the speaker. I thought, "What's going on?" I realized that the dots must be sensitive to the changes in pressure that take place when they are hit by ripples of water.

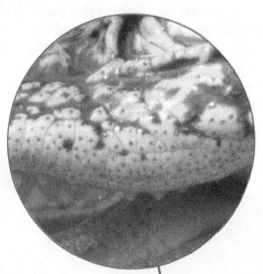

The dots that line an alligator's jaw are located where the surface of the water touches the alligator's face. They can detect and locate movements in the water.

If you look at the skull of an alligator, you can see many tiny holes in the bone where some nerves run from the alligator's face to the brain.

? Did you do any more experiments?

Oh yes, I wasn't finished yet. My hypothesis was that the dots tell the alligator where ripples in the water are coming from. To test that I was right, I had to make certain that alligators respond to ripples. Sure enough, whenever ripples in the tank reached the sensory dots, the alligator always moved toward the ripples.

I also had to rule out the possibility that the alligators were responding to sight or sound, rather than pressure changes. So I did the experiments again. I darkened the laboratory so the alligators couldn't see, and I blocked up their ears so they couldn't hear. And I got the same result. I was ready to announce my discovery. I had found a new kind of sense receptor in alligators!

? How do the dots help alligators hunt?

Alligators feed on frogs, birds, and other animals that disturb the water when they come to drink or swim. The movements of these prey animals create ripples in the water. The dots detect the ripples and help the alligator locate the disturbance that caused them. I now call the dots "dome pressure receptors," because they are shaped like little domes. Along with keen eyesight and hearing, the dome pressure receptors help alligators capture prey.

? What research are you working on now?

I am studying blind cavefish from Mexico, trying to learn whether they are blind from birth or lose their sight as they grow up. I'm also looking forward to more research on crocodilians. I want to find out how the genes of alligators with dome pressure sensors only on their faces differ from the genes of crocodilians that have pressure sensors all over their bodies.

Writing in Science

Career Link Suppose you are a reporter for a newspaper, radio, or a TV broadcast, and you've conducted this interview. Write several paragraphs about Daphne Soares, emphasizing how curiosity and accidental discoveries can play a role in a science career.

For: More on this career
Visit: PHSchool.com
Web Code: ceb-2000

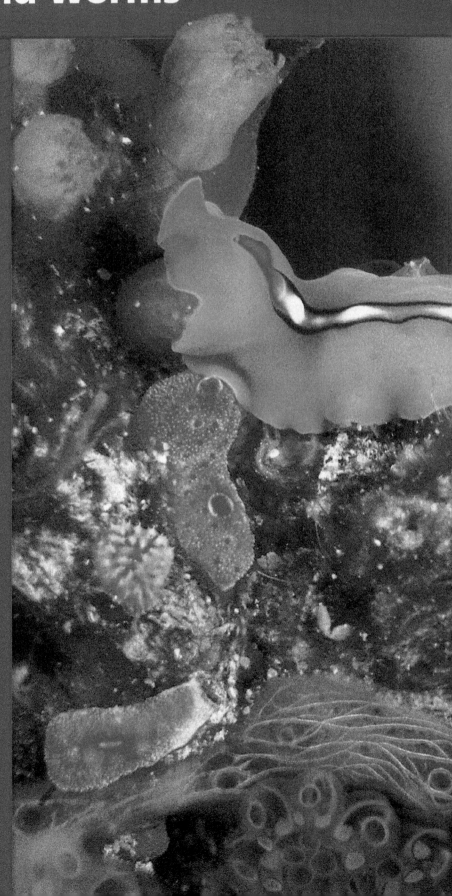

Chapter

Sponges, Cnidarians, and Worms

A purple flatworm glides along the ocean bottom.

4 ◆ B

Lab zone™ Chapter **Project**

Design and Build an Animal Habitat

Do all animals require the same things to survive? In this project, you will research what it takes to keep a class pet healthy, and then build a habitat to carry out that objective.

Your Goal To research, design, and build a habitat that will keep an animal healthy for two weeks

To complete this project, you must

- research the needs of your animal
- brainstorm various designs for a habitat that meets your animal's needs and allows you to observe its behavior
- select materials and build a prototype of your design
- test your design by having your animal live in the habitat for two weeks
- follow the safety guidelines in Appendix A

Plan It! Choose your animal. Research where it lives, and what types of climate and food it needs. Use this information to design your habitat. Brainstorm some design ideas and make sketches. Select materials to build the habitat. After your teacher approves your design, build and test the habitat.

What Is an Animal?

Reading Preview

Key Concepts
- How are animal bodies typically organized?
- What are four major functions of animals?
- How are animals classified?

Key Terms
- cell • tissue • organ
- adaptation
- sexual reproduction
- fertilization
- asexual reproduction
- phylum • vertebrate
- invertebrate

Target Reading Skill

Asking Questions Before you read, preview the red headings. In a graphic organizer like the one below, ask a *what* or *how* question for each heading. As you read, write the answers to your questions.

Structure of Animals

Question	Answer
What is a cell?	A cell is . . .

Discover Activity

Is It an Animal?

1. Carefully examine each of the organisms that your teacher gives you.
2. Decide which ones are animals. For each organism, write down the reasons for your decision. Wash your hands after handling each of the organisms.

Think It Over
Forming Operational Definitions
Use your notes about each organism to write a definition of "animal."

Your parents may have told you not to eat with your fingers, but they probably never worried that you'd eat with your feet! But animals called barnacles do just that.

A barnacle begins life as a many-legged speck that floats in the ocean. After a while, it settles its head down on a hard surface and fixes itself in place. Then it builds a hard cone around its body. To feed, the barnacle flicks its feathery feet in and out of the cone, as shown below. The feet trap tiny organisms, or living things, that float in the water.

A barnacle may look like a rock, but it is actually an animal. Animals are many-celled organisms that feed on other organisms.

A barnacle feeding (inset) ▲ and many barnacles at rest (right)

Structure of Animals

Animals are composed of many cells. A **cell** is the basic unit of structure and function in living things. **The cells of most animals are organized into higher levels of structure, including tissues, organs, and systems.** A group of similar cells that perform a specific function is called a **tissue.** One type of tissue is nerve tissue, which carries messages in the form of electrical signals from one part of the body to another. Another type of tissue is bone tissue, a hard tissue that gives bones strength.

Tissues may combine to form an **organ,** which is a group of several different tissues. For example, a frog's thigh bone is composed of bone tissue, nerve tissue, and blood. An organ performs a more complex function than each tissue could perform alone.

Groups of structures that perform the broadest functions of an animal are called systems. One example of a system is the skeletal system of a frog shown in Figure 1.

Go Online
SciLINKS NSTA

For: Links on the animal kingdom
Visit: www.SciLinks.org
Web Code: scn-0211

Reading Checkpoint What is an organ?

FIGURE 1
Levels of Organization

A frog's skeletal system has different levels of organization. **Interpreting Diagrams** *List the four levels of organization in order from smallest to largest.*

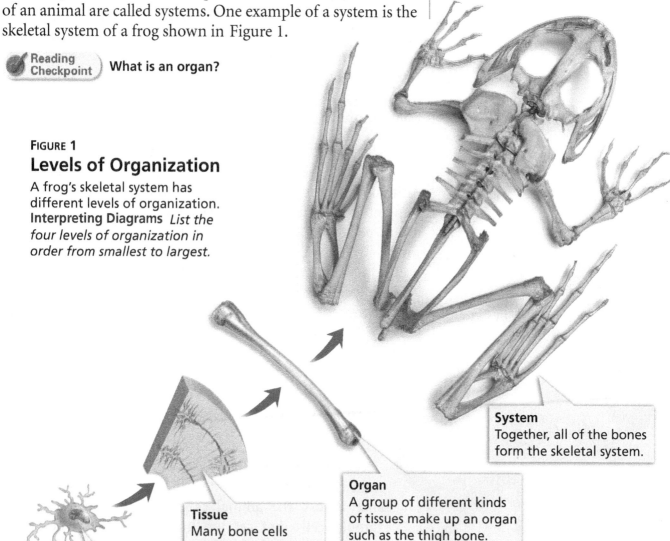

System
Together, all of the bones form the skeletal system.

Organ
A group of different kinds of tissues make up an organ such as the thigh bone.

Tissue
Many bone cells make up bone tissue.

Cells
Cells are the basic unit of animal structure.

FIGURE 2
Obtaining Food
This tarantula uses its fangs to kill a grasshopper.

Functions of Animals

From tiny worms to giant whales, animals are diverse. Animals vary not only in size but also in body structure, outward appearance, and the environments in which they live. Despite their diversity, however, all animals carry out the same basic functions. **The major functions of animals are to obtain food and oxygen, keep internal conditions stable, move, and reproduce.** Structures or behaviors that allow animals to perform these basic functions in their environments are called **adaptations.**

Obtaining Food and Oxygen An animal cannot make food for itself—it obtains food by eating other organisms. Animals may feed on plants, other animals, or a combination of plants and animals. They have adaptations that allow them to eat particular kinds of food. For example, the tarantula shown in Figure 2 has an adaptation called fangs—structures it uses to pierce other animals and suck up their juices.

Food provides animals with raw materials for growth and with energy for their bodies' activities, such as breathing and moving. Most animals take food into a cavity inside their bodies. Inside this cavity the food is digested, or broken down into substances that the animal's body can absorb and use. To release energy from food, the body's cells need oxygen. Some animals, like birds, get oxygen from air. Others, like fish, get oxygen from water.

FIGURE 3
Keeping Cool
This dog is keeping cool by getting wet and panting.

Keeping Conditions Stable Animals must maintain a stable environment within their bodies. If this balance is lost, the animal cannot survive for long. For example, cells that get too hot start to die. Therefore, animals in hot environments are adapted, meaning they have adaptations, to keep their bodies cool. Earthworms stay in moist soil during hot days, lizards crawl to shady places, and dogs pant.

Movement All animals move in some way at some point in their lives. Most animals move freely from place to place throughout their lives; for example, by swimming, walking, or hopping. Other animals, such as oysters and barnacles, move from place to place only during the earliest stage of their lives. After they find a good place to attach, these animals stay in one place.

Animal movement is usually related to meeting the basic needs of survival and reproduction. Barnacles wave feathery structures through the water and trap tiny food particles. Some geese fly thousands of miles each spring to the place where they lay eggs. And you've probably seen a cat claw its way up a tree trunk to escape from a barking dog.

Reproduction Because no individual animal lives forever, animals must reproduce. Most animals reproduce sexually. **Sexual reproduction** is the process by which a new organism develops from the joining of two sex cells—a male sperm cell and a female egg cell. The joining of an egg cell and a sperm cell is called **fertilization.** Sperm and egg cells carry information about the characteristics of the parents that produced them, such as size and color. New individuals resulting from sexual reproduction have a combination of characteristics from both parents.

Some animals can reproduce asexually as well as sexually. **Asexual reproduction** is the process by which a single organism produces a new organism identical to itself. For example, animals called sea anemones sometimes split down the middle, producing two identical organisms.

 **Reading Checkpoint** What is asexual reproduction?

Try This Activity

Get Moving
Design an animal with a new and different way of moving. Your design should help your animal obtain food or get out of danger.

1. Make and label a drawing that shows how the animal would move.
2. Using clay, aluminum cans, construction paper, pipe cleaners, and whatever other materials are available, create a three-dimensional model of your animal.
3. Compare your animal to those of other classmates. What are some similarities? What are some differences?

Making Models What features of your design help your animal obtain food or escape danger?

Figure 4
Owl Family
Baby owls are produced by sexual reproduction. **Classifying** *Which kind of reproduction involves fertilization?*

Classification of Animals

Biologists have already identified more than 1.5 million species, or distinct types, of animals. Each year they discover more. Classifying, or sorting animals into categories, helps biologists make sense of this diversity. Biologists have classified animals into about 35 major groups, each of which is called a **phylum** (FY lum) (plural *phyla*). In Figure 5 you can see some animals from the largest phyla. Notice that the phyla are arranged like branches on a tree.

FIGURE 5
Major Animal Groups

This branching tree shows one hypothesis of how the major animal groups are related. **Interpreting Diagrams** *Are flatworms more closely related to roundworms or mollusks?*

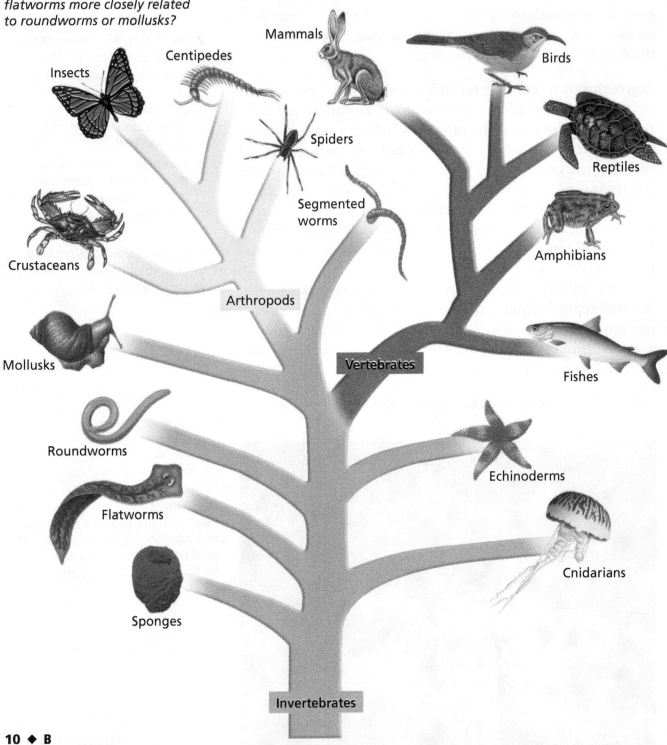

The branching pattern of the tree in Figure 5 shows how many biologists think the major groups of animals are related. For example, you can see that segmented worms are more closely related to arthropods than to sponges from their positions on the tree.

A branching tree can also show how biologists think animal life has evolved, or changed over time. This process has resulted in all the different phyla that exist today. Biologists do not know the exact way in which evolution took place. Instead, they can only make inferences on the basis of the best evidence available. Biologists hypothesize that all animals arose from single-celled ancestors.

Animals are classified according to how they are related to other animals. These relationships are determined by an animal's body structure, the way the animal develops, and its DNA. DNA is a chemical in cells that controls an organism's inherited characteristics. All **vertebrates,** or animals with a backbone, are classified in only one phylum. All the other animal phyla contain **invertebrates,** or animals without backbones. Of all the types of animals, about 97 percent are invertebrates!

 **Reading Checkpoint** What is a phylum?

Section 1 Assessment

Target Reading Skill Asking Questions Use the answers to the questions you wrote about the headings to help you answer the questions below.

Reviewing Key Concepts

1. a. **Defining** What is the basic unit of structure and function in an animal?
   b. **Sequencing** Arrange in order from simplest to most complex structure: tissue, system, cell, organ.
2. a. **Reviewing** What are four major functions of animals?
   b. **Summarizing** How do animals obtain food?
   c. **Drawing Conclusions** Why is movement important for animals?

3. a. **Defining** What is a vertebrate?
   b. **Classifying** How do biologists classify animals?
   c. **Interpreting Diagrams** According to the branching tree shown in Figure 5, are reptiles more closely related to mammals or to fishes? Explain your answer.

Writing in Science

Functional Description Write a few paragraphs about how your classroom pet or a pet at home performs the basic functions of an animal.

Animal Symmetry

Reading Preview

Key Concepts
- What is symmetry?
- What can you infer about an animal based on its symmetry?

Key Terms
- bilateral symmetry
- radial symmetry

Target Reading Skill
Comparing and Contrasting
As you read, compare and contrast the characteristics of animals with bilateral symmetry and radial symmetry in a Venn diagram like the one below. Write the similarities where the circles overlap, and write the differences on the left and right sides.

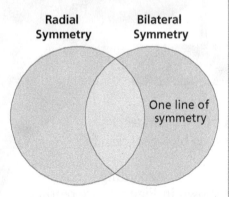

Radial Symmetry   Bilateral Symmetry

One line of symmetry

Discover Activity

How Many Ways Can You Fold It?

1. Trace the triangle onto a sheet of paper and cut it out. Then draw a circle by tracing the rim of a glass or other round object. Cut out the circle.
2. Fold the triangle so that one half matches the other. Do the same with the circle.
3. See how many different ways you can fold each figure so that the two halves are identical.

Think It Over
Classifying Name an animal whose body shape can be folded in the same number of ways as the triangle.

Have you ever stopped to look at a butterfly perched on a flower? You probably noticed that bright colors and dark lines criss-cross its wings, making a pretty pattern. Did you also see that the pattern on the left side of the butterfly is a mirror image of the pattern on the right?

The Mathematics of Symmetry

As you can see from the photo of the butterfly in Figure 7, a butterfly's body has two halves. Each half looks like a reflection of the other. **This balanced arrangement of parts, called symmetry, is characteristic of many animals.** A butterfly's symmetry contributes to its pleasing appearance. But, more important, the balanced wings help the butterfly to fly easily.

FIGURE 7
Butterfly Halves
This butterfly's body has two mirror-image halves.
Applying Concepts *What is this balanced arrangement called?*

Bilateral Symmetry

Radial Symmetry

No Symmetry

Animals have different types of symmetry, as shown in Figure 8. In the case of a fish, you can draw a line lengthwise down the middle of its body. This line is called a line of symmetry. An object has **bilateral symmetry** if there is just one line that divides it into halves that are mirror images. In contrast, objects with **radial symmetry** have many lines of symmetry that all go through a central point. For example, the sea star is circular if you look at it from the top. Any line drawn through its center can divide the sea star into two symmetrical halves. A few animals, such as most sponges, have no symmetry.

FIGURE 8
Types of Symmetry
Animals have either bilateral or radial symmetry, except for most sponges, which usually have no symmetry.

> **Reading Checkpoint** How many lines divide an animal with bilateral symmetry into halves?

Symmetry and Daily Life

Animals without symmetry tend to have simple body plans. In contrast, the bodies of animals with bilateral symmetry or radial symmetry are complex. **Depending on their symmetry, animals share some general characteristics.**

FIGURE 9
Radial Symmetry
The sea stars in this tide pool have radial symmetry.

Animals With Radial Symmetry The external body parts of animals with radial symmetry are equally spaced around a central point, like spokes on a bicycle wheel. Because of the circular arrangement of their parts, animals with radial symmetry, such as sea stars, jellyfishes, and sea urchins, do not have distinct front or back ends.

Animals with radial symmetry have several characteristics in common. All of them live in water. Most of them do not move very fast. They stay in one spot, are moved along by water currents, or creep along the bottom.

FIGURE 10
Bilateral Symmetry
Animals with bilateral symmetry, like this tiger, have a front end with sense organs that pick up information.

Animals With Bilateral Symmetry Most animals you know have bilateral symmetry, including yourself! In general, animals with bilateral symmetry are larger and more complex than those with radial symmetry. They have a front end that typically goes first as the animal moves along. These animals move more quickly and efficiently than most animals with radial symmetry. This is partly because bilateral symmetry allows for a streamlined body. In addition, most animals with bilateral symmetry have sense organs in their front ends that pick up information about what is in front of them. For example, a tiger has eyes, ears, a nose, and whiskers on its head. Swift movement and sense organs help animals with bilateral symmetry obtain food and avoid enemies.

Go Online
*SciLINKS*ₙₛₜₐ

For: Links on animal symmetry
Visit: www.SciLinks.org
Web Code: scn-0212

Reading Checkpoint Where are the sense organs of an animal with bilateral symmetry typically found?

Section 2 Assessment

Target Reading Skill Comparing and Contrasting Use the information in your Venn diagram about symmetry to help you answer Question 1 below.

Reviewing Key Concepts

1. a. **Reviewing** What is symmetry?
   b. **Comparing and Contrasting** How are bilateral symmetry and radial symmetry alike? How are they different?
   c. **Applying Concepts** What kind of symmetry does a grasshopper have? Explain.
2. a. **Identifying** What general characteristics do animals with radial symmetry share?
   b. **Summarizing** What four body characteristics do animals with bilateral symmetry usually have?
   c. **Making Generalizations** How would having sense organs in front be helpful to an animal?

At-Home Activity

Front-End Advantages With a family member, observe as many different animals as possible in a yard or at a park. Look in lots of different places, such as in the grass, under rocks, and in the air. Explain the advantages an animal with a distinct front end has. Tell the person what this type of body arrangement is called.

Sponges and Cnidarians

Reading Preview

Key Concepts
- What are the main characteristics of sponges?
- What are the main characteristics of cnidarians?
- Why are coral reefs important?

Key Terms
- larva • cnidarian • polyp
- medusa • colony • coral reef

Target Reading Skill
Comparing and Contrasting
As you read, compare and contrast sponges and cnidarians by completing a table like this one.

Sponges and Cnidarians

Feature	Sponge	Cnidarian
Body structure	Hollow bag with pores	
Cell type that traps food		
Method(s) of reproduction		

Discover Activity

How Do Natural and Synthetic Sponges Compare?

1. Examine a natural sponge, and then use a hand lens or a microscope to take a closer look. Look carefully at the holes in the sponge. Draw what you see through the lens.
2. Cut out a small piece of sponge and examine it with a hand lens. Draw what you see.
3. Repeat Steps 1 and 2 with a synthetic kitchen sponge.

Think It Over
Observing What are three ways a natural and a synthetic sponge are similar? What are three ways they are different?

Eagerly but carefully, you and the others in your group put on scuba gear as you prepare to dive into the ocean. Over the side of the boat you go. As you descend through the water, you see many kinds of fishes. When you get to the bottom, you notice other organisms, too. Some are as strange as creatures from a science fiction movie. A few of these unusual organisms may be invertebrate animals called sponges.

Sponges don't look or act like most animals you know. In fact, they are so different that for a long time, people thought that sponges were plants. Like plants, adult sponges stay in one place. But unlike most plants, sponges take food into their bodies.

Sponges

Sponges live all over the world—mostly in oceans, but also in freshwater rivers and lakes. Adult sponges are attached to hard surfaces underwater. Water currents carry food and oxygen to them and take away their waste products. Water currents also play a role in their reproduction and help transport their young to new places to live.

◀ **Diver investigating a barrel sponge**

Body Structure Sponges are invertebrate animals that usually have no body symmetry and never have tissues or organs. A sponge looks something like a hollow bag with a large opening at one end and many tiny pores covering its surface. In fact, the name of the phylum to which sponges belong—phylum Porifera—means "having pores."

Look at Figure 11. A sponge's body has different kinds of cells and structures for different functions. For example, most sponges have spikes. The network of spikes throughout the sponge supports its soft body, keeping it upright in the water. The spikes also help a sponge defend itself against an animal that might eat it, which is called a predator. The spikes can be as sharp as needles. Even so, some fish eat sponges.

Go Online
active art

For: Structure of a Sponge activity
Visit: PHSchool.com
Web Code: cep-2013

FIGURE 11

Structure of a Sponge

Structures surrounding the central cavity of a sponge are adapted for different functions.
Interpreting Diagrams *Which kind of cell in the sponge digests and distributes food?*

Collar Cell
The collar cells have whiplike structures that beat back and forth, moving water through the sponge and trapping food.

Pore
Water moves into the central cavity through small pores all over the sponge's body. It exits from a large hole at the top.

Spike
Thin spikes form a rigid frame that helps support and protect the sponge's body.

Jelly-like Cell
Among the spikes are jelly-like cells that digest and distribute food, remove wastes, and form sperm or egg cells.

FIGURE 12
Reproduction of a Sponge
The sexual reproduction of sponges involves a larval stage that moves. Adult sponges stay in one place.

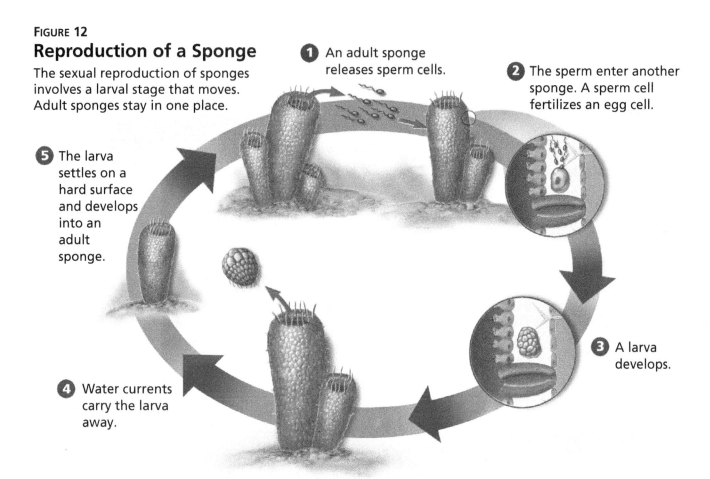

① An adult sponge releases sperm cells.

② The sperm enter another sponge. A sperm cell fertilizes an egg cell.

③ A larva develops.

④ Water currents carry the larva away.

⑤ The larva settles on a hard surface and develops into an adult sponge.

Obtaining Food and Oxygen A sponge eats tiny single-celled organisms. The sponge filters these organisms from the water moving through it. The collar cells that line the central cavity trap the tiny organisms. Jelly-like cells inside the sponge then digest, or break down, the food. Larger sponges can filter thousands of liters of water per day!

A sponge gets its oxygen from water, too. After the water moves through a sponge's pores, it passes over cells inside the sponge. Oxygen in the water then moves into the sponge's cells.

Reproduction Sponges reproduce both asexually and sexually. Budding is one form of asexual reproduction in sponges. In budding, small new sponges grow from the sides of an adult sponge. Eventually, the buds break free and begin life on their own.

Sponges reproduce sexually, too, but they do not have separate sexes. A sponge produces both sperm cells and egg cells. The sperm cells are released into the water. They enter another sponge and fertilize its eggs, as shown in Figure 12. After fertilization, a larva develops. A **larva** (plural *larvae*) is an immature form of an animal that looks very different from the adult.

 **Reading Checkpoint** What is a larva?

Math Skills

Calculating a Rate
To calculate the rate of water flow in a sponge, divide the volume of water that the sponge filters by the time it takes the water to pass through the sponge.

$$\text{Flow rate} = \frac{\text{Volume of water}}{\text{Time}}$$

For example, a marble-sized sponge filters 15.6 liters of water in a day. How many liters does it filter per hour?

$$\frac{15.6\ L}{24\ h} = 0.65\ L/h$$

Practice Problem In 4 days, a sponge filters 1,200 L. What is its rate of water flow per day?

Soak It Up!

Problem

Which sponge absorbs the most water?

Skills Focus

observing, predicting, communicating

Materials

- damp piece of cellulose sponge
- damp piece of natural sponge
- damp piece of foam sponge
- balance
- large bowl of tap water
- graduated cylinder
- beaker
- paper towel

Procedure

1. Copy the data table on a separate sheet.

2. Examine the size of the pores in each sponge. Record your observations.

3. Make a prediction about which sponge will absorb the most water. Record your prediction and give a reason.

4. Place a damp piece of cellulose sponge on a balance and measure its mass. Record the mass in the data table. Remove the sponge from the balance.

5. Repeat Step 4 with the natural sponge and then the foam sponge.

6. Submerge the cellulose sponge in a bowl of water. Squeeze it several times to remove all air bubbles. Release the sponge and let it absorb water. Then remove the sponge and place it in the beaker.

7. Squeeze out as much water as possible from the sponge into the beaker. *(Hint:* Squeeze and twist the sponge until no more drops of water come out.)

8. Pour the water from the beaker into the graduated cylinder. Measure the volume of water and record the volume in the data table. Pour the water from the graduated cylinder back into the bowl. Dry the graduated cylinder and beaker with a paper towel.

Data Table

Type of Sponge	Mass of Damp Sponge	Size of Pores	Volume of Absorbed Water	
			Total (mL)	Per Gram (mL/g)
Cellulose				
Natural				
Foam				

9. Repeat Steps 6–8 using the natural sponge and then the foam sponge. When you are finished, squeeze all the water from your sponges, and return them to your teacher.

10. Calculate the volume of water absorbed per gram of sponge, using this formula:

$$\frac{\text{Volume of absorbed water}}{\text{Mass of damp sponge}} = \text{Volume absorbed per gram}$$

Analyze and Conclude

1. **Observing** Which sponge absorbed the most water per gram of sponge? The least? Was your prediction confirmed?

2. **Drawing Conclusions** What can you conclude about the relationship between pore size and the ability of the sponge to absorb water?

3. **Predicting** How would the volume of absorbed water change if each of the sponges had twice the mass of the sponges you studied? Explain.

4. **Communicating** Natural sponges can cost more than cellulose and foam sponges. Consider that information and the results of your investigation. Which sponge would you recommend to consumers for absorbing water spills? Explain your choice.

Design an Experiment

Design an experiment to test the prediction you made in Question 3 above. Write your hypothesis as an "If ... then ..." statement. *Obtain your teacher's permission before carrying out your investigation.*

Cnidarians

Some other animals you might notice on an underwater dive are jellyfishes, corals, and sea anemones. These animals are **cnidarians** (ny DEHR ee unz), invertebrates that have stinging cells and take food into a central body cavity. **Cnidarians use stinging cells to capture food and defend themselves.**

Body Structure Cnidarians have two different body plans, which you can see in Figure 13. Notice that one form looks something like a vase and the other form looks like an upside-down bowl. Both body plans have radial symmetry, a central hollow cavity, and tentacles that contain stinging cells.

The vase-shaped body plan is called a **polyp** (PAHL ip). The sea anemone you see in Figure 13 is a polyp. A polyp's mouth opens at the top and its tentacles spread out from around the mouth. Most polyps are adapted for a life attached to an underwater surface.

The bowl-shaped body plan is called a **medusa** (muh DOO suh). The jellyfish you see in Figure 13 is a medusa. A medusa, unlike a polyp, is adapted for a swimming life. Medusas have mouths that open downward and tentacles that trail down. Some cnidarians go through both a polyp stage and a medusa stage during their lives. Others are either polyps or medusas for their entire lives.

Hydra Doing?

1.  Put a drop of water containing hydras in a small unbreakable bowl or petri dish. Allow it to sit for about 15 minutes.
2. Use a hand lens to examine the hydras as they swim. Then gently touch the tentacles of a hydra with the end of a toothpick. Watch what happens.
3. Return the hydras to your teacher. Wash your hands.

Classifying Is a hydra a polyp or a medusa? Describe its method of movement.

FIGURE 13
Cnidarian Body Plans

Cnidarians have two basic body forms, the vase-shaped polyp and the bowl-shaped medusa. **Comparing and Contrasting** *Contrast the location of the mouth in the polyp and the medusa.*

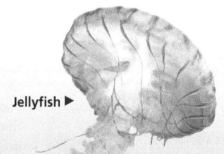
Jellyfish ▶

▼ Sea anemone

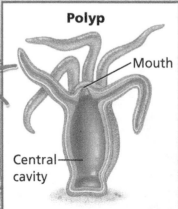
Polyp
Mouth
Central cavity

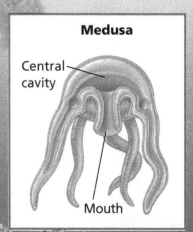
Medusa
Central cavity
Mouth

FIGURE 14
Cnidarian Attack!
A stinging cell fires when its trigger brushes against prey, such as a fish.

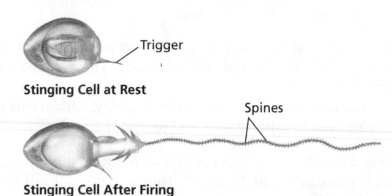

Trigger
Stinging Cell at Rest

Spines
Stinging Cell After Firing

Obtaining Food Both polyps and medusas obtain food in the same way. Cnidarians use stinging cells to catch the animals they eat, which are called prey. You can see a stinging cell in Figure 14. The cell contains a threadlike structure, which has many sharp spines. When the stinging cell touches prey, this threadlike structure explodes out of the cell and into the prey. Some stinging cells also release venom into the prey. When the prey becomes helpless, the cnidarian uses its tentacles to pull the prey into its mouth. From there, the prey passes into a hollow central body cavity, where it is digested. Undigested food is expelled through the mouth.

Movement Unlike adult sponges, many cnidarians can move to escape danger and to obtain food. Some cnidarians have muscle-like tissues that allow them to move in different ways. Jellyfishes swim through the water, and hydras turn slow somersaults. Sea anemones stretch out, shrink down, bend slowly from side to side, and often move slowly from place to place. A cnidarian's movements are directed by nerve cells that are spread out like a basketball net. This nerve net helps a cnidarian respond quickly to danger and to nearby food.

FIGURE 15
Movement of a Medusa
A medusa's nerve net signals the top part of the medusa's body to contract and relax. As the top of its body contracts, the medusa moves upward through the water.

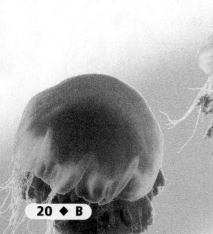

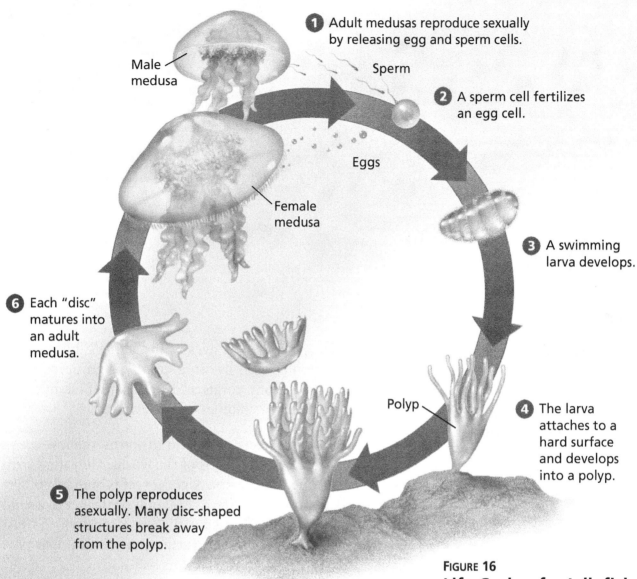

① Adult medusas reproduce sexually by releasing egg and sperm cells.

Sperm

Male medusa

② A sperm cell fertilizes an egg cell.

Eggs

Female medusa

③ A swimming larva develops.

⑥ Each "disc" matures into an adult medusa.

Polyp

④ The larva attaches to a hard surface and develops into a polyp.

⑤ The polyp reproduces asexually. Many disc-shaped structures break away from the polyp.

FIGURE 16

Life Cycle of a Jellyfish

The life cycle of a moon jelly has both a polyp and a medusa stage, and both asexual reproduction and sexual reproduction.
Interpreting Diagrams *Which form of the moon jelly (polyp or medusa) shows a form of asexual reproduction? Explain.*

Reproduction Cnidarians reproduce both asexually and sexually. For polyps such as hydras, corals, and sea anemones, budding is the most common form of asexual reproduction. Amazingly, some polyps just pull apart, forming two new polyps. Both kinds of asexual reproduction allow the numbers of polyps to increase rapidly in a short time.

Sexual reproduction in cnidarians occurs in a variety of ways. Some species of cnidarians have both sexes within one individual. In others, the sexes are separate individuals. Many cnidarians have life cycles, or a sequence of different stages of development. In Figure 16, you can see the life cycle of a moon jelly, which involves both asexual and sexual reproduction.

 Reading Checkpoint **What are two examples of asexual reproduction seen in polyps?**

◀ Coral polyps   ▼ Coral reef

FIGURE 17
Coral Reef
The massive reef surrounding this tropical island is made from the skeletal remains of the tiny cnidarians called coral (inset).

Life in a Colony

Many cnidarians spend their lives as individuals, but not all. Some species of cnidarians live in a **colony,** a group of many individual animals. Stony corals and the Portuguese man-of-war are two examples of colonies of cnidarians.

Stony Corals Coral reefs are found in warm, shallow ocean waters, mainly in tropical regions of the world. They may seem to be made of stone, but are not. A **coral reef** is built by cnidarians. At the beginning of its life, a coral polyp attaches to a solid surface. A broken shell, a sunken ship, or a rock will do just fine. After attaching to the solid surface, the coral polyp produces a hard, stony skeleton around its soft body.

The coral polyp reproduces asexually, and then its offspring reproduce asexually, too. Over time, that polyp may give rise to thousands more, each with a hard skeleton. When the polyps die, their skeletons remain behind. Over thousands of years, as live corals add their skeletons to those that have died, rocklike reefs grow up from the sea floor. The top layer of the reef is covered with hundreds of thousands of still-living coral polyps.

Coral reefs are home to more species of fishes and invertebrates than any other environment on Earth. Hundreds of sponge species live among the corals, constantly filtering water through their bodies. Worms burrow into the coral reef. Giant clams lie with their huge shells slightly open. Shrimp and crabs edge out of hiding places below the corals. At night, bright blue damselfish settle into pockets in the coral. At dawn and dusk, sea turtles, sea snakes, and sharks all visit the reef, hunting for prey. These living things interact in complex ways, creating a rich and beautiful environment.

FIGURE 18
Portuguese Man-of-War
The Portuguese man-of-war is a
tightly coordinated colony of polyps
and medusas.

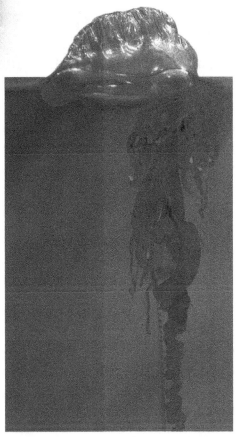

Portuguese Man-of-War Sometimes the association of individual animals in a colony is so tight that the colony acts like a single animal. The Portuguese man-of-war contains as many as 1,000 individuals that function together as one unit.

At the top of the Portuguese man-of-war is a gas-filled chamber that allows the colony to float on the surface of the ocean. Various polyps with different functions drift below. Some polyps catch prey for the colony with stinging cells. Others digest the prey. Still other polyps are adapted for reproduction.

 Reading Checkpoint **What are two examples of colonies of cnidarians?**

Section 3 Assessment

Target Reading Skill Comparing and Contrasting Use your table to quiz a partner about how sponges and cnidarians trap food. How do their methods for trapping food differ?

Reviewing Key Concepts

1. a. **Describing** What are the characteristics of a sponge?
   b. **Comparing and Contrasting** How are the cells of a sponge alike? How are they different?
2. a. **Identifying** What is one type of cell that all cnidarians have?
   b. **Sequencing** What steps are involved in how a cnidarian obtains food?
   c. **Inferring** How might a cnidarian protect itself?

3. a. **Identifying** What is a coral reef?
   b. **Summarizing** How is a coral reef built?
   c. **Making Judgments** Why is it important to protect coral reefs?

Math Practice

4. **Calculating a Rate** A very large sponge can filter 1,500 liters of water in a day. How much water can it filter per hour?

Coral Reefs in Danger

Coral reefs off the coasts of many nations are in danger. Although coral reefs are as hard as rocks, the coral animals themselves are quite delicate. Recreational divers can damage the fragile reefs. Is it possible to protect the reefs while still allowing divers to explore them?

Diving supports local businesses

The Issues

What's the Harm in Diving?

More than 1.5 million recreational divers live in the United States. With so many divers it is hard to guarantee that no harm will occur to coral reefs. Divers can cause significant damage by standing on or even touching these fragile reefs. Harm to the reefs is even more likely to occur when divers collect coral for their own enjoyment or to sell for profit. You can see brightly colored coral from the sea in jewelry and in decorations.

Should Reefs Be Further Protected?

The United States government has passed laws making it illegal, under most circumstances, to remove coral from the sea. Because a few divers break these laws, some people want to ban diving altogether. However, many divers say it's unfair to ban diving just because of a few lawbreakers.

   Many divers consider coral reefs the most exciting and beautiful places in the ocean to explore. As divers and other people visit and learn more about these delicate coral reefs, they increase others' awareness of them. Public awareness may be the best way to ensure that these rich environments are protected.

More Than a Diving Issue

Coral reefs are major tourist attractions that bring money and jobs to people in local communities. If diving were banned, local businesses would suffer significantly. Also, although divers can harm coral reefs, other human activities that result in ocean pollution, oil spills, and illegal fishing can also cause harm. In addition, natural events, such as tropical storms, changes in sea level, and changes in sea temperature, can also damage the fragile reefs.

Reefs house and protect many species of sea animals, including sponges, shrimp, sea turtles, and fishes.

What Would You Do?

1. Identify the Problem
In your own words, explain the controversy surrounding diving near coral reefs.

2. Analyze the Options
List the arguments on each side of the issue. Note the pros and cons. How well would each position protect the reefs? Who might be harmed or inconvenienced?

3. Find a Solution
Write a newspaper editorial stating your position on whether diving should be allowed near coral reefs. State your position and reasons clearly.

Go Online
PHSchool.com

For: More on coral reefs
Visit: PHSchool.com
Web Code: ceh-2010

Worms

Reading Preview

Key Concepts
- What are the three main phyla of worms?
- What are the main characteristics of each phylum of worms?

Key Terms
- parasite • host
- free-living organism
- scavenger • anus
- closed circulatory system

Target Reading Skill
Using Prior Knowledge Before you read, write what you know about worms in a graphic organizer like the one below. As you read, write what you learn.

What You Know
1. Worms are long and skinny. 2.

What You Learned
1. 2.

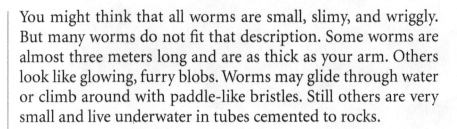

Discover Activity

What Does a Flatworm Look Like?
1. Your teacher will give you a planarian, a kind of flatworm. Pick the worm up with the tip of a small paintbrush. Place it carefully in a container. Use a dropper to cover the planarian with spring water.
2. Observe the planarian with a hand lens for a few minutes. Describe how the planarian moves. Draw a picture of the planarian.
3. Return the planarian to your teacher, and wash your hands.

Think It Over
Observing How does a planarian differ from a sponge?

You might think that all worms are small, slimy, and wriggly. But many worms do not fit that description. Some worms are almost three meters long and are as thick as your arm. Others look like glowing, furry blobs. Worms may glide through water or climb around with paddle-like bristles. Still others are very small and live underwater in tubes cemented to rocks.

Characteristics of Worms

There are many kinds of worms, all with their own characteristics. **Biologists classify worms into three major phyla—flatworms, roundworms, and segmented worms.** Flatworms belong to the phylum Platyhelminthes (plat ee HEL minth eez); roundworms belong to the phylum Nematoda; segmented worms belong to the phylum Annelida.

FIGURE 19
Giant Earthworm
A giant Gippsland earthworm can grow to be more than 1 meter long. It is one of approximately 1,000 earthworm species found in Australia.

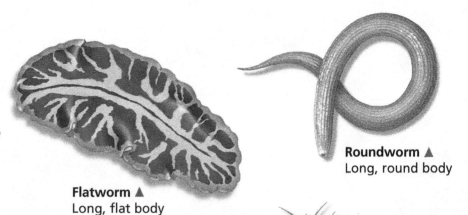

FIGURE 20
Three Phyla of Worms
The three major phyla of
worms are flatworms,
roundworms, and
segmented worms.
Observing *How are the
body shapes of these three
types of worms similar?*

Flatworm ▲
Long, flat body

Roundworm ▲
Long, round body

Segmented Worm ▲
Long, round body
made up of linked
segments

Body Structure All worms are invertebrates that have long, narrow bodies without legs. In Figure 20, you can compare the body shapes of three types of worms. Unlike sponges or cnidarians, worms have bilateral symmetry. Therefore, they have head and tail ends. In addition, they all have tissues, organs, and body systems.

Nervous System Worms are the simplest organisms with a brain, which is a knot of nerve tissue located in the head end. Because a worm's brain and some of its sense organs are located in its head end, the worm can detect objects, food, mates, and predators quickly. It can respond quickly, too. Sense organs that are sensitive to light, touch, and vibrations pick up information from the environment. The brain interprets that information and directs the animal's response. For example, if an earthworm on the surface of the ground senses the vibrations of a footstep, the worm will quickly return to its underground burrow.

Reproduction Both sexual and asexual reproduction are found in the worm phyla. In many species of worms, there are separate male and female animals, as in humans. In other species of worms, each individual has both male and female sex organs. A worm with both male and female sex organs does not usually fertilize its own eggs. Instead, two individuals mate and exchange sperm. Many worms reproduce asexually by methods such as breaking into pieces. In fact, if you cut some kinds of worms into several pieces, a whole new worm will grow from each piece.

Reading Checkpoint **What type of symmetry do worms have?**

FIGURE 21
Planarian
Planarians are free-living flatworms that live in ponds, streams, and oceans.
Comparing and Contrasting
How does a free-living organism differ from a parasite?

For: More on worms
Visit: PHSchool.com
Web Code: ced-2014

Flatworms

As you'd expect from their name, flatworms are flat. They include such organisms as tapeworms, planarians, and flukes. Although tapeworms can grow to be 10 to 12 meters long, some other flatworms are almost too small to be seen. All flatworms share certain characteristics. **Flatworms are flat and as soft as jelly.**

Many flatworms are parasites. A **parasite** is an organism that lives inside or on another organism. The parasite takes its food from its **host,** the organism in or on which it lives. Parasites may rob their hosts of food and make them weak. They may injure the host's tissues or organs, but they rarely kill their host. All tapeworms and flukes are parasites.

In contrast, some flatworms are free-living. A **free-living organism** does not live in or on other organisms. Free-living flatworms may glide over the rocks in ponds, slide over damp soil, or swim slowly through the ocean like ruffled, brightly patterned leaves.

Planarians Planarians are free-living flatworms. Planarians are **scavengers**—they feed on dead or decaying material. But they are also predators and will attack any animal smaller than they are. A planarian feeds like a vacuum cleaner. The planarian glides onto its food and inserts a feeding tube into it. Digestive juices flow out of the planarian and into the food. These juices begin to break down the food while it is still outside the worm's body. Then the planarian sucks up the partly digested bits. Digestion is completed within a cavity inside the planarian. Undigested food exits through the feeding tube.

If you look at the head of the planarian shown in Figure 21, you can see two dots. These dots are called eyespots. The eyespots can detect light but cannot see a detailed image as human eyes can. A planarian's head also has cells that pick up odors. Planarians rely mainly on smell, not light, to locate food.

Tapeworms Tapeworms are one kind of parasitic flatworm. A tapeworm's body is adapted to absorbing food from the host's digestive system. Some kinds of tapeworms can live in human hosts. Many tapeworms live in more than one host during their lifetime. You can see the life cycle of the dog tapeworm in Figure 22. Notice that this tapeworm has two different hosts—a dog and a rabbit.

 **Reading Checkpoint** How does a scavenger obtain food?

FIGURE 22
Life Cycle of a Dog Tapeworm
The tapeworm is a parasite that lives in more than one host during its life cycle.

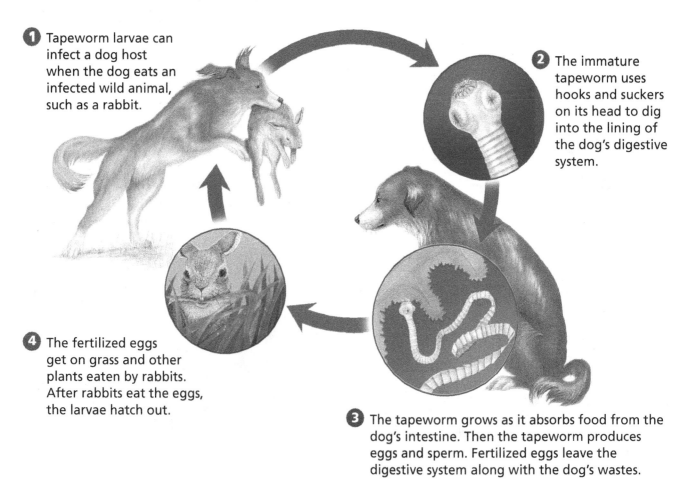

❶ Tapeworm larvae can infect a dog host when the dog eats an infected wild animal, such as a rabbit.

❷ The immature tapeworm uses hooks and suckers on its head to dig into the lining of the dog's digestive system.

❹ The fertilized eggs get on grass and other plants eaten by rabbits. After rabbits eat the eggs, the larvae hatch out.

❸ The tapeworm grows as it absorbs food from the dog's intestine. Then the tapeworm produces eggs and sperm. Fertilized eggs leave the digestive system along with the dog's wastes.

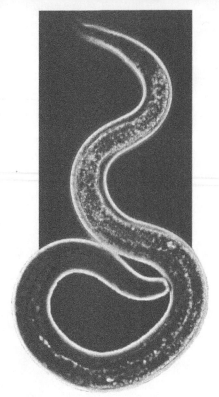

FIGURE 23
A Roundworm
The transparent body of this roundworm has been stained for better viewing under a microscope.

Roundworms

The next time you walk along a beach, consider that about a million roundworms live in each square meter of damp sand. Roundworms can live in nearly any moist environment—including forest soils, Antarctic sands, and pools of super-hot water. Most roundworms are tiny and difficult to see, but they may be the most abundant animals on Earth. Some species are free-living and some are parasites.

Unlike flatworms, roundworms have cylindrical bodies. They look like tiny strands of cooked spaghetti that are pointed at each end. **Unlike cnidarians or flatworms, roundworms have a digestive system that is like a tube, open at both ends.** Food travels in one direction through the roundworm's digestive system. Food enters at the animal's mouth, and wastes exit through an opening, called the **anus,** at the far end of the tube.

A one-way digestive system is efficient. It is something like an assembly line, with a different part of the digestive process happening at each place along the line. Digestion happens in orderly stages. First, food is broken down by digestive juices. Then the digested food is absorbed into the animal's body. Finally, wastes are eliminated. This type of digestive system enables the animal's body to absorb a large amount of the needed substances in foods.

Reading Checkpoint What is each opening at opposite ends of a roundworm's digestive tube called?

 **Math** **Analyzing Data**

Roundworm Numbers

Biologists counted all the roundworms living in a plot of soil. Then they calculated the percentage that lives in different centimeter depths of soil. Their results are graphed to the right.

1. **Reading Graphs** Where in the soil was the largest percentage of roundworms found?

2. **Calculating** What is the total percentage of roundworms found in the first 3-cm depth of soil?

3. **Drawing Conclusions** What is the relationship between the depth of the soil and the abundance of roundworms in the soil?

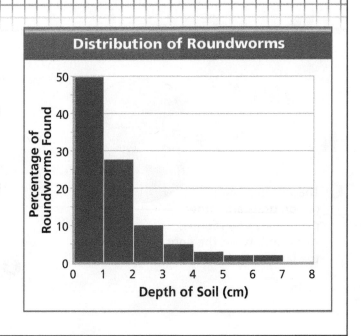

Segmented Worms

If you have ever dug in a garden, you have probably seen earthworms wriggling through the moist soil. Earthworms are segmented worms. So are leeches and some sea-floor worms.

Body Structure When you look at an earthworm, you see a body made up of a series of rings separated by grooves, something like a vacuum cleaner hose. **Earthworms and other segmented worms have bodies made up of many linked sections called segments.** On the outside, the segments look nearly identical, as you can see in Figure 24. On the inside, some organs are repeated in most segments. For example, each segment has tubes that remove wastes. Other organs, however, such as the earthworm's reproductive organs, are found only in certain segments.

All segmented worms have a long string of nerve tissue called a nerve cord and a digestive tube that run the length of the worm's body. Like roundworms, segmented worms have a one-way digestive system with two openings.

Circulatory System Segmented worms have a closed circulatory system. In a **closed circulatory system,** blood moves only within a connected network of tubes called blood vessels. In contrast, some animals, such as snails and lobsters, have an open circulatory system in which blood leaves the blood vessels and sloshes around inside the body. In both cases the blood carries oxygen and food to cells. But a closed circulatory system can move blood around an animal's body much more quickly than an open circulatory system can.

FIGURE 24
Structure of an Earthworm
An earthworm's body is divided into more than 100 segments. Some organs are repeated in most of those segments. Other organs exist in only a few segments.
Interpreting Diagrams *Name an example of a body system that runs through all of the worm's segments.*

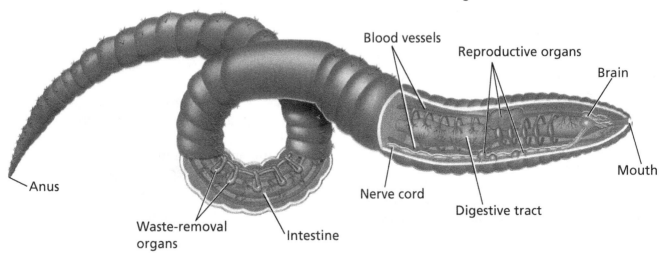

Blood vessels

Reproductive organs

Brain

Mouth

Nerve cord

Digestive tract

Anus

Waste-removal organs

Intestine

FIGURE 25
Earthworms and Garden Health
You are likely to find earthworms when you dig in garden soil.

Earthworms in the Environment Like many segmented worms, earthworms tunnel for a living. On damp nights or rainy days, they come up out of their burrows. They crawl on the surface of the ground, seeking leaves and other decaying matter that they will drag underground and eat. Staying in moist soil or damp air is important because this keeps the worm's skin moist. An earthworm obtains oxygen through moisture on its skin.

Did you know that earthworms are among the most helpful inhabitants of garden and farm soil? They benefit people by improving the soil in which plants grow. Earthworm tunnels loosen the soil, allowing air, water, and plant roots to move through it. Earthworm droppings make the soil more fertile.

 **Reading Checkpoint** Why must earthworms stay moist?

Section 4 Assessment

 Target Reading Skill Using Prior Knowledge Review your graphic organizer about worms and revise it based on what you just learned in the section.

Reviewing Key Concepts

1. a. **Listing** What are the three main phyla of worms?
   b. **Describing** What are the common characteristics of the bodies of all worms?
   c. **Explaining** How do worms get information about their environments?
2. a. **Reviewing** What are the main differences among the three main phyla of worms?
   b. **Classifying** Suppose you use a microscope to look at a tiny worm. What characteristics would you look for to classify it?

c. **Comparing and Contrasting** Compare and contrast the types of digestive systems found in worms.

Writing in Science

Interview Suppose that worms can talk, and that you are an editor for *Worm* magazine. You have been assigned to interview a tapeworm about its feeding habits. Write a transcript of your interview—your questions and the worm's answers.

Earthworm Responses

Problem

Do earthworms prefer dry or moist conditions?
Do they prefer light or dark conditions?

Skills Focus

observing, interpreting data

Materials

- plastic dropper • water • cardboard
- clock or watch • paper towels • flashlight
- 2 earthworms • storage container • tray

Procedure

1. Which environment do you think earthworms prefer—dry or moist? Record your hypothesis in your notebook.

2. Use the dropper to sprinkle water on the worms. Keep the worms moist at all times.

3. Fold a dry paper towel and place it on the bottom of one side of your tray. Fold a moistened paper towel and place it on the other side.

4. Moisten your hands. Then place the earthworms in the center of the tray. Make sure that half of each earthworm's body rests on the moist paper towel and half rests on the dry towel. Handle the worms gently.

5. Cover the tray with the piece of cardboard. After five minutes, remove the cardboard and observe whether the worms are on the moist or dry surface. Record your observations.

6. Repeat Steps 4 and 5.

7. Return the earthworms to their storage container. Moisten the earthworms with water.

8. Which do you think earthworms prefer—strong light or darkness? Record your hypothesis in your notebook.

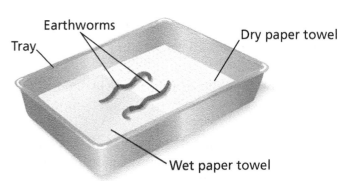

Earthworms

Tray

Dry paper towel

Wet paper towel

9. Cover the whole surface of the tray with a moistened paper towel.

10. Place the earthworms in the center of the tray. Cover half of the tray with cardboard. Shine a flashlight onto the other half.

11. After five minutes, note the locations of the worms. Record your observations.

12. Repeat Steps 10 and 11.

13. Moisten the earthworms and put them in the location designated by your teacher. Wash your hands after handling the worms.

Analyze and Conclude

1. **Observing** Which environment did the worms prefer—moist or dry? Bright or dark?

2. **Interpreting Data** Did the worms' behavior support your hypotheses?

3. **Communicating** Explain in a paragraph what knowledge or experiences helped you develop your hypotheses at the beginning of the experiments.

Design an Experiment

Do earthworms prefer a smooth or rough surface? Write your hypothesis. Then design an experiment to answer the question. *Obtain your teacher's permission before carrying out your investigation.*

① What Is an Animal?

Key Concepts

- The cells of most animals are organized into higher levels of structure, including tissues, organs, and systems.

- The major functions of animals are to obtain food and oxygen, keep internal conditions stable, move, and reproduce.

- Animals are classified according to how they are related to other animals. These relationships are determined by an animal's body structure, the way an animal develops, and its DNA.

Key Terms

cell
tissue
organ
adaptation
sexual reproduction
fertilization
asexual reproduction
phylum
vertebrate
invertebrate

② Animal Symmetry

Key Concepts

- The balanced arrangement of parts, called symmetry, is characteristic of many animals.

- Depending on their symmetry, animals share some general characteristics.

Key Terms

bilateral symmetry
radial symmetry

③ Sponges and Cnidarians

Key Concepts

- Sponges are invertebrate animals that usually have no body symmetry and never have tissues or organs.

- Cnidarians use stinging cells to capture food and defend themselves.

- Coral reefs are home to more species of fishes and invertebrates than any other environment on Earth.

Key Terms

larva
cnidarian
polyp
medusa
colony
coral reef

④ Worms

Key Concepts

- Biologists classify worms into three major phyla—flatworms, roundworms, and segmented worms.

- Flatworms are flat and soft as jelly.

- Unlike cnidarians or flatworms, roundworms have a digestive system that is like a tube, open at both ends.

- Earthworms and other segmented worms have bodies made up of many linked sections called segments.

Key Terms

parasite
host
free-living organism
scavenger
anus
closed circulatory system

Review and Assessment

Go Online
PHSchool.com

For: Self-Assessment
Visit: PHSchool.com
Web Code: cea-2010

Organizing Information

Sequencing Copy the cycle diagram about the life of a sponge onto a sheet of paper. Then complete it and add a title.

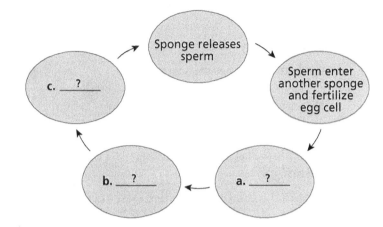

Sponge releases sperm

Sperm enter another sponge and fertilize egg cell

c. _____?_____

b. _____?_____

a. _____?_____

Reviewing Key Terms

Choose the letter of the best answer.

1. The highest level of organization in an animal is a(n)
   a. cell.   b. tissue.
   c. organ.   d. system.

2. An animal without a backbone is called a(n)
   a. vertebrate.
   b. invertebrate.
   c. larva.
   d. parasite.

3. An animal with many lines of symmetry
   a. has bilateral symmetry.
   b. has radial symmetry.
   c. has no symmetry.
   d. has a distinct head and tail end.

4. Which animal is a medusa?
   a. coral
   b. moon jelly
   c. planarian
   d. sea anemone

5. An organism that does not live in or on another organism is called a
   a. scavenger.
   b. parasite.
   c. free-living organism.
   d. host.

If the statement is true, write *true*. If it is false, change the underlined word or words to make the statement true.

6. A tissue is a group of <u>organs</u> that work together to perform a job.

7. Fishes have <u>bilateral symmetry</u>.

8. Budding is a form of <u>sexual reproduction</u>.

9. A <u>polyp</u> is an immature form of an animal that looks very different from the adult form.

10. Some tapeworms are <u>parasites</u> of dogs.

Writing in Science

Letter Suppose that you have just come back from a trip to a coral reef. Write a letter to a friend that compares corals and jellyfish. Be sure to explain how the two animals are alike and how they are different.

Discovery CHANNEL SCHOOL

Sponges, Cnidarians, and Worms
Video Preview
Video Field Trip
▶ Video Assessment

Review and Assessment

Checking Concepts

11. Explain the relationship among cells, tissues, and organs.

12. What are four key functions of animals?

13. What advantages does an animal with bilateral symmetry have over an animal with radial symmetry?

14. Compare and contrast a medusa and a polyp.

15. Are humans parasitic or free-living organisms? Explain.

16. Explain what a one-way digestive system is.

Thinking Critically

17. **Making Judgments** Suppose you check out a book from the library called *Earth's Animals*. You notice that all the animals in the book are vertebrates. Is this title a good one? Explain your reasoning.

18. **Classifying** Classify each of the following animals as having radial symmetry, bilateral symmetry, or no symmetry: sea anemones, sponges, fishes, humans, and butterflies.

19. **Comparing and Contrasting** Compare and contrast the ways in which a sponge, a planarian, and a roundworm digest their food.

20. **Relating Cause and Effect** If a disease killed off many of the earthworms in a garden, how might the plants growing in the soil be affected? Explain.

21. **Classifying** Which of the animals below is a roundworm? A sponge? A cnidarian? Describe the major characteristics of the members of these three phyla.

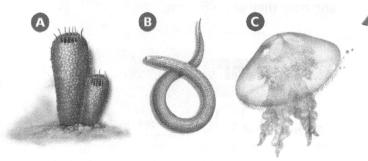

Math Practice

22. **Calculating a Rate** In 24 hours, 110 L of water pass through a sponge. What is the rate of water flow?

Applying Skills

Use the tables to answer Questions 23–25.

A scientist used a pesticide on one field and left a nearby field untreated. Next, she marked off five plots of equal size in each field. Then she dug up a cubic meter of soil beneath each plot and counted the earthworms in the soil. The tables below show her data.

Field With Pesticide		Untreated Field	
Plot	Worms per Cubic Meter	Plot	Worms per Cubic Meter
A	730	F	901
B	254	G	620
C	319	H	811
D	428	I	576
E	451	J	704

23. **Controlling Variables** Identify the manipulated and responding variables in this experiment.

24. **Calculating** Calculate the average number of worms per cubic meter in the field treated with pesticide. Then do the same for the untreated field.

25. **Drawing Conclusions** How did this pesticide affect the number of worms?

Chapter **Project**

Performance Assessment Write a summary explaining what you have learned about your animal. Describe its habitat, the food it eats, its behavior, and any surprising observations that you made. Then introduce your animal to your classmates and share what you have discovered.

Standardized Test Prep

Choose the letter of the best answer.

1. What is the correct sequence in which a stinging cell reacts to the touch of another organism?
   A trigger brushes against prey, stinging cell fires, barbs snare prey
   B barbs snare prey, stinging cell fires, barbs release prey
   C prey is paralyzed, venom enters prey, stinging cell fires
   D tentacles pull prey to mouth, prey is ingested, stinging cell fires

2. Which of the following is true of a one-way digestive system?
   F It is found in all parasites.
   G It has two openings.
   H It has one opening.
   J It is found in all parasites and has one opening.

3. Of the four animals shown below, which has the same symmetry as a jellyfish?

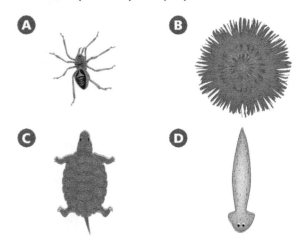

4. Imagine that the animals illustrated above are real and are resting on this page. Predict which of the animals would travel toward the top of the page if they began moving in a straight line.
   F animals A and D
   G animals A and B
   H animals B and D
   J animals A and C

5. The following terms can all be used to describe a tapeworm *except*
   A parasite
   B invertebrate
   C flatworm
   D medusa

Constructed Response

6. Compare and contrast the feeding process of a sponge with that of an earthworm. How are their feeding processes similar? How are they different?

Chapter

2

Mollusks, Arthropods, and Echinoderms

Chapter Preview

This weevil from Southeast Asia uses its impressive front legs to court females.

Discovery
CHANNEL
SCHOOL™

Mollusks, Arthropods, and Echinoderms

▶ Video Preview
Video Field Trip
Video Assessment

Lab zone™ Chapter **Project**

Going Through Changes

Most of the animals you will read about in this chapter change form during their development. In this project, you will observe firsthand how mealworms change as they develop.

Your Goal To observe how different conditions affect mealworm development

To complete this project, you must

- compare mealworm development under two different conditions
- record your mealworm observations daily for several weeks
- draw conclusions about the effects of those conditions on development
- follow the safety guidelines in Appendix A

Plan It! Find two containers, such as clean margarine tubs with lids, in which to keep the mealworms. Get some mealworm food, such as cornflakes, and a plastic spoon to transfer the food and count the mealworms. Choose two conditions, such as two different temperatures or food sources, and plan how to test the two conditions. Once you begin, record your daily observations in a data table, and sketch each stage of development.

Mollusks

Reading Preview

Key Concepts
- What are the main characteristics of mollusks?
- What are the major groups of mollusks and how do they differ?

Key Terms
- mollusk
- open circulatory system • gill
- gastropod • herbivore
- carnivore • radula • bivalve
- omnivore • cephalopod

Target Reading Skill

Comparing and Contrasting
When you compare and contrast things, you explain how they are alike and different. As you read, compare and contrast three groups of mollusks by completing a table like the one below.

Characteristics of Mollusks

Type of Mollusk	How They Obtain Food	How They Move
Gastropod		
Bivalve		
Cephalopod		

 Discover Activity

How Can You Classify Shells?

1. Your teacher will give you an assortment of shells.
2. Examine each shell carefully. Look at the shape and color of the shells and feel their inner and outer surfaces.
3. Classify the shells into groups based on the characteristics you observe.

Think It Over
Inferring How might it help an animal to have a shell? How might it be a disadvantage?

From the shells of clams, Native Americans in the Northeast once carved purple and white beads called wampum. They wove these beads into belts with complex designs that often had special, solemn significance. A wampum belt might record a group's history. When warring groups made peace, they exchanged weavings made of wampum. Iroquois women would honor a new chief with gifts of wampum strings.

The soft bodies inside the shells used to make wampum were a major source of food for Native Americans. Today, clams and similar animals, such as scallops and oysters, are still valuable sources of food for people in many parts of the world.

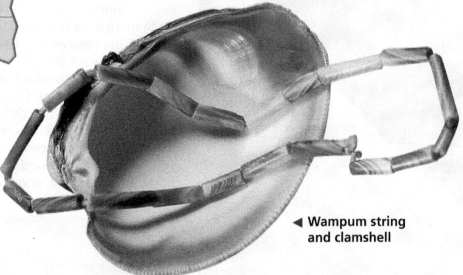

◀ **Wampum string and clamshell**

Characteristics of Mollusks

Clams, oysters, and scallops are all mollusks (phylum Mollusca). Snails and squids are mollusks, too. **Mollusks are invertebrates with soft, unsegmented bodies that are often protected by a hard outer shell. In addition to a soft body often covered by a shell, a mollusk has a thin layer of tissue called a mantle that covers its internal organs, and an organ called a foot.** In many mollusks, the mantle produces the hard shell. Depending on the type of mollusk, the foot has different functions—crawling, digging, or catching prey.

Body Structure Like segmented worms, mollusks have bilateral symmetry and a digestive system with two openings. However, unlike segmented worms, the body parts of mollusks are not usually repeated. Instead, the internal organs are located together in one area, as shown in Figure 1.

Circulatory System Most groups of mollusks have an **open circulatory system,** in which the blood is not always inside blood vessels. The heart pumps blood into a short vessel that opens into the body spaces containing the internal organs. The blood sloshes over the organs and returns eventually to the heart.

Obtaining Oxygen Most mollusks that live in water have **gills,** organs that remove oxygen from the water. The gills have tiny, hairlike structures called cilia and a rich supply of blood vessels. The cilia move back and forth, making water flow over the gills. The gills remove the oxygen from the water and the oxygen moves into the blood. At the same time, carbon dioxide, a waste gas, moves out of the blood and into the water.

 **Reading Checkpoint** Which organs of a mollusk obtain oxygen from water?

FIGURE 1
Comparing Mollusks

Although they don't look much alike at first, a snail, a clam, and a squid have the same basic body structures.

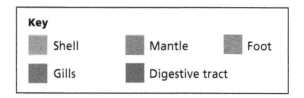

Key

■ Shell ■ Mantle ■ Foot

■ Gills ■ Digestive tract

Snail

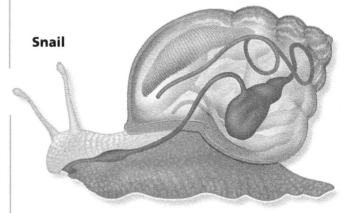

Clam

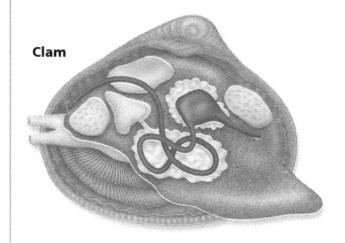

Squid

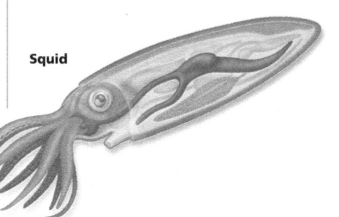

Land Snail

Sea Slug

FIGURE 2
Gastropods
Although the land snail has a shell and the sea slug does not, both are gastropods.

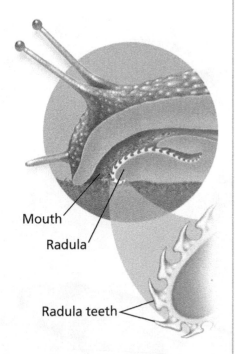
Mouth
Radula
Radula teeth

FIGURE 3
The Radula of a Snail
A snail has a food-gathering organ called a radula, which tears and scrapes up food.

Snails and Slugs

Biologists classify mollusks into groups based on their physical characteristics. These characteristics include the presence of a shell, the type of shell, the type of foot, and the type of nervous system. **The three major groups of mollusks are gastropods, bivalves, and cephalopods.**

The **gastropods** are the largest group of mollusks. They include snails and slugs, like the ones shown in Figure 2, and live nearly everywhere on Earth. They live in oceans, on rocky shores, in fresh water, and on land. **Gastropods have a single external shell or no shell at all.**

Obtaining Food Like all organisms, gastropods need food. Some gastropods are **herbivores,** animals that eat only plants. Some are scavengers that eat decaying material. Still others are **carnivores,** animals that eat only other animals.

But no matter what they eat, gastropods use an organ called a **radula** (RAJ oo luh), a flexible ribbon of tiny teeth, to obtain food. Herbivores use the radula like sandpaper to tear through plant tissues. Carnivores use their radulas in different ways. For example, a gastropod called an oyster drill uses its radula to bore a hole through an oyster's shell. Then it scrapes up the oyster's soft body tissues.

Movement A gastropod usually moves by creeping along on a broad foot. The foot may ooze a carpet of slippery mucus, which you may have seen if you've ever watched a snail move. The mucus makes it easier for the gastropod to move.

Reading
Checkpoint   **What is the function of a radula?**

Two-Shelled Mollusks

A second group of mollusks, **bivalves,** includes oysters, clams, scallops, and mussels. **Bivalves are mollusks that have two shells held together by hinges and strong muscles.** They are found in all kinds of watery environments.

Obtaining Food Like gastropods, bivalves need food. But unlike gastropods, bivalves do not have radulas. Instead, most are filter feeders that strain tiny organisms from water. Bivalves capture food as water flows over their gills. Food particles stick to mucus that covers the gills. The cilia on the gills then move the food particles into the bivalve's mouth. Most bivalves are **omnivores,** animals that eat both plants and animals.

Movement Like gastropods, bivalves don't move quickly. The larvae of most bivalves float or swim through the water. But the adults stay in one place or use their foot to move very slowly. For example, oysters and mussels attach themselves to rocks or other underwater surfaces. Clams, in contrast, move. Look at Figure 4 to see how a clam digs into mud.

Protection Sometimes an object such as a grain of sand gets stuck between a bivalve's mantle and shell. The object irritates the soft mantle. Just as you might put smooth tape around rough bicycle handlebars to protect your hands, the bivalve's mantle produces a smooth, pearly coat to cover the irritating object. Sometimes a pearl forms eventually around the object. Some oysters make beautiful pearls that are used in jewelry.

Skills Activity

Classifying

While wading in a stream, you step on a small animal with a hard covering. As you examine the animal, you discover that it has a soft body inside its shell. It may be a mollusk. What characteristics would you look for to classify the animal into a group of mollusks?

FIGURE 4
How a Clam Digs
A razor clam digs into the mud by changing the shape of its foot.
Predicting *How might the clam use its foot to move back up?*

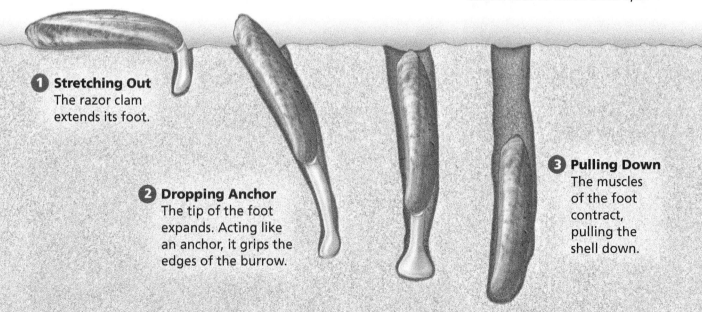

❶ Stretching Out
The razor clam extends its foot.

❷ Dropping Anchor
The tip of the foot expands. Acting like an anchor, it grips the edges of the burrow.

❸ Pulling Down
The muscles of the foot contract, pulling the shell down.

Mollusks,
Arthropods, and
Echinoderms

Video Preview
▶ Video Field Trip
Video Assessment

Octopuses and Their Relatives

Octopuses and squids are **cephalopods** (SEF uh luh pahdz). So are nautiluses and cuttlefishes. **A cephalopod is an ocean-dwelling mollusk whose foot is adapted to form tentacles around its mouth.** Unlike bivalves, not all cephalopods have shells. For example, nautiluses have an external shell, squids and cuttlefish have a small shell within the body, and octopuses have no shells. Cephalopods are the only mollusks with a closed circulatory system.

Obtaining Food Cephalopods are carnivores. A cephalopod captures prey using its muscular tentacles. Then it crushes the prey in a beak and scrapes and cuts the flesh with its radula.

A cephalopod's tentacles contain sensitive suckers, which you can see on the octopus in Figure 5. The suckers receive sensations of taste as well as touch. A cephalopod doesn't have to touch something to taste it because the suckers respond to chemicals in the water. For example, when an octopus feels beneath a rock, its tentacles may find a crab by taste before touching it.

FIGURE 5

Three Cephalopods

A nautilus, an octopus, and a squid are all cephalopods. In cephalopods, the foot is adapted to form tentacles.
Drawing Conclusions *Why is* cephalopod, *which is Greek for "head foot," a good name for members of this group?*

Octopus
Eye
Suckers
Tentacles

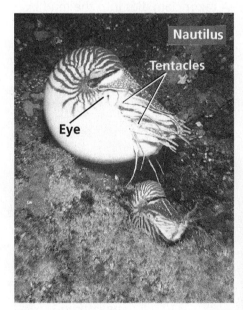

Nautilus
Tentacles
Eye

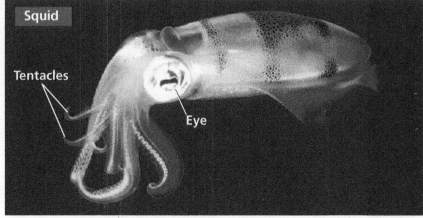

Squid
Tentacles
Eye

Nervous System Cephalopods have large eyes and excellent vision. They also have the most complex nervous system of any invertebrate. Cephalopods have large brains and can remember things they have learned. For example, in captivity, octopuses can learn when to expect deliveries of food. Some even figure out how to escape from their tanks.

Movement Cephalopods swim by jet propulsion. They squeeze a current of water out of the mantle cavity and through a tube. Then, like rockets, they shoot off in the opposite direction. By turning the tube around, they can reverse direction.

 **Reading Checkpoint** What does the foot of a cephalopod look like?

FIGURE 6
An Escaping Octopus
This octopus has figured out how to escape from a jar through a tiny hole in the lid.

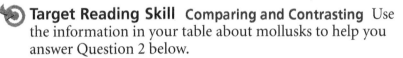

Section 1 Assessment

Target Reading Skill Comparing and Contrasting Use the information in your table about mollusks to help you answer Question 2 below.

Reviewing Key Concepts

1. a. **Listing** List the characteristics of a mollusk.
   b. **Explaining** How is a mollusk's mantle related to its shell?
   c. **Predicting** What would happen to a mollusk if the cilia on its gills did not work? Explain.
2. a. **Identifying** What are three groups of mollusks?
   b. **Classifying** What are the characteristics of the three groups of mollusks?
   c. **Comparing and Contrasting** How are the foot structures of a snail, a clam, and an octopus similar? How are they different?

At-Home Activity

Edible Mollusks Visit a local supermarket with a family member and identify any mollusks that are being sold as food. Be sure to look in places other than the fish counter, such as the canned-foods section. Discuss the parts of the mollusks that are used for food and the parts that are not edible.

SNAIL

A Snail's Pace

Problem

How do changes in the temperature of the environment affect the activity level of a snail?

Skills Focus

interpreting data, predicting

Materials

- freshwater snail
- thermometer
- ruler
- plastic petri dish
- graph paper, 2 sheets
- timer
- spring water at three temperatures: cool (9–13°C); medium (18–22°C); warm (27–31°C)

Procedure

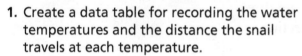

1. Create a data table for recording the water temperatures and the distance the snail travels at each temperature.

2. On one sheet of graph paper labeled *Snail*, trace a circle using the base of an empty petri dish. Divide and label the circle as shown in the illustration. On a second sheet of graph paper labeled *Data*, draw three more circles like the one in the illustration.

3. Place the petri dish over the circle on the Snail page, fill it with cool water, and record the water temperature. Then place the snail in the water just above the "S" in the circle. Handle the snail gently.

4. For five minutes, observe the snail. Record its movements by drawing a line that shows its path in the first circle on the Data page.

5. Find the distance the snail moved by measuring the line you drew. You may need to measure all the parts of the line and add them together. Record the distance in your data table.

6. Repeat Steps 3 through 5, first with medium-temperature water and then with warm water. Record the snail's paths in the second circle and third circle on the Data page.

7. Return the snail to your teacher when you are done. Wash your hands thoroughly.

8. For each temperature, compute the class average for distance traveled.

Analyze and Conclude

1. **Graphing** Make a bar graph showing the class average for each temperature.

2. **Interpreting Data** How does a snail's activity level change as temperature increases?

3. **Predicting** Do you think the pattern you found would continue at higher temperatures? Explain.

4. **Communicating** Write an e-mail to a friend describing how you conducted your experiment, any problems you ran into, and your results. Did your results help answer the question posed at the beginning of the lab? Explain your results to your friend.

Design an Experiment

Design an experiment to measure how different kinds of natural surfaces beneath the snail affect its rate of movement. Obtain three surface materials, such as fine sand, medium-grain gravel, and coarse gravel. Explain how you would modify the procedure. *Obtain your teacher's permission before carrying out your investigation.*

Arthropods

Reading Preview

Key Concepts
- What are the four major groups of arthropods and what are their characteristics?
- How do crustaceans, arachnids, and centipedes and millpedes differ?

Key Terms
- arthropod   • exoskeleton
- molting   • antenna
- crustacean   • metamorphosis
- arachnid   • abdomen

Target Reading Skill

Asking Questions Before you read, preview the red headings. In a graphic organizer like the one below, ask a *what* or a *how* question for each heading. As you read, write the answers to your questions.

Characteristics of Arthropods

Question	Answer
What is an arthropod?	

Discover Activity

Will It Bend and Move?

1. Have a partner roll a piece of cardboard around your arm to form a tube that covers your elbow. Your partner should put three pieces of tape around the tube to hold it closed—one at each end and one in the middle.
2. With the tube in place, try to write your name on a piece of paper. Then try to scratch your head.
3. Keep the tube on your arm for 10 minutes. Observe how the tube affects your ability to do things.

Think It Over
Inferring Insects and many other animals have rigid skeletons on the outside of their bodies. Why do their skeletons need joints?

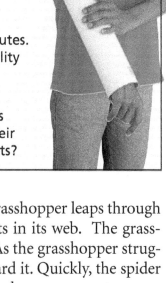

At dusk near the edge of a meadow, a grasshopper leaps through the grass. Nearby, a hungry spider waits in its web. The grasshopper leaps into the web. It's caught! As the grasshopper struggles to free itself, the spider rushes toward it. Quickly, the spider wraps the grasshopper in silk. The grasshopper cannot escape. Soon it will become a tasty meal for the spider.

The spider and grasshopper are both **arthropods,** or members of the arthropod phylum (phylum Arthropoda). Animals such as crabs, lobsters, centipedes, and scorpions are also arthropods.

FIGURE 7
A Spider at Work
This spider wraps its prey, a grasshopper, in silk. Both animals are arthropods.

Characteristics of Arthropods

Arthropods are classified into four major groups. **The major groups of arthropods are crustaceans, arachnids, centipedes and millipedes, and insects.** All arthropods share certain characteristics. **Arthropods are invertebrates that have an external skeleton, a segmented body, and jointed attachments called appendages.** Wings, mouthparts, and legs are all appendages. Jointed appendages are such a distinctive characteristic that arthropods are named for it. *Arthros* means "joint" in Greek, and *podos* means "foot" or "leg."

Arthropods share some characteristics with many other animals, too. They have bilateral symmetry, an open circulatory system, and a digestive system with two openings. In addition, most arthropods reproduce sexually.

Outer Skeleton If you were an arthropod, you would have a waterproof covering. This waxy covering is called an **exoskeleton,** or outer skeleton. It protects the animal and helps prevent evaporation of water. Water animals are surrounded by water, but land animals need a way to keep from drying out. Arthropods may have been the first animals to live on land. Their exoskeletons probably enabled them to do this because they keep the arthropods from drying out.

As an arthropod grows larger, its exoskeleton cannot expand. The growing arthropod is trapped within its exoskeleton, like a knight in armor that is too small. Arthropods solve this problem by occasionally shedding their exoskeletons and growing new ones that are larger. The process of shedding an outgrown exoskeleton is called **molting.** After an arthropod has molted, its new skeleton is soft for a time. During that time, the arthropod has less protection from danger than it does after its new skeleton has hardened.

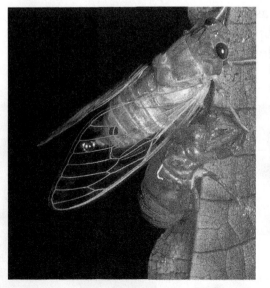

FIGURE 9
A Molting Cicada
This cicada has just molted. You can see its old exoskeleton hanging on the leaf just below it.
Applying Concepts *Why must arthropods molt?*

Comparisons of the Largest Arthropod Groups				
Characteristic	Crustaceans	Arachnids	Centipedes and Millipedes	Insects
Number of body sections	2 or 3	2	2	3
Pairs of legs	5 or more	4	Many	3
Pairs of antennae	2	None	1	1

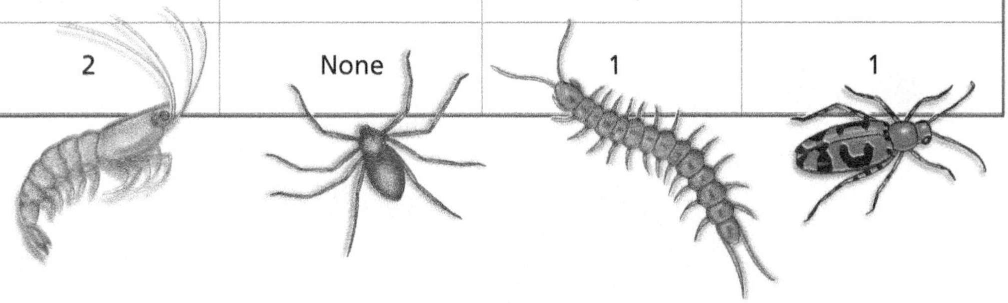

FIGURE 10
Members of the largest arthropod groups differ in several characteristics. **Interpreting Tables** *Which group of arthropods has no antennae?*

Segmented Body The bodies of arthropods are segmented. A segmented body plan is easiest to see in centipedes and millipedes, which have bodies made up of many identical-looking segments. In fact, their bodies look something like the bodies of earthworms. You can also see segments on the tails of shrimp and lobsters. In some groups of arthropods, several body segments become joined into distinct sections. An arthropod may have up to three sections—a head, a midsection, and a hind section.

Jointed Appendages Just as your fingers are appendages attached to your palms, many arthropods have jointed appendages attached to their bodies. The joints in the appendages give the animal flexibility and enable it to move. If you did the Discover activity, you saw how important joints are for allowing movement. Arthropod appendages tend to be highly specialized tools used for moving, obtaining food, reproducing, and sensing the environment. For example, arthropods use legs to walk and wings to fly. In addition, most arthropods have appendages called antennae (singular *antenna*). An **antenna** is an appendage attached to the head that contains sense organs.

Diversity Scientists have identified more species of arthropods—over one million—than all other species of animals combined! There are probably many others that have not yet been discovered. Look at Figure 10 to compare some characteristics of the four major groups of arthropods.

 **Reading Checkpoint** What does an antenna do?

Go Online
*SC*LINKS_TM **NSTA**

For: Links on arthropods
Visit: www.SciLinks.org
Web Code: scn-0222

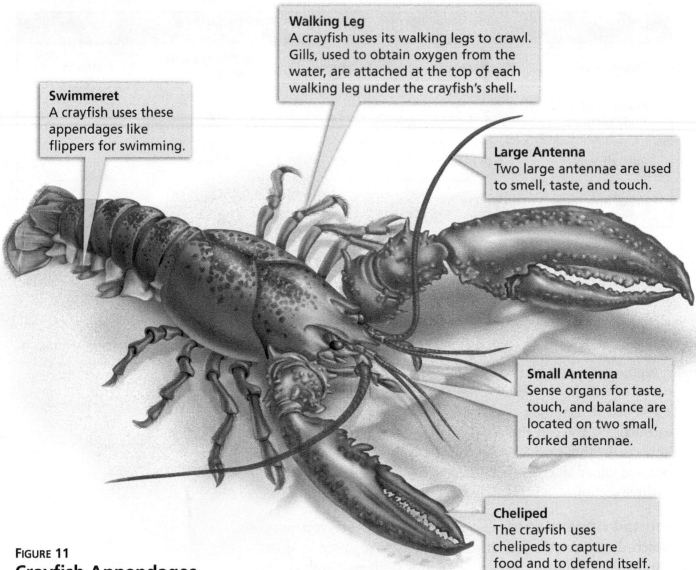

Walking Leg
A crayfish uses its walking legs to crawl. Gills, used to obtain oxygen from the water, are attached at the top of each walking leg under the crayfish's shell.

Swimmeret
A crayfish uses these appendages like flippers for swimming.

Large Antenna
Two large antennae are used to smell, taste, and touch.

Small Antenna
Sense organs for taste, touch, and balance are located on two small, forked antennae.

Cheliped
The crayfish uses chelipeds to capture food and to defend itself.

FIGURE 11
Crayfish Appendages
A crayfish's appendages are as varied as the tools on a Swiss army knife. The appendages are adapted for different functions.
Interpreting Diagrams *What functions do the chelipeds serve?*

Crustaceans

If you've ever eaten shrimp cocktail or crab cakes, you've dined on **crustaceans** (krus TAY shunz). Crayfish and lobsters are other familiar crustaceans. Crustaceans thrive in freshwater lakes and rivers, and even in puddles that last a long time. You can find them in the deepest parts of oceans and along coastlines. A few, like the pill bug, live in damp places on land.

Body Structure Crustaceans share certain characteristics. **A crustacean is an arthropod that has two or three body sections, five or more pairs of legs, and two pairs of antennae.** Each crustacean body segment has a pair of legs or another type of appendage attached to it. The various types of appendages function differently, as you can see in Figure 11.

The appendages attached to the head of a crayfish include two pairs of antennae that are used for smelling, tasting, touching, and keeping balance. The crayfish uses most of its leg appendages for walking. However, it uses its first pair of legs, called chelipeds, for obtaining food and defending itself.

Obtaining Oxygen and Food Because crustaceans live in watery environments, most have gills to obtain oxygen. The gills are located beneath the shell of a crustacean. Water containing oxygen reaches the gills as a crustacean moves along in its environment.

Crustaceans obtain food in many ways. Some are scavengers that eat dead plants and animals. Others are predators, eating animals they have killed. The pistol shrimp is a predator with an appendage that moves with such force that it stuns its prey. Krill, which are shrimplike crustaceans that live in cold ocean waters, are herbivores that eat plantlike microorganisms. In turn, krill are eaten by predators such as fishes, penguins, seals, and even great blue whales, the world's largest animals.

Life Cycle Most crustaceans, such as crabs, barnacles, and shrimp, begin their lives as microscopic, swimming larvae. The bodies of these larvae do not resemble those of adults. Crustacean larvae develop into adults by **metamorphosis** (met uh MAWR fuh sis), a process in which an animal's body undergoes dramatic changes in form during its life cycle.

 **Reading Checkpoint** What organs does a crustacean use to obtain oxygen?

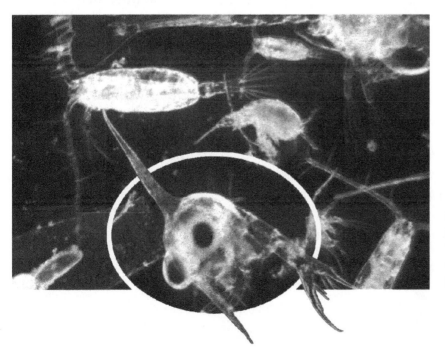

FIGURE 12
Crab Larva
This larva of a crab floats in the ocean with other microscopic animals.

Try This Activity

Pill Bugs—Wet or Dry?

1. Line a box with aluminum foil. Tape down two paper towels side by side in the box. Tape a strip of masking tape between the two towels. Moisten one of the paper towels. Keep the other towel dry.

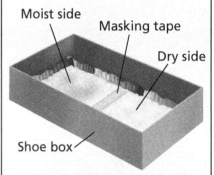

2. Put ten pill bugs on the masking tape. Then put a lid on the box.

3. After 5 minutes, lift the lid and count the pill bugs on the dry towel, the moist towel, and the masking tape. Record your results in a data table.

4. Repeat Steps 2 and 3 two more times. Then average the results of the three trials. Wash your hands after handling the pill bugs.

Interpreting Data Do pill bugs prefer a moist or a dry environment?

FIGURE 13
Red Knee Tarantula
This red knee tarantula lives in an underground burrow. The spider uses fangs to inject venom into its prey.

Arachnids

Spiders, mites, ticks, and scorpions are the **arachnids** (uh RAK nidz) that people most often meet. **Arachnids are arthropods with two body sections, four pairs of legs, and no antennae.** Their first body section is a combined head and midsection. The hind section, called the **abdomen,** is the other section. The abdomen contains the reproductive organs and part of the digestive system.

Spiders Spiders are probably the most familiar, most feared, and most fascinating kind of arachnid. All spiders are predators, and most of them eat insects. Some, such as tarantulas and wolf spiders, run down their prey. Others, such as golden garden spiders, spin sticky webs to trap their prey.

Spiders have hollow fangs through which they inject venom into their prey. Spider venom turns the tissues of the prey into mush. Later the spider uses its fangs like drinking straws, and sucks in the food. In spite of what some people might think, spiders rarely bite people. When spiders do bite, their bites are often painful but not life-threatening. However, the bite of a brown recluse or a black widow may require hospital care.

FIGURE 14
Dust Mite
This microscopic dust mite feeds on dead skin and hair shed by humans. **Classifying** *Would you describe the mite as a carnivore, scavenger, or filter feeder? Why?*

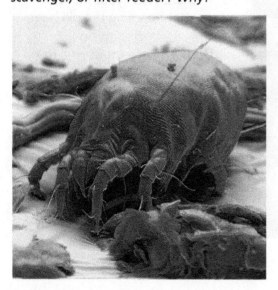

Mites If chiggers have ever given you an itchy rash, you've had an unpleasant encounter with tiny arachnids called mites. Chiggers and many other mites are parasites. Ear mites, for example, give dogs and cats itchy ears. Mites are everywhere. Even the cleanest houses have microscopic dust mites. If you are allergic to dust, you may actually be allergic to the exoskeletons of dust mites. In addition to living in dry areas, mites also live in fresh water and in the ocean.

 Reading Checkpoint) **What kind of arachnid is a chigger?**

FIGURE 15
Scorpion
A scorpion is a carnivore that injects venom from a stinger at the end of its abdomen.

Scorpions

Scorpions live mainly in hot climates, and are usually active at night. During the day, scorpions hide in cool places—under rocks and logs, or in holes in the ground, for example. At the end of its abdomen, a scorpion has a spinelike stinger. The scorpion uses the stinger to inject venom into its prey, which is usually a spider or an insect.

Ticks

Ticks are parasites that live on the outside of a host animal's body. Nearly every kind of land animal has a species of tick that sucks its blood. Some ticks that attack humans can carry diseases. Lyme disease, for example, is spread by the bite of an infected deer tick. You can see an enlarged deer tick to the right. In reality, a deer tick is just a few millimeters long.

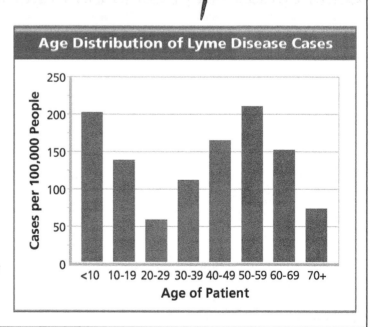

◀ Deer tick

Math Analyzing Data

Lyme Disease Cases

The graph shows the numbers of cases of Lyme disease by age group reported by Connecticut during one year. Use the graph to answer the questions.

1. **Reading Graphs** What variable is plotted on the y-axis? What does the first bar tell you?

2. **Interpreting Data** Which age group is least at risk for Lyme disease? Explain.

3. **Interpreting Data** Which two age groups are most at risk?

4. **Calculating** Suppose a particular school in Connecticut has 1,000 students ranging in age from 10 to 19. About how many of these students would you expect to get Lyme disease per year?

Age Distribution of Lyme Disease Cases

Cases per 100,000 People (y-axis): 0, 50, 100, 150, 200, 250

Age of Patient (x-axis): <10, 10-19, 20-29, 30-39, 40-49, 50-59, 60-69, 70+

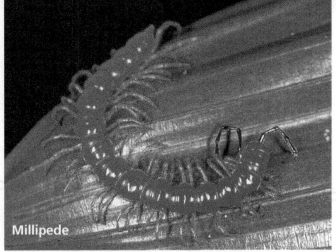

Centipede

Millipede

FIGURE 16
Centipede and Millipede
Both centipedes and millipedes
have many pairs of legs.
Interpreting Photographs *How
many pairs of legs does each
segment of the centipede have?*

Centipedes and Millipedes

**Centipedes and millipedes are arthropods with two body
sections and many pairs of legs.** The two body sections are a
head with one pair of antennae, and a long abdomen with
many segments. Centipedes have one pair of legs attached to
each segment. Some centipedes have more than 100 segments.
In fact, the word *centipede* means "hundred feet." Centipedes
are swift predators that inject venom into their prey.

Millipedes, which may have more than 80 segments, have two
pairs of legs on each segment—more legs than any other arthropod. Though *millipede* means "thousand feet," they don't have
quite that many legs. Most millipedes are scavengers that graze on
partly decayed leaves. When they are disturbed, millipedes can
curl up into a ball, protected by their tough exoskeleton. Some will
also squirt an awful-smelling liquid at a potential predator.

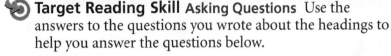

Section **2** **Assessment**

Target Reading Skill Asking Questions Use the
answers to the questions you wrote about the headings to
help you answer the questions below.

Reviewing Key Concepts

1. **a. Naming** What are the major groups of arthropods?
   b. Summarizing How are all arthropods alike?
   c. Applying Concepts Some restaurants serve soft-
   shelled crab. What do you think happened to the crab
   just before it was caught?

2. **a. Identifying** What are the characteristics of a
   crustacean?
   b. Reviewing Describe the body structure of an
   arachnid.
   c. Comparing and Contrasting How are centipedes and
   millipedes alike? How are they different?

Writing in Science

Observation Write about an
arthropod that you have observed.
Describe details about its physical
appearance, its movements, and
any other behaviors that you
observed.

Insects

Reading Preview

Key Concepts
- What are the main characteristics of insects?
- What is one way insects are adapted to obtain particular types of food?
- What are two types of metamorphosis that insects undergo?

Key Terms
- insect • thorax
- complete metamorphosis
- pupa
- gradual metamorphosis
- nymph

Target Reading Skill

Sequencing A sequence is the order in which a series of events or steps in a process occurs. As you read, make a cycle diagram that shows the steps in the complete metamorphosis of an insect. Write each step in a separate circle.

Complete Metamorphosis

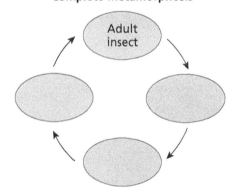

 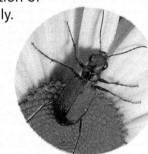

Discover Activity

What Characteristics Do Insects Share?

1. Your teacher will give you a collection of insects. Observe the insects carefully.
2. Note the physical characteristics of each insect's body covering. Count the number of body sections.
3. Count the number of legs, wings, and antennae on each insect. Then return the insects to your teacher and wash your hands.

Think It Over
Inferring Compare the legs and the wings of two different species of insect. How is each insect adapted to move?

What do you do if you want to avoid being noticed? You keep perfectly quiet and you don't do anything that will attract attention. You might even wear clothes that help you to blend into the environment—a tactic called camouflage. The thorn insect is a master of camouflage. Not only does it look like a thorn, but it acts like one, too, staying quite still unless a predator like a bird comes too close. Then it springs away to safety.

Other kinds of insects have different camouflage tactics. For example, some caterpillars look like bird droppings, and others look and act like twigs. Plant hoppers may gather in clusters that look like yellow blossoms. And many kinds of moths resemble dead leaves.

Thorn insect ▶

Graphing

Use the data to make a circle graph that shows the percentage of total insect species in each group. (See the Skills Handbook.)

Insect Groups

Group	Number of Species
Ants, bees, and wasps	115,000
Beetles and weevils	350,000
Butterflies and moths	178,000
Flies and mosquitoes	110,000
Other insect groups	147,000

Body Structure

Moths are **insects,** as are caterpillers, plant hoppers, dragonflies, cockroaches, and bees. You can identify insects, like other arthropods, by counting their body sections and legs. **Insects are arthropods with three body sections, six legs, one pair of antennae, and usually one or two pairs of wings.** The three body sections are the head, thorax, and abdomen, as you can see in Figure 17.

Head Most of an insect's sense organs, such as the eyes and antennae, are located on the head. Insects usually have two large compound eyes. These eyes contain many lenses, which are structures that focus light to form images. Compound eyes are especially keen at seeing movement. Most insects also have small simple eyes that can distinguish between light and darkness.

Thorax An insect's midsection, or **thorax,** is the section to which wings and legs are attached. Most species of insects can fly once they are adults. Insects are the only invertebrates that can fly. By flying, insects can travel long distances to find mates, food, and new places to live. Being able to fly also enables insects to escape from many predators.

Abdomen Inside the abdomen are many of the insect's internal organs. Small holes on the outside of the abdomen lead to a system of tubes inside the insect. These tubes allow air, which contains oxygen, to enter the body. The oxygen in the air travels directly to the insect's cells.

Reading Checkpoint What are the three sections of an insect's body?

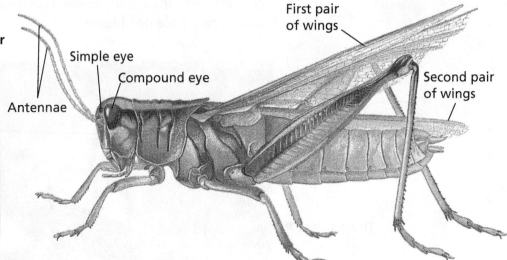

FIGURE 17
Structure of a Grasshopper
A grasshopper's body, like that of every insect, has three sections.

First pair of wings

Simple eye

Compound eye

Antennae

Second pair of wings

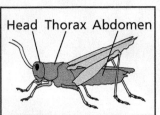

Head Thorax Abdomen

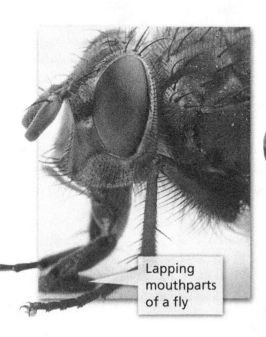
Lapping mouthparts of a fly

Sucking mouthparts of a butterfly

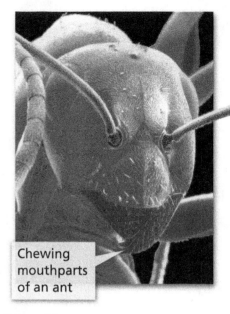
Chewing mouthparts of an ant

FIGURE 18
Diversity of Mouthparts
The mouthparts of this fly, butterfly, and wood ant are very different in their structure.
Inferring *Could a butterfly eat an ant's food? Explain.*

Obtaining Food

The rule seems to be this: If it is living, or if it once was living, some kind of insect will eat it. You probably know that many insects eat parts of plants, such as leaves or nectar. But insects also eat products that are made from plants, such as paper. If you open a very old book, watch for book lice. These tiny insects live in old books, chewing crooked tunnels through the pages.

Insects may feed on animals, too. Some, like fleas and mosquitoes, feed on the blood of living animals. Others, like dung beetles, feed on animal droppings. Still others, like burying beetles, feed on the decaying bodies of dead animals.

An insect's mouthparts are adapted for a highly specific way of getting food. You can see some of these adaptations in Figure 18. Some flies have a sponge-like mouthpart that they use to lap up decaying flesh. A butterfly's mouthparts are shaped like a coiled tube, which can be uncoiled and used like a drinking straw to suck up nectar from flowers. Most ants have sharp-edged mouthparts that can cut through seeds, wood, and other foods.

Reading Checkpoint **How does a butterfly obtain food?**

Life Cycle

Insects begin life as tiny, hard-shelled, fertilized eggs. After they hatch, insects begin a process of metamorphosis that eventually produces an adult insect. **Each insect species undergoes either complete metamorphosis or gradual metamorphosis.**

Go Online
PHSchool.com

For: More on insect metamorphosis
Visit: PHSchool.com
Web Code: ced-2023

FIGURE 19
Insect Metamorphosis

Depending on the species, most insects develop into adults through complete metamorphosis or gradual metamorphosis.

1 Egg
Female fireflies lay their eggs in moist places. The eggs of fireflies glow in the dark.

2 Larva
The eggs hatch into larvae that feed on snails and slugs.

Complete
Metamorphosis

4 Adult
When its development is complete, an adult firefly crawls out of its pupal case and unfurls its wings. Adult fireflies flash their light to attract mates.

3 Pupa
After a time, the firefly larva becomes a pupa. Inside the protective pupal case, wings, legs, and antennae form.

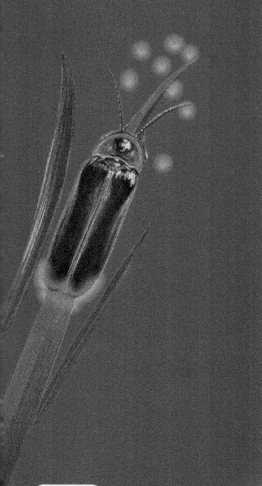

Complete Metamorphosis In Figure 19 you can see that an insect with **complete metamorphosis** has four different stages: egg, larva, pupa, and adult. Eggs hatch into larvae. The larvae, such as the caterpillars of butterflies and the grubs of beetles, usually look something like worms. Larvae are specialized for eating and growing. After a time, a larva enters the next stage of the process and becomes a **pupa** (PYOO puh). As a pupa, the insect is enclosed in a protective covering.

Although the pupa does not eat and moves very little, it is not resting. Major changes in body structure are taking place in this stage, as the pupa becomes an adult insect. Beetles, butterflies, flies, and ants all undergo complete metamorphosis.

Gradual Metamorphosis In contrast, the second type of metamorphosis, called **gradual metamorphosis**, has no distinct larval stage. An egg hatches into a stage called a **nymph** (nimf), which usually looks like the adult insect without wings. A nymph may molt several times before becoming an adult. Grasshoppers, termites, cockroaches, and dragonflies go through gradual metamorphosis.

 Reading Checkpoint **What is gradual metamorphosis?**

④ Adult
The adult grasshopper emerges from the final molt equipped with full-sized wings. Once its wings have hardened, the adult flies off to mate and begin the cycle again.

① Egg
A female grasshopper uses the tip of her abdomen to jab holes in the soil where she lays her eggs.

Gradual Metamorphosis

② Nymph
Eggs hatch into nymphs that look much like miniature adults, except that they have no wings, or only small ones.

③ Larger Nymph
A nymph feeds until its exoskeleton becomes too tight, and then it molts. The nymph molts four or five times before becoming an adult.

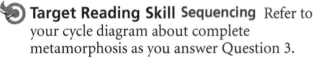

Section 3 Assessment

Target Reading Skill Sequencing Refer to your cycle diagram about complete metamorphosis as you answer Question 3.

Reviewing Key Concepts

1. a. **Identifying** What characteristics do insects share?
   b. **Interpreting Diagrams** Look at Figure 17. To which body section are a grasshopper's wings attached?
   c. **Making Generalizations** Suppose the adaptation of wings was suddenly lost in all insects. Predict what would happen to the number and diversity of insects.
2. a. **Naming** Name a type of insect that has chewing mouthparts.
   b. **Reviewing** What are three ways that the mouthparts of insects are adapted for obtaining food?

3. a. **Listing** List the stages of gradual metamorphosis and the stages of complete metamorphosis.
   b. **Interpreting Diagrams** Look at Figure 19. How are complete metamorphosis and gradual metamorphosis different?
   c. **Applying Concepts** Why is a nymph more likely than a larva to eat the same food as its parents?

> **Lab zone** **At-Home Activity**
>
> **Bug Hunt** Walk with a family member in your backyard or neighborhood. Search the undersides of leaves, under woodchips or rocks, and other likely places for insects. Show your family member what distinguishes an insect from other kinds of arthropods.

What's Living in the Soil?

Problem

What kinds of animals live in soil and leaf litter?

Skills Focus

observing, classifying

Materials

- 2-liter plastic bottle
- large scissors
- trowel
- cheesecloth
- large rubber band
- gooseneck lamp
- hand lens
- large, wide-mouthed jar
- small jar
- coarse steel wool
- fresh sample of soil and leaf litter

Procedure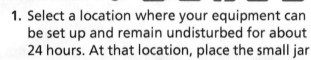

1. Select a location where your equipment can be set up and remain undisturbed for about 24 hours. At that location, place the small jar inside the center of the large jar as shown in the photograph on page 61.

2. Use scissors to cut a large plastic bottle in half. **CAUTION:** *Cut in a direction away from yourself and others.* Turn the top half of the bottle upside down to serve as a funnel.

3. Insert a small amount of coarse steel wool into the mouth of the funnel to keep the soil from falling out. Do not pack the steel wool too tightly. Leave spaces for small organisms to crawl through. Place the funnel into the large jar as shown in the photograph.

4. Using the trowel, fill the funnel with soil and surface leaf litter. When you finish, wash your hands thoroughly.

5. Look closely to see whether the soil and litter are dry or wet. Record your observation.

6. Make a cover for your sample by placing a piece of cheesecloth over the top of the funnel. Hold the cheesecloth in place with a large rubber band. Immediately position a lamp about 15 cm above the funnel, and turn on the light. Allow this setup to remain undisturbed for about 24 hours. **CAUTION:** *Hot light bulbs can cause burns. Do not touch the bulb.*

7. When you are ready to make your observations, turn off the lamp. Leave the funnel and jar in place while making your observations. Use a hand lens to examine each organism in the jar. **CAUTION:** *Do not touch any of the organisms.*

8. Use a data table like the one shown to sketch each type of organism and to record other observations. Be sure to include evidence that will help you classify the organisms. (*Hint:* Remember that some animals may be at different stages of metamorphosis.)

9. Examine the soil and leaf litter, and record whether this material is dry or wet.

10. When you are finished, follow your teacher's directions about returning the organisms to the soil. Wash your hands with soap.

Data Table				
Sketch of Organism	Number Found	Size	Important Characteristics	Probable Phylum

Analyze and Conclude

1. **Observing** Describe the conditions of the soil environment at the beginning and end of the lab. What caused the change?

2. **Classifying** What types of animals did you collect in the small jar? What characteristics did you use to identify each type of animal? Which types of animals were the most common?

3. **Developing Hypotheses** Why do you think the animals moved down the funnel away from the soil?

4. **Inferring** Using what you have learned about arthropods and other animals, make an inference about the role that each animal you collected plays in the environment.

5. **Communicating** Develop a field guide that categorizes and describes the types of animals you found in your soil sample. Include sketches and brief descriptions of the animals.

Design an Experiment

What kinds of organisms might live in other soil types—for example, soil at the edge of a pond, dry sandy soil, or commercially prepared potting soil? Design an experiment to answer this question.

Insect Ecology

Reading Preview

Key Concepts
- Why are insects important in food chains?
- What are two other ways insects interact with their environments?
- What are some ways used to control insect pests?

Key Terms
- food chain • ecology
- producer • consumer
- decomposer • pollinator
- pesticide
- biological control

Target Reading Skill

Building Vocabulary Using a word in a sentence helps you think about how best to explain the word. After you read the section, reread the paragraphs that contain definitions of Key Terms. Use all the information you have learned to write a meaningful sentence using the Key Term.

Discover **Activity**

What Materials Carry Pollen Best?

1. Use an eraser to transfer some pollen between two flowers your teacher gives you.
2. Next, use a cotton swab to do the same. Did the eraser or cotton swab transfer pollen better?

Think It Over
Inferring How might its ability to transfer pollen between flowers affect an insect's role in the environment?

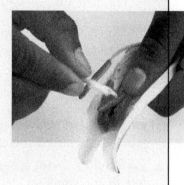

In a meadow, a caterpillar munches the leaves of a plant. Later that day, a bird eats the caterpillar. Years later, after the bird has died, a beetle eats the dead bird. The plant, caterpillar, bird, and beetle are all part of one food chain. A **food chain** is a series of events in which one organism eats another and obtains energy. The study of food chains and other ways that organisms interact with their environment is called **ecology.**

Insects and the Food Chain

A food chain starts with a **producer**—an organism that makes its own food. Most producers, such as grass and other plants, use energy from sunlight to make their food. In a food chain, producers are food for consumers. A **consumer** is an organism that obtains energy by eating other organisms. Some consumers, like caterpillars, eat producers, and some eat other consumers. Decomposers, such as carrion beetles, also play a role in food chains. A **decomposer** breaks down the wastes and dead bodies of other organisms. In a food chain insects may play the roles of consumer and decomposer. In addition, some insects are prey for other consumers.

Insects as Consumers of Plants The roles of insects in a food chain are shown in Figure 20. **Insects play key roles in food chains because of the many different ways that they obtain food and then become food for other animals.**

Many insects are consumers of plants. Perhaps you have tried growing tomato plants and seen how fat green caterpillars ate up the leaves. In fact, insects eat about 20 percent of the crops grown for humans. Insects eat most species of wild plants, too. Some insects eat the leaves of plants, while others eat the sap, bark, roots, and other parts of plants.

Insects as Prey Insects play another role in food chains—they are prey for many animals. That is, other consumers eat insects. Many fishes and birds eat insects to survive. For example, the main source of food for trout and bass is insects. Indeed, that's why people use lures called "flies" to catch fishes like these. The lures look like the mayflies and stoneflies these fishes normally eat. Some species of birds feed their young, called chicks, only insects. And the chicks are big eaters! A single swallow chick, for example, may consume about 200,000 insects before it leaves the nest.

Percentage

A percentage is a ratio that compares a number to 100. If 25 percent of 900,000 insect species eat other insects, how many insect-eating species are there? Set up a proportion and solve it.

$$\frac{\text{Insect-eating species}^{X}}{900,000 \text{ insect species}} = \frac{25\%}{100\%}$$

Insect-eating species = 225,000

Practice Problem A swallow chick eats 200,000 insects. If 12 percent of the insects are beetles, how many beetles does it eat?

$$\frac{\text{beetles}}{200,000} = \frac{12}{100}$$

$$100X = 2400000$$

$$X = 24,000$$

FIGURE 20

Insects in a Food Chain

In a food chain, some insects are consumers of plants. Some insects are prey for other consumers. Other insects are decomposers.

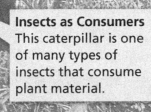

Insects as Decomposers
This carrion beetle feeds on the tissues of a dead bird.

Insects as Prey
Caterpillars and other insects are consumed by other types of animals, such as birds.

Insects as Consumers
This caterpillar is one of many types of insects that consume plant material.

Insects as Decomposers In a food chain some insects play the role of decomposers by breaking down the wastes and bodies of dead organisms. For example, in some tropical food chains, termites may break down up to one third of the dead wood, leaves, and grass produced there every year. In other food chains, flies and dung beetles break down animal droppings, called manure. By doing this, the buildup of manure from large animals is prevented.

The substances that insect decomposers break down enrich the soil. In addition, insect decomposers may burrow and nest in the ground. By doing so, these insects expose soil to oxygen from the air and mix up the nutrients in the soil.

• Tech & Design in History •

Products From Insects

Over the last few thousand years, insects have supplied humans with some important products.

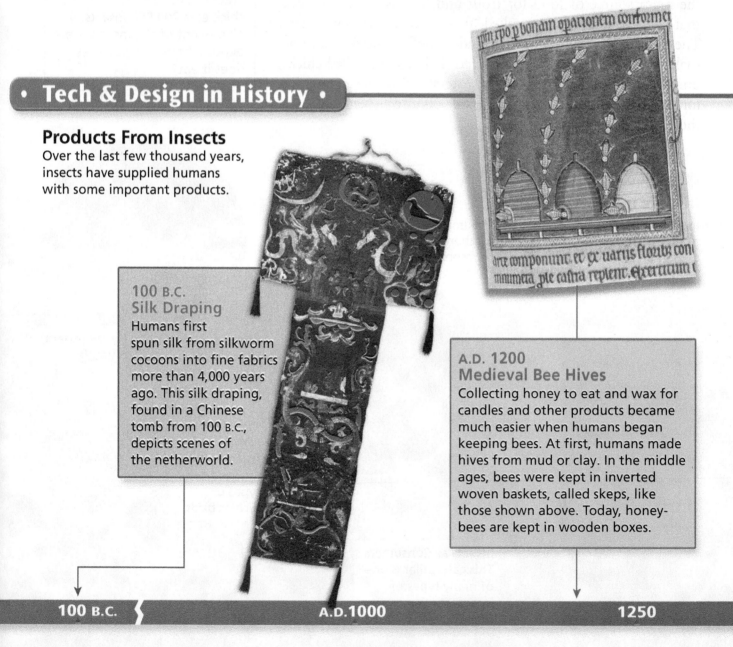

100 B.C.
Silk Draping
Humans first spun silk from silkworm cocoons into fine fabrics more than 4,000 years ago. This silk draping, found in a Chinese tomb from 100 B.C., depicts scenes of the netherworld.

A.D. 1200
Medieval Bee Hives
Collecting honey to eat and wax for candles and other products became much easier when humans began keeping bees. At first, humans made hives from mud or clay. In the middle ages, bees were kept in inverted woven baskets, called skeps, like those shown above. Today, honeybees are kept in wooden boxes.

100 B.C.   **A.D. 1000**   **1250**

Insects as Food for Humans Did you know that insects were an important source of nutrition for prehistoric humans? Even today, insects are collected and eaten by people in many parts of the world. In some Mexican villages, dried grasshoppers are ground up and mixed with flour to make tortillas. In other parts of the world, the larvae of certain species of beetles are roasted over an open fire. Ants, crickets, and cicadas are just a few of the other types of insects eaten by humans.

Maybe you are thinking, "Yuck! I'd never eat an insect." Even if you'd never allow an insect on your dinner plate, you are likely to have used the products of insects in other aspects of your daily life. You can see some of the major uses of insect products through history in the timeline below.

 **Reading Checkpoint** What is an animal that breaks down wastes and dead organisms called?

Writing in Science

Research and Write
Research one of the products described in the timeline below. Then write an advertisement for the product. Include information about the species of insect used to develop the product, and details about how the product is made.

**1518
Cochineal Dye**
Explorer Hernando Cortez reported the use of the red dye, cochineal, in Mexico. The dye is extracted from a tiny cactus-eating insect called the cochineal scale. Today, humans use the dye to color some textiles, foods, and cosmetics.

**1920s
Shellac Records**
Humans make shellac from a waxy substance secreted by the lac scale insect. Shellac has been used to seal furniture, polish floors, and coat records. Shellac was especially important to the record industry in the 1920s and 1930s (until synthetic vinyl came along in the 1940s).

**1980s
Firefly Light**
Since the 1980s, scientists have used the light-producing chemicals from fireflies in many applications, including the study of genes and diseases.

1500	1750	2000

FIGURE 21
A Bee as a Pollinator
This bee is getting dusted with yellow pollen as it drinks nectar from the flower. **Observing** *On which of the bee's structures can you observe pollen grains?*

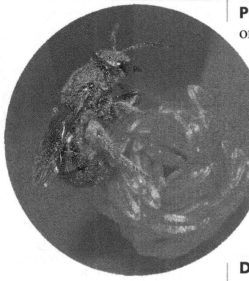

Other Interactions

Besides eating and being eaten, insects interact in other ways with the living things in their environments. **Two ways insects interact with other living things are by moving pollen among plants and by spreading disease-causing organisms.**

Pollen Carriers Have you ever seen a bee crawling into a flower on a warm summer day? Have you wondered what it is doing? The bee is helping itself to the plant's nectar and pollen, which are food for bees. But plants also need to share their pollen with other plants. Pollen contains cells that become sperm cells, allowing plants to reproduce. When the bee crawls into a flower to obtain its food, it gets dusted with pollen, as shown in Figure 21. Then, as the bee enters the next flower, some of the pollen on its body is left in the second flower. An animal that carries pollen among plants is called a **pollinator.** Bees are pollinators, and so are many beetles and flies. Without pollinators, some plants cannot reproduce.

Disease Carriers Not all interactions between insects and other living things have happy endings. While some insects transfer pollen, others spread diseases to both plants and animals, including humans. Insects that spread diseases include some mosquitoes and fleas. These insects often have sucking mouthparts that pierce the skin of their prey, providing an opening for the disease-causing organisms to enter. Diseases that are carried by insects include malaria, which is spread by mosquitoes. Malaria causes high fevers and can be treated with medicines today.

 **Reading Checkpoint** What is a pollinator?

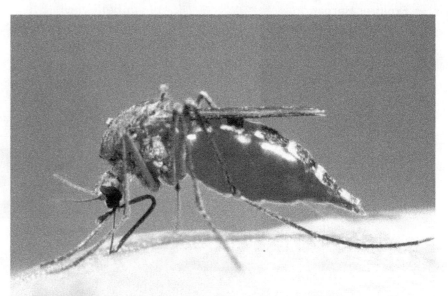

FIGURE 22
Disease-Causing Mosquito
A mosquito like the one shown here can spread disease-causing organisms such as malaria among humans.

Controlling Pests

Some insects are harmful, even though they don't spread diseases. Harmful insects are called pests. **To try to control pests, people use chemicals, traps, and living things, including other insects.** Chemicals that kill pests are called **pesticides.** However, pesticides also kill pollinators, such as bees, and can harm other animals.

What are the alternatives to pesticides? Biologists are using their knowledge of insect ecology to develop new pest controls. One such control is a trap that attracts mosquitoes in a way similar to how humans attract mosquitoes. Another control is to surround crops with wild plants that are bad-tasting or even poisonous to the harmful insect.

People may prefer to use biological controls. A **biological control** is a natural predator or disease released into an area to fight a harmful insect. For example, ladybugs, which eat other insects, have been introduced to some areas where crops grow to control aphids. Aphids are tiny insects that damage plants by sucking plant sap.

FIGURE 23
Biological Control
Ladybugs are used as biological control agents against aphids. Here, one ladybug consumes its prey.

> **Reading Checkpoint** What is a chemical intended to kill pest insects called?

Section 4 Assessment

Target Reading Skill Building Vocabulary Use your sentences to help answer the questions.

Reviewing Key Concepts

1. **a. Defining** What is a food chain?
   b. Interpreting Photographs What three roles do insects play in the food chain shown in Figure 20?
2. **a. Reviewing** Besides their role in food chains, what are two other ways insects interact with their environment?
   b. Summarizing What effect do pollinators have on their environment?
   c. Predicting What would a world without pollinators be like?

3. **a. Reviewing** How can insect pests be controlled?
   b. Comparing and Contrasting How are the effects of using biological controls similar to the effects of using pesticides? How are they different?
   c. Applying Concepts Some insect species are harmful only in areas of the world where they do not normally live but have been accidentally released. Why might this be?

Math Practice

4. **Percentage** Suppose 33 percent of the 50 tons of wood produced in one year by a forest is consumed by termites and other insects. How many tons do the insects eat?

$$\frac{X}{50} = \frac{33}{100}$$

$$1650 = 100X$$
$$165 = X$$

Battling Pest Insects

It's hard to believe that insects can cause much harm. But some species, such as the cotton boll weevil, can devastate crops. Boll weevils eat cotton bolls, the part of the plant that produces cotton fibers. Other insects, such as some mosquitoes, spread diseases. To control insect pests, people often use pesticides—chemicals or substances that kill insects or alter their life processes.

What Are Pesticides?

Since ancient times, people have used substances such as sulfur to kill pests. In the 1900s, people began developing new chemicals to battle harmful insects. Today, most pesticides used in the United States are synthetic—made by people in laboratories. On average, it takes about 15 years and about 20 million dollars to develop a new pesticide. That time includes obtaining approval from the Environmental Protection Agency, which oversees pesticide use. Once on the market, pesticides can work to kill insects in a variety of ways. They might attack the physical, chemical, or biological processes of the pests.

How Pesticides Work
Pesticides kill insects in a variety of ways. People may select one or more pesticides to attack a particular pest.

Attack the Gut
Pesticides that contain certain bacteria and viruses can attack the gut lining, killing the insect.

Paralyze the Nervous System
Pesticides that interfere with signals in the brain can cause convulsions, paralysis, and death.

Boll weevil on a cotton boll

Problems With Pesticides

Using pesticides has increased food production worldwide. However, the technology of pesticides has drawbacks. Pesticides that kill harmful insects can also kill helpful insects, such as bees. In large doses, these chemicals are also toxic to humans and pets. Even low levels of chemicals can build up and affect animals in the food chain. Rain can carry pesticides into rivers and lakes and pollute water supplies. The best pesticides target only pests and do not stay in the environment for a long time.

Applying the Pesticide
One way to apply pesticides is by using an airplane to spray crops.

Destroy the Exoskeleton
Pesticides can cause the exoskeleton to become so thin that the insect dies while molting. Pesticides can also absorb the waxy coating, leading to water loss and death.

Disrupt the Life Cycle
Certain pesticides prevent larvae from maturing into adults.

Interfere With Reproduction
Pesticides that are oils can smother and kill insect eggs. Other pesticides sterilize adult insects.

Weigh the Impact

1. Identify the Need
Why do people use pesticides?

2. Research
Using the Internet, research different insects affecting major crops in your state. Choose one pest insect. Find out the methods used in controlling it. Are there alternatives to pesticides?

3. Write
Write a proposal to your governor for insect control in your state. Use your research and notes to explain how your method works.

Go Online
PHSchool.com

For: More on pesticides
Visit: PHSchool.com
Web Code: ceh-2020

Echinoderms

Reading Preview

Key Concepts
- What are the main characteristics of echinoderms?
- What are the major groups of echinoderms?

Key Terms
- echinoderm • endoskeleton
- water vascular system
- tube feet

 Target Reading Skill

Previewing Visuals When you preview, you look ahead at the material to be read. Preview Figure 24. Then write two questions that you have about the diagram in a graphic organizer like the one below. As you read, answer your questions.

Water Vascular System

Q.	What are tube feet?
A.	
Q.	

Discover Activity

How Do Sea Stars Hold On?

1. Use a plastic dropper and water to model how a sea star moves and clings to surfaces. Fill the dropper with water, and then squeeze out most of the water.
2. Squeeze the last drop of water onto the inside of your arm. Then, while squeezing the bulb, touch the tip of the dropper into the water drop. With the dropper tip against your skin, release the bulb.
3. Hold the dropper by the tube and lift it slowly, paying attention to what happens to your skin.

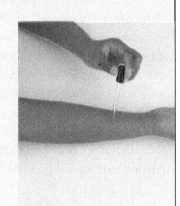

Think It Over
Predicting Besides moving and clinging to surfaces, what might sea stars use their suction structures for?

While exploring a rocky beach one day, you see what looks like a dill pickle at the bottom of a tide pool. You think it might be a plant or a rock covered with green slime. But as you look more closely, the pickle begins to crawl very slowly. This amazing creature is a sea cucumber, a relative of sea stars.

Characteristics of Echinoderms

Sea cucumbers, sea stars, sea urchins, and sand dollars are all **echinoderms** (ee KY noh durmz), members of the phylum Echinodermata. **Echinoderms are invertebrates with an internal skeleton and a system of fluid-filled tubes called a water vascular system.** All echinoderms live in salt water.

Body Structure The skin of most echinoderms is stretched over an internal skeleton, or **endoskeleton,** made of hardened plates. These plates give the animal a bumpy texture. Adult echinoderms have a unique kind of radial symmetry in which the body parts, usually in multiples of five, are arranged like spokes on a wheel.

Movement The internal system of fluid-filled tubes in echinoderms is called the **water vascular system.** You can see a sea star's water vascular system in Figure 24. Portions of the tubes in this system can contract, or squeeze together, forcing water into structures called **tube feet.** This process is something like how you move water around in a water balloon by squeezing different parts of the balloon.

The tube feet stick out from the echinoderm's sides or underside. The ends of tube feet are sticky. When filled with water, they act like small, sticky suction cups. The stickiness and suction enable the tube feet to grip the surface beneath the echinoderm. Most echinoderms use their tube feet to move along slowly and to capture food.

Reproduction and Life Cycle Almost all echinoderms are either male or female. Eggs are usually fertilized in the water, after a female releases her eggs and a male releases his sperm. The fertilized eggs develop into tiny, swimming larvae that look very different from the adults. The larvae eventually undergo metamorphosis and become adult echinoderms.

> **Reading Checkpoint** What are the functions of an echinoderm's tube feet?

Go Online
active art

For: Water Vascular System activity
Visit: PHSchool.com
Web Code: cep-2025

FIGURE 24
A Water Vascular System
Echinoderms, such as this sea star, have a water vascular system that helps them move and catch food.
Interpreting Diagrams *Where does water enter the water vascular system?*

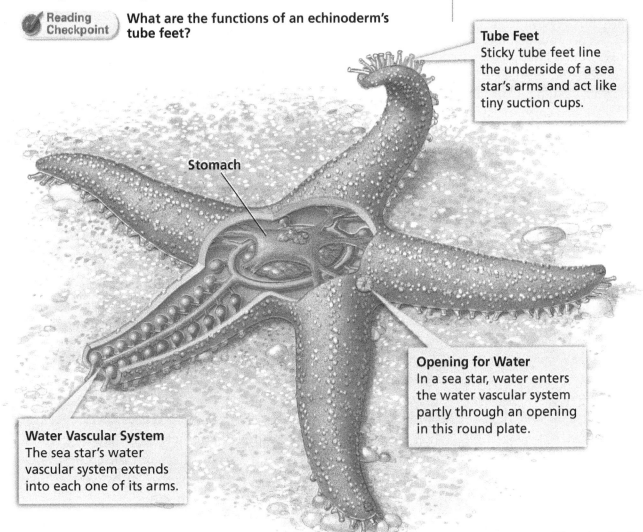

Tube Feet
Sticky tube feet line the underside of a sea star's arms and act like tiny suction cups.

Stomach

Opening for Water
In a sea star, water enters the water vascular system partly through an opening in this round plate.

Water Vascular System
The sea star's water vascular system extends into each one of its arms.

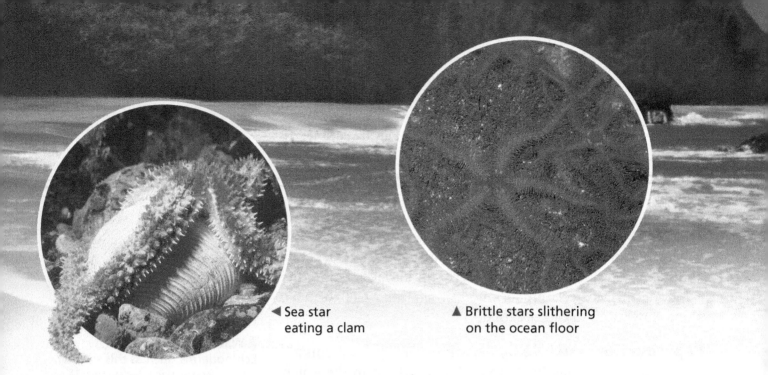

◀ Sea star
eating a clam

▲ Brittle stars slithering
on the ocean floor

Diversity of Echinoderms

Echinoderms are diverse in their appearance, but all have radial symmetry and are found in the ocean. **Interpreting Photographs** *Why is echinoderm, which means "spiny skinned," a good name for this group?*

Diversity of Echinoderms

There are four major groups of echinoderms: sea stars, brittle stars, sea urchins, and sea cucumbers. The members of these groups share many characteristics, but look quite different. They also have different ways of feeding and moving.

Sea Stars Sea stars are predators that eat mollusks, crabs, and even other echinoderms. Sea stars use their tube feet to move across the ocean bottom. They also use their tube feet to capture prey. A sea star will grasp a clam with all five arms. Then it pulls on the tightly closed shells with its tube feet. When the shells open, the sea star forces its stomach out through its mouth and into the opening between the clam's shells. Digestive chemicals break down the clam's tissues, and the sea star sucks in the partially digested body of its prey.

Brittle Stars Unlike a sea star's arms, a brittle star's arms are long and slender, with flexible joints. The tube feet, which have no suction cups, are used for catching food but not for moving. Instead, brittle stars slither along the ocean bottom by waving their long arms in a snakelike motion against the ocean floor.

Sea Urchins Unlike sea stars and brittle stars, sea urchins have no arms. Moveable spines cover and protect their bodies, so they look something like a pincushion. These spines cover a central shell that is made of plates joined together. To move, sea urchins use bands of tube feet that extend out between the spines. They scrape and cut their food, such as seaweed, with five teethlike structures that they project from their mouths.

▲ Sea urchins eating seaweed

▲ Sea cucumber crawling on the ocean floor

Sea Cucumbers As you might expect from their name, sea cucumbers look a little bit like the cucumbers you eat. These animals can be red, brown, blue, or green. Underneath their leather-like skin, their bodies are soft, flexible, and muscular. Sea cucumbers have rows of tube feet on their underside, enabling them to crawl slowly along the ocean floor where they live. At one end of a sea cucumber is a mouth surrounded by tentacles. The sea cucumber, which is a filter feeder, can lengthen its tentacles to sweep food toward its mouth.

 **Reading Checkpoint** How does a sea cucumber move?

Section 5 Assessment

 Target Reading Skill Previewing Visuals Refer to your questions and answers about Figure 24 to help you answer Question 1 below.

Reviewing Key Concepts

1. a. **Reviewing** What characteristics do echinoderms have?
   b. **Summarizing** How does an echinoderm use its tube feet to grip a surface?
   c. **Inferring** Why is movement using tube feet slow?

2. a. **Identifying** Identify the four major groups of echinoderms.
   b. **Comparing and Contrasting** Compare and contrast how sea stars and sea urchins feed.
   c. **Predicting** Would a sea star be able to eat clams without using its tube feet? Explain.

Writing in Science

Comparison Paragraph In a paragraph, compare and contrast how sea stars, brittle stars, and sea urchins move.

Chapter 2

Study Guide

① Mollusks

Key Concepts

- In addition to a soft body often covered by a shell, a mollusk has a thin layer of tissue called a mantle that covers its internal organs, and an organ called a foot.
- The three major groups of mollusks are gastropods, bivalves, and cephalopods.
- Gastropods are mollusks that have a single external shell or no shell at all.
- Bivalves are mollusks that have two shells held together by hinges and strong muscles.
- A cephalopod is an ocean-dwelling mollusk whose foot is adapted to form tentacles around its mouth.

Key Terms

mollusk	gill	radula
open	gastropod	bivalve
circulatory	herbivore	omnivore
system	carnivore	cephalopod

② Arthropods

Key Concepts

- The major groups of arthropods are crustaceans, arachnids, centipedes and millipedes, and insects.
- Arthropods are invertebrates that have an external skeleton, a segmented body, and jointed attachments called appendages.
- A crustacean is an arthropod that has two or three body sections, five or more pairs of legs, and two pairs of antennae.
- Arachnids are arthropods with two body sections, four pairs of legs, and no antennae.
- Centipedes and millipedes are arthropods with two body sections and many pairs of legs.

Key Terms

arthropod	antenna	arachnid
exoskeleton	crustacean	abdomen
molting	metamorphosis	

③ Insects

Key Concepts

- Insects are arthropods with three body sections, six legs, one pair of antennae, and usually one or two pairs of wings.
- An insect's mouthparts are adapted for a highly specific way of getting food.
- Each insect species undergoes either complete metamorphosis or gradual metamorphosis.

Key Terms

insect	pupa
thorax	gradual
complete	metamorphosis
metamorphosis	nymph

④ Insect Ecology

Key Concepts

- Insects play key roles in food chains because of the many different ways that they obtain food and then become food for other animals.
- Two ways insects interact with other living things are by moving pollen among plants and by spreading disease-causing organisms.
- To try to control pests, people use chemicals, traps, and living things, including other insects.

Key Terms

food chain	
ecology	pollinator
producer	pesticide
consumer	biological control
decomposer	

⑤ Echinoderms

Key Concepts

- Echinoderms are invertebrates with an internal skeleton and a system of fluid-filled tubes called a water vascular system.
- There are four major groups of echinoderms: sea stars, brittle stars, sea urchins, and sea cucumbers.

Key Terms

echinoderm	water vascular system
endoskeleton	tube feet

Review and Assessment

Organizing Information

Concept Mapping Copy the concept map about the classification of arthropods onto a sheet of paper. Then complete it and add a title. (For more on Concept Mapping, see the Skills Handbook.)

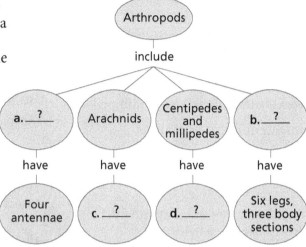

Arthropods
include
a. ___?___ | Arachnids | Centipedes and millipedes | b. ___?___
have | have | have | have
Four antennae | c. ___?___ | d. ___?___ | Six legs, three body sections

Reviewing Key Terms

Choose the letter of the best answer.

1. An animal that eats other animals is a(n)
   a. carnivore.
   b. omnivore.
   c. filter feeder.
   d. herbivore.

2. Mollusks with two shells are known as
   a. cephalopods.
   b. gastropods.
   c. bivalves.
   d. sea stars.

3. An arthropod's antennae are located on its
   a. head.
   b. thorax.
   c. abdomen.
   d. mantle.

4. To obtain oxygen from their environments, mollusks and crustaceans use which organ?
   a. radula
   b. lungs
   c. gills
   d. legs

5. The shedding of an outgrown exoskeleton is called
   a. complete metamorphosis.
   b. incomplete metamorphosis.
   c. molting.
   d. reproduction.

6. At which stage of development would an insect be enclosed in a cocoon?
   a. egg
   b. larva
   c. pupa
   d. adult

7. One example of a biological control is
   a. catching pest insects in traps.
   b. making and selling honey by raising bees in hives.
   c. killing pest insects with pesticides.
   d. introducing a pest insect's natural predator.

8. An echinoderm has
   a. a radula.
   b. tube feet.
   c. antennae.
   d. an exoskeleton.

Writing in Science

News Report As a television reporter, you are covering a story about a giant squid that has washed up on the local beach. Write a short news story describing the discovery. Be sure to describe how scientists classified the animal as a squid.

Discovery
CHANNEL
SCHOOL

Mollusks, Arthropods, and Echinoderms
Video Preview
Video Field Trip
▶ Video Assessment

Review and Assessment

Checking Concepts

9. Explain how a snail uses its radula.

10. How is a cephalopod's nervous system different from that of other mollusks?

11. Describe four things that a crayfish can do with its appendages.

12. How are centipedes different from millipedes?

13. How are insects different from other arthropods?

14. Identify two reasons why insects sometimes must be controlled.

15. How is an echinoderm's radial symmetry different from that of a jellyfish?

Thinking Critically

16. **Comparing and Contrasting** Compare and contrast bivalves and cephalopods.

17. **Classifying** Which phylum does each of the animals below belong to? Explain your answer.

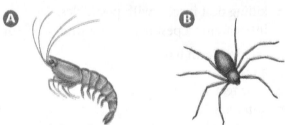

18. **Applying Concepts** Explain why the development of a lion, which grows larger as it changes from a tiny cub to a 90 kg adult, is not metamorphosis.

19. **Drawing Conclusions** A rancher imports dung beetles from Africa to help control manure build-up from cattle. Later, he observes that the pastures are producing more grass for the cattle to eat. What conclusion could the rancher draw about the dung beetles?

20. **Making Judgments** Do you think pesticides should be used to kill insect pests? Explain.

21. **Comparing and Contrasting** How is a spider's method of obtaining food similar to that of a sea star? How is it different?

Math Practice

22. **Percentage** Of approximately 150,000 species of mollusks, 27 percent are gastropods. About how many species of gastropods are there?

Applying Skills

Use the data table to answer Questions 23–25.
The following data appeared in a book on insects.

Flight Characteristics

Type of Insect	Wing Beats (per second)	Flight Speed (kilometers per hour)
Hummingbird moth	85	17.8
Bumblebee	250	10.3
Housefly	190	7.1

23. **Graphing** Use the data to make two bar graphs: one showing the three insect wing-beat rates and another showing the flight speeds.

24. **Interpreting Data** Which of the three insects has the highest wing-beat rate? Which insect flies the fastest?

25. **Drawing Conclusions** Based on the data, is there a relationship between the rate at which an insect beats its wings and the speed at which it flies? Explain. What factors besides wing-beat rate might affect flight speed?

Lab zone Chapter **Project**

Performance Assessment Prepare a display to show how you set up your experiment and what your results were. Construct and display graphs to show the data you collected. Include pictures of the mealworms in each stage of development. Write your conclusion of how the experimental conditions affected the growth and development of the mealworms. Also suggest some possible explanations for your results.

Standardized Test Prep

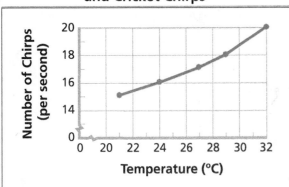
Choose the letter of the best answer.

1. An animal that has a soft, unsegmented body surrounded by a hard outer shell is most likely
   A an earthworm.
   B a cnidarian.
   C a mollusk.
   D an arthropod.

2. Which animal feature most likely evolved as an adaptation to provide direct protection from a predator's attack?
   F a snail's radula
   G a sea urchin's spines
   H a crayfish's antennae
   J an insect's thorax

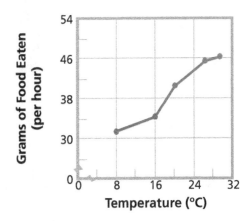

3. Examine the information in the graph above. Which is the best title for the graph?
   A Effect of Caterpillar Feeding Rate on Temperature
   B Caterpillar Behavior and Temperature
   C Respiration Rate and Temperature
   D Relationship of Temperature and Caterpillar Feeding Rate

4. What is the most reasonable prediction for what the feeding rate would be at 32°C?
   F 60 g/hr
   G 46 g/hr
   H 40 g/hr
   J 0 g/hr

Constructed Response

5. In a certain small country, mosquitoes are very common. The mosquitoes spread a disease that is deadly to humans. The government decides to spray the entire country with a pesticide that will kill all mosquitoes and other flying insects as well. How is this action likely to affect the food chain?

Chapter

3

Fishes, Amphibians, and Reptiles

interactive Textbook

The fishes in this school are named "sweetlips." ▶

Lab zone™ Chapter **Project**

Animal Adaptations

How does an animal capture food, escape from predators, or obtain oxygen? To help answer these questions, you will create models of three different animals and show how each is adapted to its environment.

Your Goal To make three-dimensional models of a fish, an amphibian, and a reptile that show how each is adapted to carry out one life function in its environment

To complete this project, you must

● select one life function to show

● build a three-dimensional model of each type of animal, showing the adaptations each has for carrying out the function you selected

● make a poster that explains how each animal's adaptation is suited to its environment

● follow the safety guidelines in Appendix A

Plan It! Pair up with a classmate and share what you already know about fishes, amphibians, and reptiles. Answer the following questions: Where do these animals live? How do they move around? How do they protect themselves?

Decide on the life function you will show. As you read about these types of animals, make your models showing the adaptations the animals have for carrying out the functions.

What Is a Vertebrate?

Discover Activity

How Is an Umbrella Like a Skeleton?

1. Open an umbrella. Turn it upside down and examine how it is made.
2. Now close the umbrella and watch how the braces and ribs collapse.
3. Think of what would happen if you removed the ribs from the umbrella and then tried to use it during a rainstorm.

Think It Over
Inferring What is the function of the ribs of an umbrella? How are the ribs of the umbrella similar to the bones in your skeleton? How are they different?

Look backward in time, into an ocean 530 million years ago. There you see a strange-looking creature—a jawless fish—that is about as long as your index finger. The creature is swimming with a side-to-side motion, like a flag flapping in the wind. Its tail fin is broad and flat. Tiny armorlike plates cover its small body. Its eyes are set wide apart. If you could see inside the animal, you would notice that it has a backbone. You are looking at one of the earliest vertebrates at home in an ancient sea.

Characteristics of Chordates

Vertebrates like the ancient jawless fish are a subgroup in the phylum Chordata. All members of this phylum are called **chordates** (KAWR dayts). Most chordates, including fishes, amphibians, such as frogs, and reptiles, such as snakes, are vertebrates. So are birds and mammals. But a few chordates are invertebrates. **At some point in their lives, chordates will have a notochord, a nerve cord that runs down their back, and slits in their throat area.**

Notochord The phylum name Chordata comes from the **notochord,** a flexible rod that supports a chordate's back. Some chordates, like the lancelet shown in Figure 1, have notochords all their lives. In contrast, in vertebrates, part or all of the notochord is replaced by a backbone.

▼ Ancient jawless fish

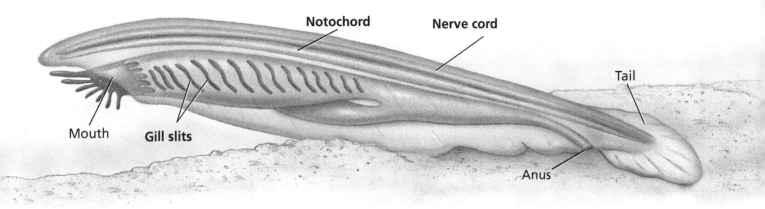

Mouth Gill slits Notochord Nerve cord Tail Anus

FIGURE 1
Characteristics of a Lancelet
This lancelet shows the characteristics of a chordate: a notochord that helps support its body, a nerve cord down its back, and gill slits.

Nerve Cord in Back In addition to having a notochord, all chordates have a nerve cord that runs down their back. Your spinal cord is such a nerve cord. The nerve cord is the connection between the brain and the nerves, on which messages travel back and forth. Many other groups of animals—arthropods and segmented worms, for example—have nerve cords, but their nerve cords do not run down their backs.

Slits in Throat Area At some point in their lives, chordates have slits in their throat area called pharyngeal (fuh RIN jee ul) slits, or gill slits. Some chordates, including fishes, keep these slits as part of their gills for their entire lives. But in many vertebrates, including humans, pharyngeal slits disappear before birth.

 **What is a notochord?**

Characteristics of Vertebrates

Most chordates are vertebrates. In addition to the characteristics shared by all chordates, vertebrates share certain other characteristics. **A vertebrate has a backbone that is part of an internal skeleton.** This endoskeleton supports the body and allows it to move.

Backbone A vertebrate's backbone, which is also called a spine, runs down the center of its back. You can see in Figure 2 that the backbone is formed by many similar bones called **vertebrae** (singular *vertebra*). The vertebrae are lined up in a row like beads on a string. Joints, or movable connections between the vertebrae, give the spine flexibility. You can bend over and tie your shoes because your backbone has flexibility. Each vertebra has a hole in it that allows the spinal cord to pass through it. The spinal cord fits into the vertebrae like fingers fit into rings.

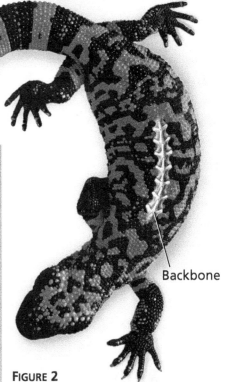

Backbone

FIGURE 2
The Backbone of a Lizard
The backbone of this gila monster has flexibility. **Predicting** *Could the backbone bend if the vertebrae did not have joints?*

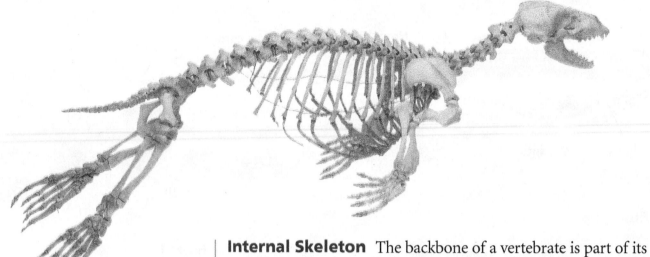

FIGURE 3
The Skeleton of a Seal
This seal's skeleton has adaptations for swimming. Long, flat bones support the flippers. The flat skull helps the seal move smoothly through the water.

Go Online
SciLINKS NSTA

For: Links on vertebrates
Visit: www.SciLinks.org
Web Code: scn-0231

Internal Skeleton The backbone of a vertebrate is part of its endoskeleton. This endoskeleton protects the internal organs of the body, helps give the body shape, and gives muscles a place to attach. In addition to the backbone, a vertebrate's endoskeleton includes the skull and ribs. The skull protects the brain. The ribs attach to the vertebrae and protect the heart, lungs, and other internal organs. Many vertebrates, like the seal shown in Figure 3, also have arm and leg bones adapted for movement.

A vertebrate's endoskeleton has several characteristics. Unlike an arthropod's exoskeleton, an endoskeleton doesn't need to be replaced as the animal grows. It also forms an internal frame that supports the body against the downward pull of gravity, while allowing easy movement. Because of these characteristics, vertebrates can grow bigger than animals with exoskeletons or no skeletons at all.

 **Reading Checkpoint** What does an endoskeleton protect?

Keeping Conditions Stable

One characteristic that differs among the major groups of vertebrates is the way they control their body temperature. **The body temperature of most fishes, amphibians, and reptiles is close to the temperature of their environment. In contrast, birds and mammals have a stable body temperature that is often warmer than their environment.**

Ectotherms Fishes, amphibians, and reptiles are ectotherms. An **ectotherm** is an animal whose body does not produce much internal heat. Its body temperature changes depending on the temperature of its environment. For example, when a turtle is lying on a sunny riverbank, it has a higher body temperature than when it is swimming in a cool river. Ectotherms are sometimes called "coldblooded." This term is misleading because their blood is often quite warm.

Woma python ►

▼ Emperor penguins

Endotherms In contrast to a turtle, a beaver would have the same body temperature whether it is in cool water or on warm land. The beaver is an example of an **endotherm**—an animal whose body regulates its own temperature by controlling the internal heat it produces. An endotherm's body temperature usually does not change much, even when the temperature of its environment changes. Birds and mammals, such as beavers, are endotherms.

Endotherms also have other adaptations, such as sweat glands and fur or feathers, for maintaining their body temperature. On hot days, some endotherms sweat. As the sweat evaporates, the animal is cooled. On cool days, fur or feathers keep endotherms warm. Because endotherms can keep their body temperatures stable, they can live in a greater variety of environments than ectotherms can.

FIGURE 4
Temperature Regulation
On a cool, sunny morning, a woma python raises its body temperature by basking in the sun. In contrast, an emperor penguin stays warm by producing internal heat.
Inferring *Which animal is an endotherm?*

Section ① Assessment

 Target Reading Skill Building Vocabulary Use your definitions to help answer the questions.

Reviewing Key Concepts

1. a. **Listing** List three characteristics of chordates.
   b. **Comparing and Contrasting** In chordates, how does the notochord of a vertebrate differ from that of an invertebrate?
   c. **Explaining** An earthworm has a nerve cord that runs along its body. Is an earthworm a chordate? Explain.
2. a. **Identifying** What characteristic do only vertebrates have?
   b. **Describing** Describe a backbone.
   c. **Relating Cause and Effect** What gives a backbone flexibility?

3. a. **Summarizing** What is the difference between an ectotherm and an endotherm?
   b. **Making Generalizations** Would an ectotherm or an endotherm be more active on a cold night? Explain your answer.

At-Home Activity

Bumpy Back Rub Have members of your family feel the tops of the vertebrae running down the center of their backs. Then have them feel the hard skull beneath the skin on their foreheads. Tell them about the functions of the backbone and skull.

Soaking Up Those Rays

Problem

How do some lizards control their body temperatures in the extreme heat of a desert?

Skills Focus

interpreting data, predicting

Materials

• paper • pencil

Procedure

1. The data below were collected by scientists studying how lizards control their body temperature. Examine the data.
2. Copy the data table into your notebook.
3. Organize the data in the diagrams by filling in the table, putting the appropriate information in each column. Begin by writing a brief description of each type of lizard behavior.
4. Complete the data table using the information in the diagrams.

Analyze and Conclude

1. **Interpreting Data** Describe how the lizard's body temperature changed between 6 A.M. and 9 P.M.
2. **Inferring** What are three sources of heat that caused the lizard's body temperature to rise during the day?
3. **Interpreting Data** During the hottest part of the day, what were the air and ground temperatures? Why do you think the lizard's temperature remained below 40°C?
4. **Predicting** Predict what the lizard's body temperature would have been from 9 P.M. to 6 A.M. Explain your prediction.
5. **Predicting** Predict what would happen to your own body temperature if you spent a brief period outdoors in the desert at noon. Predict what your temperature would be if you spent time in a burrow at 7 P.M. Explain your predictions.

6 A.M.–7 A.M.
Emerging from burrow
Air temperature **20°C**
Ground temperature **28°C**
Body temperature **25°C**

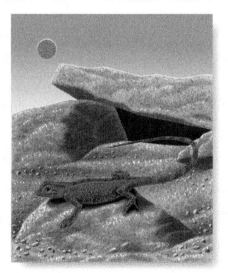

7 A.M.–9 A.M.
Basking (lying on ground in sun)
Air temperature **27°C**
Ground temperature **29°C**
Body temperature **32.6°C**

9 A.M.–12 NOON
Active (moving about)
Air temperature **27°C**
Ground temperature **30.8°C**
Body temperature **36.6°C**

Data Table

Activity	Description of Activity	Time of Day	Air Temperature (°C)	Ground Temperature (°C)	Body Temperature (°C)
1. Emerging		6 a.m.	20	28	25
2. Basking		7 a.m.	27	29	32.6
3. Active		9 a.m	32	30.8	36.6
4. Retreat		12 noon	40.3	53.8	39.5
5. Stilting		2:30 P.M.	34.2	47.4	39.5
6. Retreat		6 P.M.	25	26	25

6. **Drawing Conclusions** Based on what you learned from the data, explain why it is misleading to say that an ectotherm is a "cold-blooded" animal.

7. **Communicating** Write a paragraph explaining why it is helpful to organize data in a data table before you try to interpret the data.

More to Explore

Make a bar graph of the temperature data. Explain what the graph shows you. How does this graph help you interpret the data about how lizards control their body temperature in the extreme heat of a desert?

.

12 NOON–2:30 P.M.
Retreat to burrow
Air temperature **40.3°C**
Ground temperature **53.8°C**
Body temperature **39.5°C**

2:30 P.M.–6 P.M.
Stilting (belly off ground)
Air temperature **34.2°C**
Ground temperature **47.4°C**
Body temperature **39.5°C**

6 P.M.–9 P.M.
Retreat to burrow
Air temperature **25°C**
Ground temperature **26°C**
Body temperature **25°C**

Fishes

Reading Preview

Key Concepts
- What are the characteristics of most fishes?
- What are the major groups of fishes and how do they differ?

Key Terms
- fish • cartilage • swim bladder

Target Reading Skill
Previewing Visuals Before you read, preview Figure 12. Then write two questions that you have about the diagram in a graphic organizer like the one below. As you read, answer your questions.

Structure of a Fish

Q.	What is a swim bladder?
A.	
Q.	

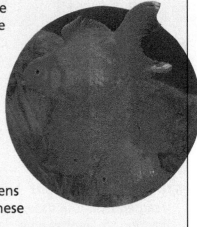

Discover Activity

How Does Water Flow Over a Fish's Gills?
1. Closely observe a fish in an aquarium for a few minutes. Note how frequently the fish opens its mouth.
2. Notice the flaps on each side of the fish's head behind its eyes. Observe how the flaps open and close.
3. Observe the movements of the mouth and the flaps at the same time. Note any relationship between the movements of these two structures.

Think It Over
Observing What do the flaps on the sides of the fish do when the fish opens its mouth? What role do you think these two structures play in a fish's life?

In the warm waters of a coral reef, a large spotted fish called a graysby hovers in the water, barely moving. A smaller striped fish called a goby swims up to the graysby. Then, like a vacuum cleaner moving over a rug, the goby swims slowly over the larger fish, eating dead skin and tiny parasites. The goby even cleans inside the graysby's mouth and gills. Both fishes benefit from this cleaning. The graysby gets rid of unwanted materials, and the goby gets a meal.

Gobies cleaning a ▶
graysby

Water flow

Gills

Blood vessels in gills

Two-chambered heart

Blood vessels in body

Key
■ Oxygen-rich blood
■ Oxygen-poor blood

FIGURE 5
Respiration and Circulation
Water flows into the mouth of this fish and then over its gills. Oxygen moves into the blood and is delivered to the cells of the fish.
Interpreting Diagrams *Where does oxygen get into the blood of a fish?*

Characteristics of Fishes

Both the goby and the graysby it cleans are fishes. A **fish** is a vertebrate that lives in water and uses fins to move. **In addition to living in water and having fins, most fishes are ectotherms, obtain oxygen through gills, and have scales.** Scales are thin, overlapping plates that cover the skin.

Fishes make up the largest group of vertebrates. Nearly half of all vertebrate species are fishes. In addition, fishes have been on Earth longer than any other kind of vertebrate.

Obtaining Oxygen Fishes get their oxygen from water. As a fish swims, it opens its mouth and takes a gulp of water, as you observed if you did the Discover Activity. The water, which contains oxygen, moves through openings in the fish's throat region that lead to the gills. Gills, which look like tiny feathers, have many blood vessels within them. As water flows over the gills, oxygen moves from the water into the fish's blood. At the same time, carbon dioxide, a waste product, moves out of the blood and into the water. After flowing over the gills, the water flows out of the fish through slits beneath the gills.

Circulatory System From the gills, the blood travels throughout the fish's body, supplying the body cells with oxygen. Like all vertebrates, fishes have a closed circulatory system. The heart of a fish has two chambers, or inner spaces. The heart of a fish pumps blood in one loop—from the heart to the gills, from the gills to the rest of the body, and back to the heart. You can trace this path in Figure 5.

▲ Skeleton

FIGURE 6
Fins of an Angelfish
The skeleton of a fish shows that the fins have bony support. The fins of this angelfish act like paddles as the fish moves through the water.

Movement Fins help fishes swim. Look at the fins on the angelfish in Figure 6. Each fin has a thin membrane stretched across bony supports. Like a canoe paddle, a fin provides a large surface to push against the water. The push allows for faster movement through the water. If you have ever swum wearing a pair of swim fins, you probably noticed how fast you moved through the water. Most of the movements of fishes are related to obtaining food, but some are related to reproduction.

Reproduction Most fishes have external fertilization. In external fertilization, the eggs are fertilized outside the female's body. The male hovers close to the female and spreads a cloud of sperm cells over the eggs she releases. The young develop outside the female's body.

In contrast, some fishes, such as sharks and guppies, have internal fertilization. In internal fertilization, eggs are fertilized inside the female's body. The young develop inside her body. When they are mature enough to live on their own, she gives birth to them.

> **Reading Checkpoint** What is the structure of a fin?

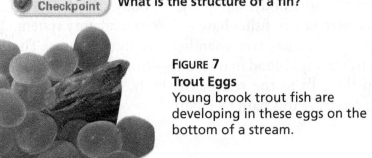

FIGURE 7
Trout Eggs
Young brook trout fish are developing in these eggs on the bottom of a stream.

Nervous System The nervous system and sense organs of fishes help them find food and avoid predators. Most fishes can see much better in water than you can. Keen senses of touch, smell, and taste also help fishes capture food. Some fishes have taste organs in unusual places. For example, the catfish shown in Figure 8 tastes with its whiskers.

Jawless Fishes

Fishes have lived on Earth longer than any other kind of vertebrate. Fishes are organized into three main groups based on the structures of their mouths and the types of skeletons they have. **The major groups of fishes are jawless fishes, cartilaginous fishes, and bony fishes.**

Jawless fishes are unlike other fishes in that they have no jaws and no scales. Jaws are hinged bony structures that allow animals to open and close their mouths. Instead of jaws, jawless fishes have mouths containing structures for scraping, stabbing, and sucking their food. Their skeletons are made of **cartilage,** a tissue that is more flexible than bone.

Hagfishes and lampreys are the only kinds of jawless fishes that exist today. Hagfishes look like large, slimy worms. They crawl into the bodies of dead or dying fishes and use their rough tongues to scrape decaying tissues. Many lampreys are parasites of other fishes. They attach their mouths to healthy fishes and then suck in the tissues and blood of their victims. If you look at the lamprey's mouth in Figure 9, you can probably imagine the damage it can do.

FIGURE 8
A Catfish
The whiskers of a catfish have many taste buds. To find food, the catfish drags its whiskers along muddy lake or river bottoms.

FIGURE 9
A Lamprey
Lampreys have eel-shaped bodies. They use sharp teeth and suction-cup mouths to feed on other fishes. **Classifying** *To which group of fishes do lampreys belong?*

 Reading Checkpoint **What material makes up the skeleton of a jawless fish?**

▲ Mouth

FIGURE 10
Blue-Spotted Ray
This ray is a cartilaginous fish
that lives on the ocean floor.

Cartilaginous Fishes

Sharks, rays, and skates are cartilaginous (kahr tuh LAJ uh nuhs) fishes. **The cartilaginous fishes have jaws and scales, and skeletons made of cartilage.** The pointed, toothlike scales that cover their bodies give their skin a texture that is rougher than sandpaper.

Obtaining Oxygen Most sharks cannot pump water over their gills. Instead, they rely on swimming or currents to keep water moving across their gills. For example, when sharks sleep, they position themselves in currents that send water over their gills.

Rays and skates are not as active as sharks. They spend a lot of time partially buried in the sand of the ocean floor. During this time, they take in water through small holes located behind their eyes. Water leaves through gill openings on their undersides.

Obtaining Food Cartilaginous fishes are usually carnivores. Rays and skates hunt on the ocean floor, crushing mollusks, crustaceans, and small fishes with their teeth. Sharks will attack and eat nearly anything that smells like food. They can smell and taste even a tiny amount of blood—as little as one drop in 115 liters of water! Although sharks have a keen sense of smell their eyesight is poor. Because they see poorly, sometimes they swallow strange objects. Indeed, one shark was found to have a raincoat and an automobile license plate in its stomach.

The mouth of a shark contains jagged teeth arranged in rows. Most sharks use only the first couple of rows for feeding. The remaining rows are replacements. If a shark loses a front-row tooth, a tooth behind it moves up to replace it.

FIGURE 11
Great White Shark
This great white shark has a familiar
shark trait—many sharp teeth.

FIGURE 12
Structure of a Bony Fish
This yellow perch has the characteristics of a bony fish. **Interpreting Diagrams** *What are the functions of fins?*

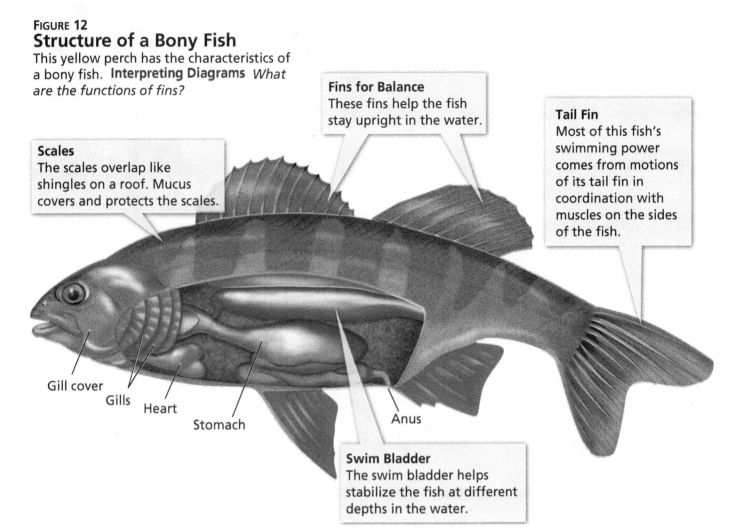

Fins for Balance
These fins help the fish stay upright in the water.

Tail Fin
Most of this fish's swimming power comes from motions of its tail fin in coordination with muscles on the sides of the fish.

Scales
The scales overlap like shingles on a roof. Mucus covers and protects the scales.

Gill cover

Gills   Heart

Stomach

Anus

Swim Bladder
The swim bladder helps stabilize the fish at different depths in the water.

Bony Fishes

Most familiar kinds of fishes, such as trout, tuna, and gold-fishes, are bony fishes. **A bony fish has jaws, scales, a pocket on each side of the head that holds the gills, and a skeleton made of hard bones.** Each gill pocket is covered by a flap that opens to release water.

The major structures of a bony fish are shown in Figure 12. Notice that a bony fish has an organ called a **swim bladder,** which is an internal, gas-filled sac that helps the fish stay stable at different depths in the water. Gas levels in the swim bladder are adjusted after the fish reaches its desired depth. By adjusting these levels, the fish can stay at a depth without using a lot of energy.

Bony fishes make up about 95 percent of all fish species. They live in both salt water and fresh water. Some live in the dark depths of the ocean. Others thrive in light-filled waters, such as those around coral reefs. Figure 13 on the next page shows some of the great variety of bony fishes.

Observing
Put on your goggles and dis-posable gloves. Place a pre-served fish on newspaper on your desk and examine it closely. Note its size and shape, and the number and locations of its fins. Lift the gill cover and observe the gills with a hand lens. Use your observations to make a diagram of the fish. Wash your hands when you are finished.

 **Reading Checkpoint**) **Which organ helps a bony fish maintain its position in the water?**

FIGURE 13
Diversity of Bony Fishes
These photographs show just a few species of bony fishes.

Anemone Fish ▶
A sea anemone's tentacles can be deadly to other fishes, but they don't harm the anemone fish.

Balloonfish ▶
When threatened, a balloonfish swallows large amounts of water or air to make itself into a spiny ball.

▼ **Sockeye Salmon**
Sockeye salmon are Pacific Ocean fishes that migrate from ocean to inland lakes to reproduce.

◀ **Sea Dragon** The leafy sea dragon is well camouflaged in weedy bays and lagoons.

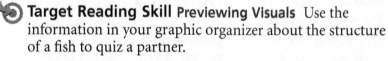

Section 2 Assessment

Target Reading Skill Previewing Visuals Use the information in your graphic organizer about the structure of a fish to quiz a partner.

Reviewing Key Concepts

1. a. **Reviewing** What are the main characteristics of fishes?
   b. **Explaining** Why do fishes have gills?
   c. **Applying Concepts** What would happen to a goldfish that could not open its mouth? Explain.
2. a. **Identifying** What are three major groups of fishes?
   b. **Classifying** Into which group of fishes would you classify a fish with jaws and a skeleton made of cartilage?
   c. **Comparing and Contrasting** How do sharks and hagfishes obtain food?

Writing in Science

Wanted Poster Design a "Wanted" poster for a lamprey. Present the lamprey as a "criminal of the ocean." Include the lamprey's physical characteristics, feeding habits, and any other details that will allow people to track down this fish.

Home Sweet Home

Problem

What features does an aquarium need for fish to survive in it?

Skills Focus

observing, making models

Materials

- gravel • metric ruler • guppies • snails
- guppy food • dip net
- tap water • thermometer • water plants
- aquarium filter • aquarium heater
- rectangular aquarium tank (15 to 20 liters) with cover

Procedure

1. Wash the aquarium tank with lukewarm water—do not use soap. Then place it on a flat surface in indirect sunlight.

2. Rinse the gravel and spread it over the bottom of the tank to a depth of about 3 cm.

3. Fill the tank about two-thirds full with tap water. Position several water plants in the tank by gently pushing their roots into the gravel. Wash your hands after handling the plants.

4. Add more water until the level is about 5 cm from the top.

5. Place the filter in the water and turn it on. Insert an aquarium heater into the tank and turn it on. Set the temperature to 25°C. **CAUTION:** *Do not touch electrical equipment with wet hands.*

6. Allow the water to "age" by letting it stand for two days. Aging allows the chlorine to evaporate.

7. When the water has aged and is at the proper temperature, add guppies and snails to the tank. Include one guppy and one snail for each 4 liters of water. Cover the aquarium. Wash your hands after handling the animals.

8. Observe the aquarium every day for two weeks. Feed the guppies a small amount of food daily. Look for evidence that the fishes and snails have adapted to their new environment. Also look for the ways they carry out their life activities, such as feeding and respiration. Record your observations.

9. Use a dip net to keep the gravel layer clean and to remove any dead plants or animals.

Analyze and Conclude

1. **Observing** How does the aquarium meet the following needs of the organisms living in it: (a) oxygen supply, (b) proper temperature, and (c) food?

2. **Inferring** What happens to the oxygen that the fishes take in from the water in this aquarium? How is that oxygen replaced?

3. **Making Models** How is an aquarium like a guppy's natural environment? How is it different?

4. **Communicating** Write an e-mail to a friend or relative in which you summarize the record you made during the two weeks you observed the aquarium.

Design an Experiment

Write a one-page procedure for adding a second kind of fish to the aquarium. Include a list of questions that you would need to have answered before you could carry out your plan successfully. (Success would be marked by both types of fishes surviving together in the tank.) *Obtain your teacher's permission before carrying out your investigation.*

Amphibians

Reading Preview

Key Concepts
- What are the main characteristics of amphibians?
- What are some adaptations of adult amphibians for living on land?

Key Terms
- amphibian • tadpole • lung
- atrium • ventricle • habitat

Target Reading Skill

Sequencing As you read, make a cycle diagram like the one below that shows the different stages of a frog's metamorphosis during its life cycle. Write each step of the process in a separate circle.

Frog Metamorphosis

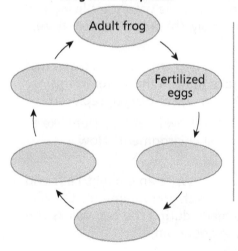

Adult frog

Fertilized eggs

Spring peeper ▶

Discover Activity

What's the Advantage of Being Green?

1. Count out 20 dried yellow peas and 20 green ones. Mix them up in a paper cup.
2. Cover your eyes. Have your partner gently scatter the peas onto a large sheet of green paper.
3. Uncover your eyes. Have your partner keep time while you pick up as many peas, one at a time, as you can find in 15 seconds.
4. When 15 seconds are up, count how many peas of each color you picked up.
5. Repeat Steps 2 through 4, but this time you scatter the peas and keep time while your partner picks up the peas.
6. Compare your results with those of your partner and your classmates.

Think It Over

Inferring Many frogs are green, as are their environments. What advantage does a frog have in being green?

What's that sound coming from the pond? Even 1 kilometer away you can hear the shrill calls of frogs called spring peepers on this damp spring night. By the time you reach the pond, the calls are ear-splitting. You might think that the frogs must be huge to make such a loud sound. But each frog is smaller than the first joint of your thumb! In the beam of your flashlight, you see the puffed-up throats of the males, vibrating with each call. Female peepers bound across roads and swim across streams to mate with the noisy males.

What Is an Amphibian?

A frog is one kind of amphibian; toads and salamanders are other kinds. An **amphibian** is a vertebrate that is ectothermic and spends its early life in water. Indeed, the word *amphibian* means "double life," and amphibians have exactly that. **After beginning their lives in water, most amphibians spend their adulthood on land, returning to water to reproduce.**

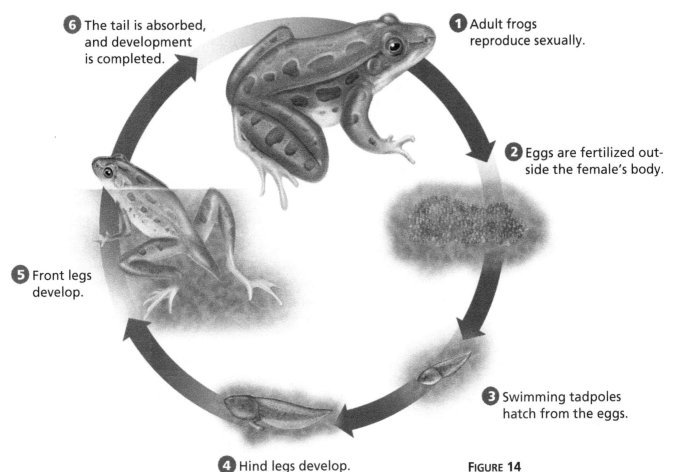

6 The tail is absorbed, and development is completed.

1 Adult frogs reproduce sexually.

2 Eggs are fertilized outside the female's body.

5 Front legs develop.

3 Swimming tadpoles hatch from the eggs.

4 Hind legs develop.

FIGURE 14
Life Cycle of a Frog
During its metamorphosis from tadpole to adult, a frog's body undergoes a series of dramatic changes. **Applying Concepts** *How do these changes prepare a frog for living on land?*

Groups of Amphibians The two major groups of amphibians are salamanders and frogs and toads. You can distinguish between the groups by the presence of a tail in the adults. Salamanders keep their tails in adulthood, while almost all frogs and toads do not.

Reproduction and Development Amphibians have a life cycle that suits the "double lives" they lead. Eggs are fertilized internally in most salamanders and externally in most frogs and toads. Fertilized eggs develop in water. After a few days, larvae wriggle out of a jelly that coats the eggs and begin a free-swimming, fishlike life.

The larvae of most amphibians grow and eventually undergo metamorphosis. You can trace the process of frog metamorphosis in Figure 14. The larva of a frog or a toad is called a **tadpole.**

Unlike tadpoles, the larvae of salamanders look like adults. Most salamander larvae undergo a metamorphosis in which they lose their gills. However, the changes are not as dramatic as those that happen during a frog or toad's metamorphosis.

 Reading Checkpoint **What is a frog larva called?**

Go Online
PHSchool.com

For: More on the frog life cycle
Visit: PHSchool.com
Web Code: ced-2033

Living on Land

Once an amphibian becomes an adult and moves onto land, its survival needs change. It must now get its oxygen from the air, not the water. Fins no longer help it move. **The respiratory and circulatory systems of adult amphibians are adapted for life on land. In addition, adult amphibians have adaptations for obtaining food and moving.**

Obtaining Oxygen Amphibian larvae use gills to obtain oxygen from the water they live in. During metamorphosis, most amphibians lose their gills and develop lungs. **Lungs** are organs of air-breathing vertebrates in which oxygen gas and carbon dioxide gas are exchanged between the air and the blood. Oxygen and carbon dioxide are also exchanged through the thin, moist skins of adult amphibians.

Circulatory System A tadpole's circulatory system has a single loop and a heart with two chambers, like that of a fish. In contrast, the circulatory system of many adult amphibians has two loops and a heart with three chambers. You can trace the path of blood through an amphibian in Figure 15. The two upper chambers of the heart, called **atria** (singular *atrium*), receive blood. One atrium receives oxygen-rich blood from the lungs, and the other receives oxygen-poor blood from the rest of the body. From the atria, blood moves into the lower chamber, the **ventricle,** which pumps blood out to the lungs and body. Oxygen-rich and oxygen-poor blood mix in the ventricle.

Go Online
active art

For: Respiration and Circulation activity
Visit: PHSchool.com
Web Code: cep-2032

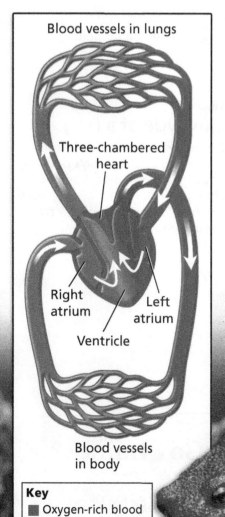

Blood vessels in lungs

Three-chambered heart

Right atrium

Left atrium

Ventricle

Blood vessels in body

Key
- Oxygen-rich blood
- Oxygen-poor blood

FIGURE 15
Respiration and Circulation
This adult salamander has lungs and a double-loop circulatory system. **Interpreting Diagrams**
What kind of blood is in the ventricle?

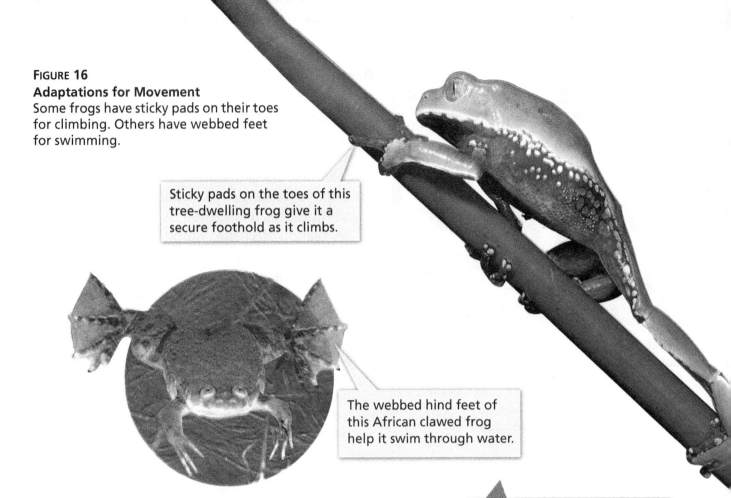

FIGURE 16
Adaptations for Movement
Some frogs have sticky pads on their toes for climbing. Others have webbed feet for swimming.

Sticky pads on the toes of this tree-dwelling frog give it a secure foothold as it climbs.

The webbed hind feet of this African clawed frog help it swim through water.

Obtaining Food Although most tadpoles are herbivores, most adult salamanders, frogs, and toads are carnivores that feed on small animals. Frogs and toads usually wait for their prey to come close. But salamanders, unlike frogs and toads, actively stalk and ambush their prey.

Frogs and toads have camouflage that helps them obtain food. Most frogs and toads are brownish-green, making them hard to see in their environment. In the Discover Activity, you learned that it is hard to see something green against a green background.

Movement A vertebrate that lives on land needs a strong skeleton to support its body against the pull of gravity. In addition, a land animal needs some way of moving. Fins work in water, but they don't work on land. Most adult amphibians have strong skeletons and muscular limbs adapted for moving on land.

Salamanders usually crawl in their environments, but frogs and toads have adaptations for other kinds of movements. Perhaps you've tried to catch a frog or a toad only to have it leap away from you. The legs of frogs and toads have adaptations for leaping. Leaping requires powerful hind-leg muscles and a skeleton that can absorb the shock of landing. The feet of frogs and toads have adaptations, too, as you can see in Figure 16.

Lab zone Try This Activity

Webbing Along

1. Fill a sink or pail with water.

2. Spread your fingers and put your hand into the water just far enough so that only your fingers are under water. Drag your fingers back and forth through the water.

3. Now dry your hand and cover it with a small plastic bag. Secure the bag around your wrist with a rubber band.

4. Repeat Step 2. Note any difference in the way in which your fingers push the water.

Making Models Use your model to explain how a frog's webbed feet help it move through water.

FIGURE 17
Golden Frog
Golden frogs, like the one shown here, are rarely seen anymore in their native habitat—the rain forests of Panama. **Relating Cause and Effect** *What are two possible causes for the decrease in the number of golden frogs?*

Amphibians in Danger Worldwide, amphibian populations are decreasing. One reason for the decrease is the destruction of amphibian habitats. An animal's **habitat** is the specific environment in which it lives. When a swamp is filled in or a forest is cut, an area that was moist becomes drier. Few amphibians can survive for long in dry, sunny areas. But habitat destruction does not account for the whole problem of population decrease. Amphibians are declining even in areas where their habitats have not been damaged. Because their skins are delicate and their eggs lack shells, amphibians are especially sensitive to changes in their environment. Poisons in the environment, such as pesticides and other chemicals, can pollute the waters that amphibians need to live and reproduce. Even small amounts of these chemicals can weaken adult amphibians, kill amphibian eggs, or cause tadpoles to become deformed.

 **Reading Checkpoint** What is a habitat?

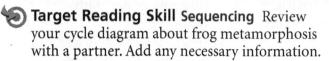

Section 3 Assessment

Target Reading Skill **Sequencing** Review your cycle diagram about frog metamorphosis with a partner. Add any necessary information.

Reviewing Key Concepts

1. **a. Defining** What is an amphibian?
   b. Summarizing What are three main characteristics of amphibians?
   c. Comparing and Contrasting How is the metamorphosis of a salamander different from the metamorphosis of a frog?
2. **a. Reviewing** What are four adaptations of adult amphibians for living on land?
   b. Describing What are three adaptations frogs and toads have for moving? How does each adaptation help the amphibian survive in its environment?
   c. Sequencing How does blood move in the circulatory system of an amphibian? (*Hint:* Start with blood leaving the ventricle of the heart.)

Writing in Science

Web Site Design the home page of a Web site that introduces people to amphibians. First, come up with a catchy title for your Web site. Then, design your home page, the first page people will see. Consider these questions as you come up with your design: What information will you include? What will the illustrations or photos show? What links to specific topics relating to amphibians will you have?

Reptiles

Reading Preview

Key Concepts
- What are some adaptations that allow reptiles to live on land?
- What are the characteristics of each of the three main groups of reptiles?
- What adaptation helped dinosaurs survive before they became extinct?

Key Terms
- reptile
- kidney
- urine
- amniotic egg

Target Reading Skill

Identifying Main Ideas As you read the information under the heading titled Adaptations for Life on Land, write the main idea in a graphic organizer like the one below. Then write three supporting details that give examples of the main idea.

Main Idea

Reptiles are adapted to conserve water.		
Detail	Detail	Detail

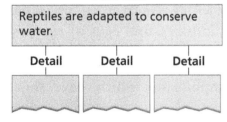

Discover Activity

How Do Snakes Feed?

1. To model how a snake feeds, stretch a sock cuff over a grapefruit "prey" by first pulling on one side and then on the other. Work the grapefruit down into the "stomach." A snake's jawbones can spread apart like the sock cuff.

2. Remove the grapefruit and put a rubber band around the sock about 8 centimeters below the opening. The rubber band represents the firmly joined jawbones of a lizard. Now try to repeat Step 1.

Think It Over
Inferring What is the advantage of having jawbones like a snake's?

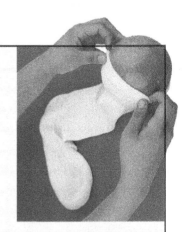

The king cobra of Southeast Asia is the world's longest venomous snake. It can grow to more than 4 meters long. When it encounters a predator, a king cobra flattens its neck and rears up. Its ropelike body sways back and forth, and its tongue flicks in and out.

A king cobra's fearsome behavior in response to a predator contrasts with the gentle way it treats its eggs. King cobras are one of the few snakes that build nests. The female builds a nest of grass and leaves on the forest floor. She lays her eggs inside the nest and guards them until they hatch.

King cobra ▶

FIGURE 18
A Desert Tortoise
The tough, scaly skin of this desert
tortoise helps it survive in a dry
environment.

Adaptations for Life on Land

Like other reptiles, king cobras lay their eggs on land rather
than in water. A **reptile** is an ectothermic vertebrate that has
lungs and scaly skin. In addition to snakes such as the king
cobra, lizards, turtles, and alligators are also reptiles. Unlike
amphibians, reptiles can spend their entire lives on dry land.

The ancestors of modern reptiles were the first vertebrates
adapted to life completely out of water. Reptiles get their oxygen from air and breathe entirely with lungs. Reptiles that live
in water, such as sea turtles, evolved from reptiles that lived on
land. So, even though they live in water, they still breathe with
lungs and come ashore to lay eggs.

You can think of a land animal as a pocket of water held
within a bag of skin. To thrive on land, an animal must have
adaptations that keep the water within the "bag" from evapo-
rating in the dry air. **The skin, kidneys, and eggs of reptiles
are adapted to conserve water.**

Skin and Kidneys Unlike amphibians, which have thin,
moist skin, reptiles have dry, tough skins covered with scales.
This scaly skin protects reptiles and helps keep water in their
bodies. Another adaptation that helps keep water inside a reptile's body is its **kidneys,** which are organs that filter wastes
from the blood. The wastes are then excreted in a watery fluid
called **urine.** The kidneys of reptiles concentrate the urine so
that the reptiles lose very little water.

Go Online
PHSchool.com

For: More on reptiles
Visit: PHSchool.com
Web Code: ced-2034

Reading
Checkpoint   What are two functions of a reptile's skin?

An Egg With a Shell Reptiles have internal fertilization and lay their eggs on land. While still inside a female's body, fertilized eggs are covered with membranes and a leathery shell. Unlike an amphibian's egg, a reptile's egg has a shell and membranes that protect the developing embryo and help keep it from drying out. An egg with a shell and internal membranes that keep the embryo moist is called an **amniotic egg.** Pores in the shell let oxygen gas in and carbon dioxide gas out.

Look at Figure 19 to see the membranes of a reptile's egg. One membrane holds a liquid that surrounds the embryo. The liquid protects the embryo and keeps it moist. A second membrane holds the yolk, or food for the embryo. A third membrane holds the embryo's wastes. Oxygen and carbon dioxide are exchanged across the fourth membrane.

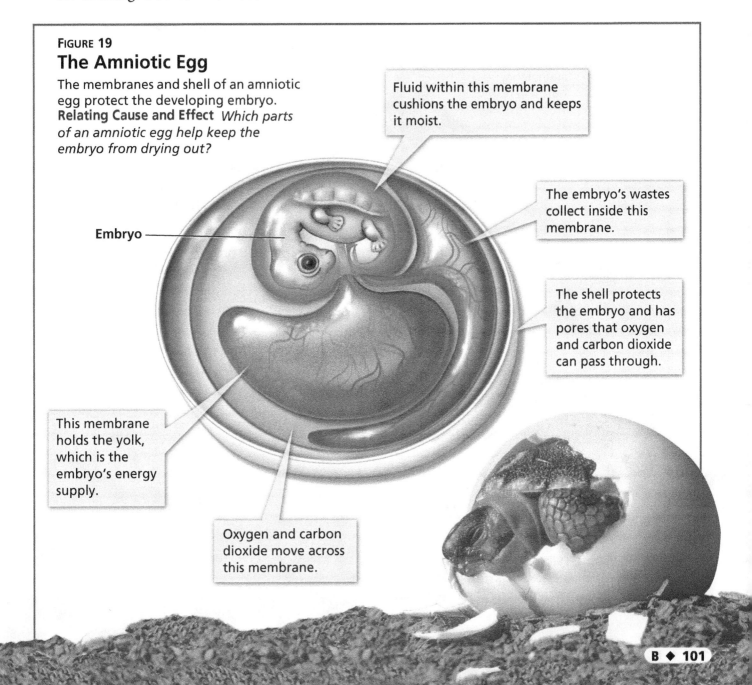

FIGURE 19
The Amniotic Egg
The membranes and shell of an amniotic egg protect the developing embryo.
Relating Cause and Effect *Which parts of an amniotic egg help keep the embryo from drying out?*

Fluid within this membrane cushions the embryo and keeps it moist.

The embryo's wastes collect inside this membrane.

The shell protects the embryo and has pores that oxygen and carbon dioxide can pass through.

Embryo

This membrane holds the yolk, which is the embryo's energy supply.

Oxygen and carbon dioxide move across this membrane.

Lizards and Snakes

Most reptiles alive today are either lizards or snakes. These two groups of reptiles share some important characteristics. **Both lizards and snakes are reptiles that have skin covered with overlapping scales.** As they grow, they shed their skin and scales, replacing the worn ones with new ones. Most lizards and snakes live in warm areas.

Lizards differ from snakes in an obvious way. Lizards have four legs, usually with claws on the toes, and snakes have no legs. In addition, lizards have long tails, external ears, movable eyelids, and two lungs. In contrast, snakes have streamlined bodies, no external ears, and no eyelids, and most have only one lung. You can see the characteristics of a lizard in Figure 20.

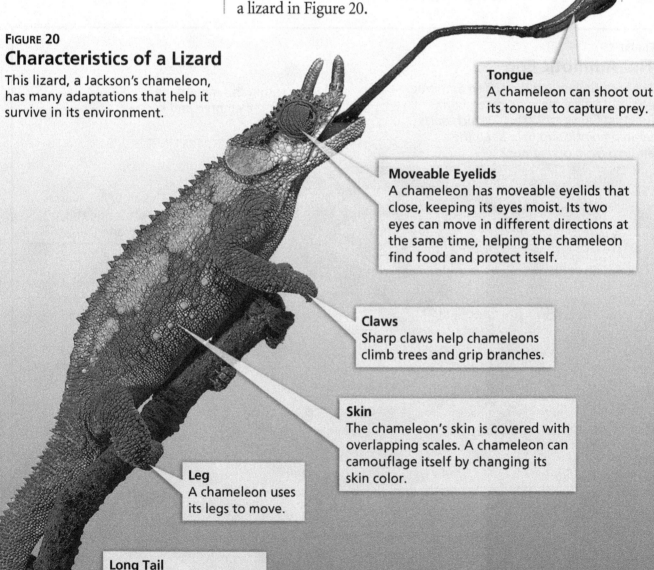

FIGURE 20

Characteristics of a Lizard

This lizard, a Jackson's chameleon, has many adaptations that help it survive in its environment.

Tongue
A chameleon can shoot out its tongue to capture prey.

Moveable Eyelids
A chameleon has moveable eyelids that close, keeping its eyes moist. Its two eyes can move in different directions at the same time, helping the chameleon find food and protect itself.

Claws
Sharp claws help chameleons climb trees and grip branches.

Skin
The chameleon's skin is covered with overlapping scales. A chameleon can camouflage itself by changing its skin color.

Leg
A chameleon uses its legs to move.

Long Tail
A chameleon coils its tail tightly around branches, giving it extra grip.

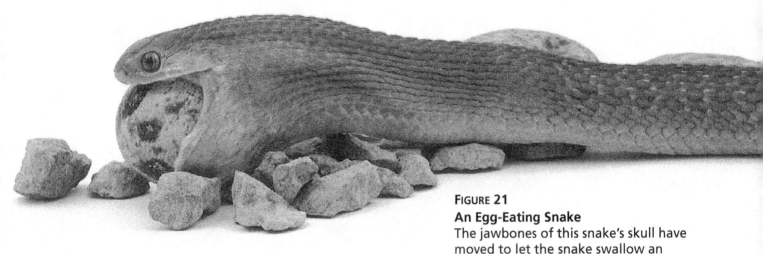

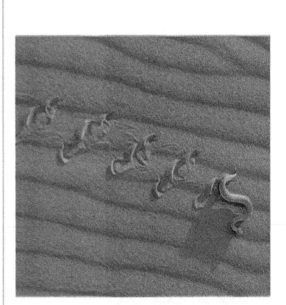

Obtaining Food A few lizards are herbivores that eat leaves. Most lizards, however, are carnivores that capture their prey by jumping at it. While some large lizards will eat frogs and birds, most smaller lizards are adapted to hunt insects. For example, chameleons have sticky tongues adapted for snaring insects.

All snakes are carnivores. Most snakes feed on small animals, such as mice, but some eat large prey. If you did the Discover Activity, you learned that a snake's jawbones can spread wide apart. In addition, the bones of a snake's skull can move to let the snake swallow an animal larger in diameter than itself. Snakes capture their prey in different ways. For example, some snakes have long, curved front teeth for hooking slippery prey. Other snakes, such as rattlesnakes and copperheads, have venom glands attached to hollow teeth called fangs. When these snakes bite their prey, venom flows down through the fangs and enters the prey.

Movement While lizards walk and run using their legs, snakes cannot move in this way. If you've ever seen a snake slither across the ground, you know that when it moves, its long, thin body bends into curves. Snakes move by contracting, or shortening, bands of muscles that are connected to their ribs and their backbones. Alternate contractions of muscles on the right and left sides produce a slithering side-to-side motion. Instead of slithering, sidewinder snakes, like the one shown in Figure 22, lift up their bodies as they move.

 **Reading Checkpoint** How do lizards move?

FIGURE 22
A Sidewinder Snake
This sidewinder snake lifts loops of its body off the desert sand as it moves along. Only a small part of its body touches the sand at one time.

Alligator

Crocodile

FIGURE 23
Alligator and Crocodile
Alligators and crocodiles are the largest reptiles still living on earth. They are similar in many ways, including appearance.
Comparing and Contrasting *How can you tell the difference between an alligator and a crocodile?*

Discovery
CHANNEL
SCHOOL

Fishes, Amphibians, and Reptiles

Video Preview
▶ Video Field Trip
Video Assessment

Alligators and Crocodiles

If you walk along a lake in Florida, you just might see an alligator swimming silently in the water. Most of its body lies beneath the surface, but you can see its large, bulging eyes above the surface. Alligators, crocodiles, and their relatives are the largest living reptiles. **Both alligators and crocodiles are large, carnivorous reptiles that care for their young.** So, how do you tell an alligator from a crocodile? Alligators have broad, rounded snouts, with only a few teeth visible when their mouths are shut. In contrast, crocodiles have pointed snouts, with most of their teeth visible when their mouths are shut.

Obtaining Food Alligators and crocodiles are carnivores that often hunt at night. They have several adaptations for capturing prey. They use their strong, muscular tails to swim rapidly. Their jaws are equipped with many large, sharp, and pointed teeth. Their jaw muscles are extremely strong when biting down. Although alligators will eat dogs, raccoons, and deer, they usually do not attack humans.

Reproduction Unlike most other reptiles, crocodiles and alligators care for their eggs and newly hatched young. After laying eggs, the female stays near the nest. From time to time, she comes out of the water and crawls over the nest to keep it moist. After the tiny alligators or crocodiles hatch, the female scoops them up in her huge mouth. She carries them from the nest to a nursery area in the water where they will be safer. For as long as a year, she will stay near her young until they can feed and protect themselves.

 **Reading Checkpoint** When do alligators and crocodiles hunt?

The Sex Ratio of Newly Hatched Alligators

The temperature of the developing eggs of the American alligator affects the sex ratio of the young. (Sex ratio is the number of females compared with the number of males.) The graph on the right shows the numbers of young of each sex that hatched from eggs in which the young developed at different temperatures.

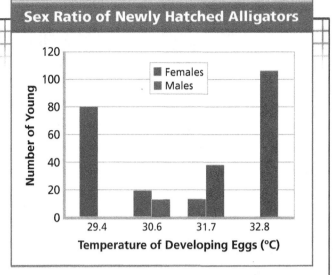

Sex Ratio of Newly Hatched Alligators

1. **Reading Graphs** At which temperature(s) did only females hatch?

2. **Drawing Conclusions** What effect does the temperature of developing eggs have on the sex of the baby alligators?

3. **Calculating** If 100 eggs developed at 31.7°C, about how many of the young would be male?

Turtles

Turtles live in the ocean, in fresh water, and on land. Turtles that live on land are commonly called "tortoises." **A turtle is a reptile whose body is covered by a protective shell that includes the ribs and the backbone.** The bony plates of the shell are covered by large scales made from the same material as the skin's scales. Some turtles have shells that are large enough to cover the whole body. A box turtle, for example, can draw its head, legs, and tail inside its shell for protection. Other turtles, like the snapping turtle, have much smaller shells. Turtle shells may be hard or as soft as pancakes.

Turtles feed in a variety of ways, but all have a sharp-edged beak instead of teeth for tearing food. Some turtles are carnivores, such as the largest turtles, the leatherbacks. Leatherbacks feed mainly on jellyfishes. Their tough skin protects them from the effects of the stinging cells. Other turtles, such as the Galápagos tortoise, are herbivores. They feed mainly on cacti, using their beaks to scrape off the prickly spines before swallowing the cactus.

Reading Checkpoint What are turtles that live on land called?

FIGURE 24
A Galápagos Tortoise
The Galápagos tortoise lives on land, where it eats mainly cacti.

Extinct Reptiles—The Dinosaurs

Millions of years ago, huge turtles and fish-eating reptiles swam in the oceans. Flying reptiles soared through the skies. Snakes and lizards basked on warm rocks. And there were dinosaurs of every description. Unlike today's reptiles, some dinosaurs may have been endothermic. Some dinosaurs, such as *Brachiosaurus* in Figure 25, were the largest land animals that ever lived.

Dinosaurs were the earliest vertebrates that had legs positioned directly beneath their bodies. This adaptation allowed them to move more easily than animals such as salamanders and lizards, whose legs stick out from the sides of their bodies. Most herbivorous dinosaurs, such as *Brachiosaurus*, walked on four legs. Most carnivores, such as the huge *Tyrannosaurus rex*, ran on two legs.

Dinosaurs became extinct, or disappeared from Earth, about 65 million years ago. No one is certain why. Today, it's only in movies that dinosaurs shake the ground with their footsteps. But the descendants of dinosaurs may still exist. Some biologists think that birds descended from certain small dinosaurs.

 **Reading Checkpoint** **Give an example of a dinosaur that ran on two legs.**

FIGURE 25
Brachiosaurus
Brachiosaurus grew to be more than 22.5 meters long—longer than two school buses put together end to end. **Inferring** *What advantage did a long neck give* Brachiosaurus?

Section 4 Assessment

 Target Reading Skill Identifying Main Ideas Use the information in your graphic organizer to help you answer Question 1 below.

Reviewing Key Concepts

1. a. **Defining** What is a reptile?
   b. **Explaining** What are three adaptations that allow reptiles to survive on land?
   c. **Predicting** What might happen to a reptile egg if part of its shell were removed?
2. a. **Identifying** What are the three main groups of reptiles?
   b. **Classifying** A gecko is a small reptile that has no shell protecting its body. It uses its legs to climb trees. Into which reptile group would you classify the gecko?
   c. **Comparing and Contrasting** Compare and contrast how alligators and turtles obtain food.

3. a. **Reviewing** When did the dinosaurs become extinct?
   b. **Interpreting Diagrams** What adaptation did the dinosaur in Figure 25 have that helped it survive?
   c. **Inferring** What advantage might a dinosaur that was an endotherm have had over other reptiles?

Writing in Science

Product Label Write a "packaging label" that will be pasted onto the eggshell of a reptile. Include on your label a list of the contents of the shell and a one-paragraph description of the egg's ability to survive in a dry environment.

Vertebrate History in Rocks

Reading Preview

Key Concepts
- Where are fossils most frequently found?
- What can scientists learn from studying fossils?

Key Terms
- fossil   • sedimentary rock
- paleontologist

Target Reading Skill

Asking Questions Before you read, preview the red headings. In a graphic organizer like the one below, ask *what* and *how* questions for each heading. As you read, write the answers to your questions.

Vertebrate History in Rocks

Question	Answer
How do fossils form?	Fossils form by . . .

Discover Activity

What Can You Tell From an Imprint?

1. Flatten some modeling clay into a thin sheet on a piece of paper.
2. Firmly press two or three small objects into different areas of the clay. The objects might include such things as a key, a feather, a postage stamp, or a flower. Don't let anyone see the objects you are using.
3. Carefully remove the objects from the clay, leaving only the objects' imprints.
4. Exchange your imprints with a partner. Try to identify the objects that made the imprints.

Think It Over
Observing What types of objects made the clearest imprints? If those imprints were fossils, what could you learn about the objects by looking at their "fossils"? What couldn't you learn?

Millions of years ago, in an ancient pond, some fishes died and their bodies settled into the mud on the bottom. Soon heavy rains fell, and more mud washed into the pond, covering the fishes. The soft tissues of the fishes decayed, but their bones remained. After many thousands of years, the mud hardened into rock, and the bones became the fossils shown here.

Fossilized fishes ▶

Go Online

SciLINKS NSTA

For: Links on fossils
Visit: www.SciLinks.org
Web Code: scn-0235

What Are Fossils?

A **fossil** is the hardened remains or other evidence of a living thing that existed a long time ago. Sometimes a fossil is an imprint in rock, such as an animal's footprint or the outline of a leaf. Other fossils are the remains of bones, shells, skeletons, or other parts of living things. Fossils are made when a chemical process takes place over time, during which an organism's tissues are replaced by hard minerals. Because most living tissues decay rapidly, only a very few organisms are preserved as fossils.

Fossils are found most frequently in sedimentary rock. Hardened layers of sediments make up **sedimentary rock.** Sediments contain particles of clay, sand, mud, or silt.

Science and **History**

Discovering Vertebrate Fossils

People have been discovering fossils since ancient times. Here are some especially important fossil discoveries.

**1677
Dinosaur-Bone
Illustration**
Robert Plot, the head of a museum in England, published a book that had an illustration of a huge fossilized thighbone. Plot thought that the bone belonged to a giant human, but it probably was the thighbone of a dinosaur.

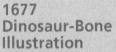

1811 Sea Reptile
Along the cliffs near Lyme Regis, England, 12-year-old Mary Anning discovered the fossilized remains of the giant sea reptile now called *Ichthyosaurus*. Mary became one of England's first professional fossil collectors.

**1822
Dinosaur Tooth**
In a quarry near Lewes, England, Mary Ann Mantell discovered a strange-looking tooth embedded in stone. Her husband Gideon drew the picture of the tooth shown here. The tooth belonged to the dinosaur *Iguanodon*.

1670   1760   1820

How do sediments build up into layers? Have you ever washed a dirty soccer ball and seen sand and mud settle in the sink? If you washed a dozen soccer balls, the sink bottom would be covered with layers of sediments. Sediments build up in many ways. For example, wind can blow a thick layer of sand onto dunes. Sediments can also form when muddy water stands in an area for a long time. Muddy sediment in the water eventually settles to the bottom and builds up.

Over a very long time, layers of sediments can be pressed and cemented together to form rock. As sedimentary rock forms, traces of living things that have been trapped in the sediments are sometimes preserved as fossils.

 Reading Checkpoint) **How does sedimentary rock form?**

Writing in Science

Research and Write If you could interview the person who discovered one of the fossils, what questions would you ask about the fossil and how it was found? Write a list of those questions. Then use reference materials to try to find the answers to some of them.

**1861
Bird Bones**
A worker in a stone quarry in Germany found *Archaeopteryx*, a feathered, birdlike animal that also had many reptile characteristics.

**1902
*Tyrannosaurus***
A tip from a local rancher sent Barnum Brown, a fossil hunter, to a barren, rocky area near Jordan, Montana. There Brown found the first relatively complete skeleton of *Tyrannosaurus rex.*

1964 *Deinonychus*
In Montana, paleontologist John Ostrom discovered the remains of a small dinosaur, *Deinonychus*. This dinosaur was probably a predator that could move rapidly. This fossil led scientists to hypothesize that dinosaurs may have been endotherms.

**1991
Dinosaur Eggs in China**
Digging beneath the ground, a farmer on Green Dragon Mountain in China uncovered what may be the largest nest of fossil dinosaur eggs ever found. A paleontologist chips carefully to remove one of the eggs from the rock.

1880   **1940**   **2000**

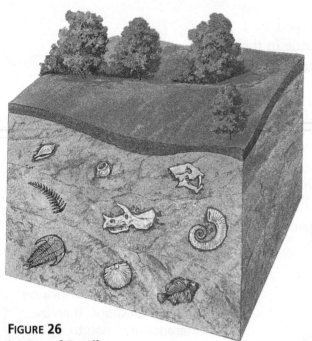

FIGURE 26
Layers of Fossils
Fossils most often form in layers of sedimentary rock.
Interpreting Diagrams *Which rock layer probably contains the oldest fossils?*

Interpretation of Fossils

What information can scientists learn from fossils? **Paleontologists** (pay lee un TAHL uh jists), the scientists who study extinct organisms, examine fossil structure and make comparisons to present-day organisms. **By studying fossils, paleontologists can infer how animals changed over time.** One important piece of information that paleontologists can learn from a fossil is its approximate age.

A Fossil's Age One method for estimating a fossil's age takes advantage of the process in which sediments form. Think about sediments settling out of water—the lowest layers are deposited first, and newer sediments settle on top of the older layers. Therefore, fossils in higher layers of rock are often younger than fossils in lower layers.

However, rock layers can become tilted or even turned upside down by events such as earthquakes. So, a fossil's position in rock is not always a good indication of its age. Scientists usually rely on other methods to help determine a fossil's age. For example, fossils—and the rocks in which they are found—contain some radioactive chemical elements. These radioactive elements decay, or change into other chemical elements, over a known period of time. The more there is of the decayed form of the element, the older the fossil.

Using Fossils Paleontologists have used fossils to determine a likely pattern of how vertebrates changed over time. You can see in Figure 27 that this pattern of vertebrate evolution looks something like a branching tree. Fossils show that the first vertebrates to live on Earth were fishes. Fishes first appeared on Earth about 530 million years ago. Amphibians, which appeared on Earth about 380 million years ago, are descended from fishes. Then, about 320 million years ago, amphibians gave rise to reptiles. Both mammals and birds, which you will learn about in the next chapter, are descended from reptiles. Based on the age of the oldest mammal fossils, mammals first lived on Earth about 220 million years ago. Birds were the latest group of vertebrates to arise. Their oldest fossils show that birds first appeared on Earth 150 million years ago.

 Reading Checkpoint **What is a paleontologist?**

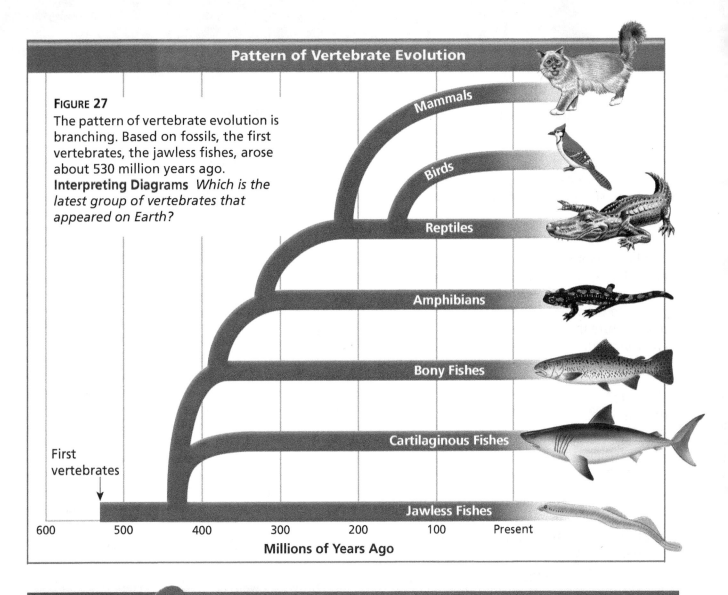

Pattern of Vertebrate Evolution

FIGURE 27
The pattern of vertebrate evolution is branching. Based on fossils, the first vertebrates, the jawless fishes, arose about 530 million years ago.
Interpreting Diagrams *Which is the latest group of vertebrates that appeared on Earth?*

Mammals

Birds

Reptiles

Amphibians

Bony Fishes

Cartilaginous Fishes

First vertebrates

Jawless Fishes

| 600 | 500 | 400 | 300 | 200 | 100 | Present |

Millions of Years Ago

Section 5 Assessment

Target Reading Skill Asking Questions Use your graphic organizer to answer the questions below.

Reviewing Key Concepts

1. a. Identifying Where are fossils most often found?
   b. Describing What are some types of fossils?
   c. Inferring How might a small fish that dies in a muddy pool become a fossil?
2. a. Reviewing What can be learned from studying fossils?
   b. Summarizing How does the measurement of radioactive elements help scientists calculate a fossil's age?
   c. Interpreting Diagrams Look at Figure 27. About how much time passed between the first appearance of vertebrates and the time birds appeared?

Lab zone At Home Activity

Sedimentary Newspaper? If your family keeps newspapers in a stack, check the dates of the newspapers in the stack with a family member. Are the newspapers in any kind of order? If the oldest ones are on the bottom and the newest are on the top, you can relate this to the way in which sediments are laid down. Ask family members to imagine that two fossils were trapped in different newspapers. Explain which fossil would probably be older.

1 What Is a Vertebrate?

Key Concepts

- At some point in their lives, chordates will have a notochord, a nerve cord that runs down their back, and slits in their throat area.

- A vertebrate has a backbone that is part of an internal skeleton.

- The body temperature of most fishes, amphibians, and reptiles is close to the temperature of their environment. In contrast, birds and mammals have a stable body temperature that is often warmer than their environment.

Key Terms

chordate	ectotherm
notochord	endotherm
vertebra	

2 Fishes

Key Concepts

- In addition to living in water and having fins, most fishes are ectotherms, obtain oxygen through gills, and have scales.

- The major groups of fishes are jawless fishes, cartilaginous fishes, and bony fishes.

- Jawless fishes are unlike other fishes in that they have no jaws and no scales.

- Cartilaginous fishes have jaws and scales, and skeletons made of cartilage.

- A bony fish has jaws, scales, a pocket on each side of the head that holds the gills, and a skeleton made of hard bone.

Key Terms
fish
cartilage
swim bladder

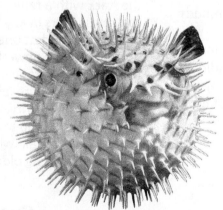

3 Amphibians

Key Concepts

- After beginning their lives in water, most amphibians spend their adulthood on land, returning to water to reproduce.

- The respiratory and circulatory systems of adult amphibians are adapted for life on land. In addition, adult amphibians have adaptations for obtaining food and moving.

Key Terms

amphibian	lung	ventricle
tadpole	atrium	habitat

4 Reptiles

Key Concepts

- The skin, kidneys, and eggs of reptiles are adapted to conserve water.

- Both lizards and snakes are reptiles that have skin covered with overlapping scales.

- Both alligators and crocodiles are large, carnivorous reptiles that care for their young.

- A turtle is a reptile whose body is covered by a protective shell that includes the ribs and the backbone.

- Dinosaurs were the earliest vertebrates that had legs positioned directly beneath their bodies.

Key Terms

reptile	kidney
urine	amniotic egg

5 Vertebrate History in Rocks

Key Concepts

- Fossils are found most frequently in sedimentary rock.

- By studying fossils, paleontologists can infer how a species changed over time.

Key Terms

fossil	sedimentary rock
paleontologist	

Review and Assessment

Organizing Information

Identifying Main Ideas Copy the graphic organizer about reptiles onto a sheet of paper. Then complete it.

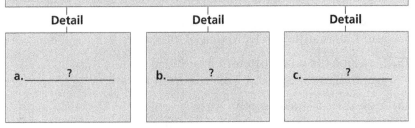

Main Idea

The larvae of amphibians are adapted for life in water, and adult amphibians are adapted for life on land.

Detail	Detail	Detail
a. _____ ?	b. _____ ?	c. _____ ?

Reviewing Key Terms

Choose the letter of the best answer.

1. Vertebrates are a subgroup of
   a. chordates.
   b. fishes.
   c. amphibians.
   d. reptiles.

2. A fish
   a. is an endotherm.
   b. has fins.
   c. has lungs.
   d. has a three-chambered heart.

3. A tadpole is the larva of a
   a. fish.
   b. salamander.
   c. frog or toad.
   d. lizard or snake.

4. A reptile
   a. is an endotherm.
   b. lays eggs.
   c. has a swim bladder.
   d. has a thin skin.

5. Layers of clay, sand, mud, or silt harden and become
   a. radioactive chemicals.
   b. sedimentary rock.
   c. fossils.
   d. dinosaur bones.

If the statement is true, write *true.* If it is false, change the underlined word or words to make the statement true.

6. A <u>notochord</u> is replaced by a backbone in many vertebrates.

7. A bony fish uses its <u>gills</u> to stabilize its position in the water.

8. <u>Amphibians</u> obtain oxygen through gills and have scales.

9. An <u>amniotic egg</u> is a characteristic of reptiles.

10. <u>Paleontologists</u> are scientists who study fossils.

Writing in Science

Description Suppose you are a journalist for a nature magazine and you have spent a week observing crocodiles. Write a paragraph describing how crocodiles obtain their food.

Discovery CHANNEL SCHOOL™

Fishes, Amphibians, and Reptiles
Video Preview
Video Field Trip
▶ Video Assessment

Review and Assessment

Checking Concepts

11. Describe the main characteristics of chordates.

12. How do fishes reproduce?

13. Describe the life cycle of a frog.

14. How is the circulatory system of an adult amphibian different from that of a fish?

15. Describe the adaptations of an adult amphibian for obtaining oxygen from the air.

16. How does a snake move?

17. Explain how the structure of a reptile's egg protects the embryo inside.

18. Describe two methods that scientists use to determine the age of a fossil.

Thinking Critically

19. **Relating Cause and Effect** Explain why an endoskeleton allows vertebrates to grow larger than animals without endoskeletons.

20. **Interpreting Diagrams** How does blood move in the circulatory system shown below?

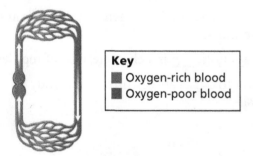

Key
- Oxygen-rich blood
- Oxygen-poor blood

21. **Applying Concepts** Imagine that you are in a hot desert with a wet paper towel. You must keep the towel from drying out. What strategy can you copy from reptiles to keep the towel from drying out?

22. **Inferring** A scientist discovers a fossilized fish with a body streamlined for fast movement, a large tail fin, and sharp, pointed teeth. What could the scientist infer about the type of food that this fish ate and how it obtained its food? On what evidence is the inference based?

Applying Skills

Use the graph to answer Questions 23–25.

A scientist performed an experiment on five goldfishes to test the effect of water temperature on "breathing rate"—the rate at which the fishes open and close their gill covers. The graph shows the data that the scientist obtained at four different temperatures.

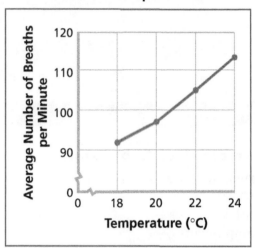

23. **Controlling Variables** Identify the manipulated variable and the responding variable in this experiment.

24. **Interpreting Data** How does the breathing rate at 18°C compare to the breathing rate at 22°C?

25. **Drawing Conclusions** Based on the data shown, what is the relationship between water temperature and fish breathing rate?

Lab zone Chapter **Project**

Performance Assessment Display your models in a creative and interesting way—for example, show the models in action and show details of the animals' habitats. Also display your poster. List all the adaptations you learned from your classmates' presentations. How did constructing a three-dimensional model help you understand the characteristics of these groups?

Standardized Test Prep

Choose the letter of the best answer.

1. If you monitored the body temperature of a snake in four different air temperatures, what would you notice about its body temperature?
   A It rises or falls with the air temperature.
   B It always stays at about 37°C .
   C It is higher than the air temperature.
   D It is lower than the air temperature.

Characteristics of Observed Animals

Animal	Skeleton	Scales	Outer Covering of Egg
1	Bone	None	Clear jelly
2	Bone	Yes	Leathery shell
3	Bone	Yes	Thin, moist membrane
4	Cartilage	Yes	No eggs observed

2. A scientist observed four different animals and recorded her data in the table shown above. Which of the animals is most likely a reptile?
   F Animals 1 and 3
   G Animal 2
   H Animal 3
   J Animal 4

3. Based on the data in the table above, what kind of animal can you infer Animal 3 might be?
   A amphibian
   B bony fish
   C cartilaginous fish
   D reptile

4. Suppose you are conducting an experiment that requires you to handle live bullfrogs. Which laboratory safety procedure should you carry out at the conclusion of each work session?
   F Carefully clean the bullfrog's container.
   G Put on gloves.
   H Wash your hands thoroughly.
   J Turn the heat on.

Constructed Response

5. Explain why amphibians can be said to have a "double life." Be sure to include details describing the two different phases in the life of a typical amphibian.

Chapter 4

Birds and Mammals

Chapter Preview

Interactive Textbook

A three-toed sloth hangs from a tree branch in Costa Rica.

Chapter **Project**

Bird Watch

One of the best ways to learn about animals is to watch them in action. In this project, you'll watch birds and other animals that visit a bird feeder. You will discover how they eat and interact. What you observe may raise new questions for you to answer.

Your Goal To make detailed observations of the birds and other animals that appear at a bird feeder

To complete this project, you must

- observe the feeder regularly for at least two weeks and use a field guide to identify the kinds of birds that visit the feeder
- make detailed observations of how the birds at your feeder eat
- describe the most common kinds of bird behavior
- follow the safety guidelines in Appendix A

Plan It! Begin by sharing knowledge about the birds in your area with some classmates. What kinds of birds can you expect to see? What types of foods do birds eat? Then, using this knowledge, start observing your feeder. Record all your observations in detail in your notebook. After completing your observations, you will interpret your data and observations and make graphs and charts for your display.

Birds

Reading Preview

Key Concepts
- What are the main characteristics of birds?
- How are birds adapted to their environments?

Key Terms
- bird • contour feather
- down feather • crop • gizzard

Target Reading Skill

Previewing Visuals When you preview, you look ahead at the material to be read. Preview Figure 1. Then write two questions that you have about the diagram in a graphic organizer like the one below. As you read, answer your questions.

Adaptations for Flight

Q.	How are birds adapted for flight?
A.	
Q.	

Discover Activity

What Are Feathers Like?

1. Observe the overall shape and structure of a feather. Then use a hand lens to examine the many hairlike barbs that project out from the feather's central shaft.

2. Gently separate two barbs in the middle of the feather. Rub the separated edges with your fingertip. How do they feel?

3. Use the hand lens to examine the edges of the two separated barbs. Draw a diagram of what you observe.

4. Rejoin the two separated barbs by gently pulling outward from the shaft. Then wash your hands.

Think It Over
Observing Once the barbs have been separated, is it easy to rejoin them? How might this be an advantage to the bird?

One day in 1861, in a limestone quarry in what is now Germany, Hermann von Meyer was inspecting rocks. Meyer, a fossil hunter, spotted something dark in a rock. It was the blackened imprint of a feather! Excited, he began searching for a fossil of an entire bird. He eventually found it—a skeleton surrounded by the imprint of many feathers. The fossil was given the scientific name *Archaeopteryx* (ahr kee AHP tur iks), meaning "ancient winged thing."

Paleontologists think that *Archaeopteryx* lived about 145 million years ago. *Archaeopteryx* didn't look much like the birds you know. It looked more like a reptile with wings. Unlike any modern bird, *Archaeopteryx* had a long, bony tail and a mouth full of teeth. But, unlike a reptile, it had feathers and wings. Paleontologists think that *Archaeopteryx* and modern birds descended from some kind of reptile, possibly a dinosaur.

◀ **A model of *Archaeopteryx***

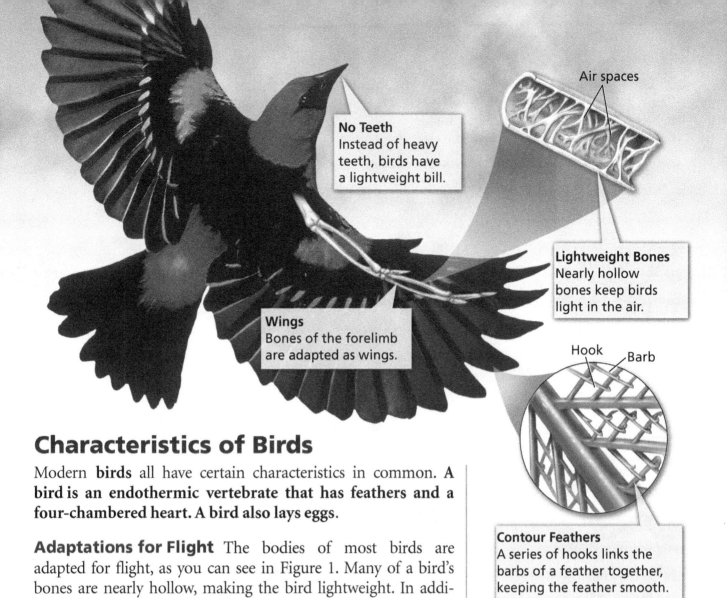

No Teeth
Instead of heavy teeth, birds have a lightweight bill.

Air spaces

Lightweight Bones
Nearly hollow bones keep birds light in the air.

Wings
Bones of the forelimb are adapted as wings.

Hook

Barb

Contour Feathers
A series of hooks links the barbs of a feather together, keeping the feather smooth.

FIGURE 1
Adaptations for Flight
The bodies of most birds have adaptations for flight.
Interpreting Diagrams *Which of these adaptations make birds light?*

Characteristics of Birds

Modern **birds** all have certain characteristics in common. **A bird is an endothermic vertebrate that has feathers and a four-chambered heart. A bird also lays eggs**.

Adaptations for Flight The bodies of most birds are adapted for flight, as you can see in Figure 1. Many of a bird's bones are nearly hollow, making the bird lightweight. In addition, the bones of a bird's forelimbs form wings. Flying birds have large chest muscles that move the wings. Finally, feathers help birds fly. Birds are the only animals with feathers.

Feathers are not all the same. If you have ever picked up a feather, it was probably a contour feather. A **contour feather** is one of the large feathers that give shape to a bird's body. The long contour feathers that extend beyond the body on the wings and tail are called flight feathers. When a bird flies, these feathers help it balance and steer. You can see in Figure 1 that a contour feather consists of a central shaft and many small hairlike projections, called barbs. Hooks hold the barbs together. When birds fly, their barbs may pull apart, "unzipping" their feathers. Birds often pull the feathers through their bills to "zip" the barbs back together again.

In addition to contour feathers, birds have short, fluffy **down feathers** that are specialized to trap heat and keep the bird warm. Down feathers are found right next to the bird's skin, at the base of the contour feathers. Down feathers are soft and flexible, unlike contour feathers.

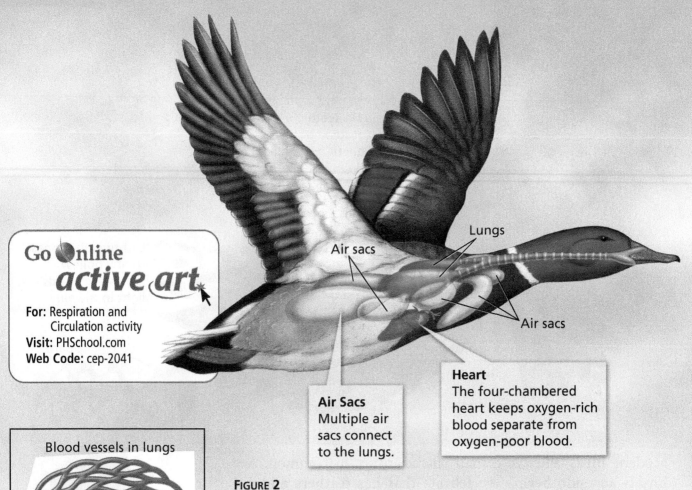

Lungs

Air sacs

Air sacs

Go Online
active art

For: Respiration and
Circulation activity
Visit: PHSchool.com
Web Code: cep-2041

Air Sacs
Multiple air
sacs connect
to the lungs.

Heart
The four-chambered
heart keeps oxygen-rich
blood separate from
oxygen-poor blood.

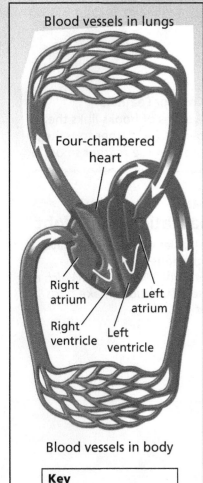

Blood vessels in lungs

Four-chambered
heart

Right
atrium

Left
atrium

Right
ventricle

Left
ventricle

Blood vessels in body

Key
■ Oxygen-rich blood
■ Oxygen-poor blood

FIGURE 2
Respiration and Circulation
Air sacs and a four-chambered heart help birds
obtain oxygen and move it to their cells.
Applying Concepts *Why is a four-chambered
heart efficient?*

Obtaining Oxygen Flying uses a lot of energy. Therefore,
cells must receive plenty of oxygen to release the energy con-
tained in food. Birds have a highly efficient way to get oxygen
into their bodies and to their cells. Birds have a system of air
sacs in their bodies. This system connects to the lungs. The air
sacs enable birds to obtain more oxygen from each breath of air
than other animals can.

The circulatory systems of birds are also efficient at getting
oxygen to the cells. Birds have hearts with four chambers—two
atria and two ventricles. Trace the path of blood through a
bird's two-loop circulatory system in Figure 2. The right side of
a bird's heart pumps oxygen-poor blood to the lungs, where
oxygen is picked up. Oxygen-rich blood returns to the left side
of the heart, which pumps it to the cells.

The advantage of a four-chambered heart over a three-
chambered heart is that oxygen-rich blood does not mix with
oxygen-poor blood. Therefore, blood carried to the cells of the
body has plenty of oxygen.

Obtaining Food Birds must obtain a lot of food to provide the energy needed for flight. To capture, grip, and handle food, birds mainly use their bills. Bills are shaped to help birds feed quickly and efficiently. For example, the pointy, curved bill of a hawk acts like a meat hook to pull off bits of its prey. In contrast, a duck's bill acts like a kitchen strainer, separating out seeds and tiny animals from muddy pond water.

After a bird eats its food, digestion begins. Each organ in a bird's digestive system is adapted to process food. Many birds have an internal storage tank, or **crop,** for storing food inside the body after swallowing it. Find the crop in Figure 3. The crop is connected to the stomach.

The stomach has two parts. In the first part, food is bathed in chemicals that begin to break it down. Then the food moves to a thick-walled, muscular part of the stomach called the **gizzard.** The gizzard squeezes and grinds the partially digested food. Remember that birds do not have teeth. The gizzard does the same grinding function for birds that your teeth do for you. The gizzard may contain small stones that the bird has swallowed. These stones help grind the food by rubbing against it and crushing it.

 **Reading Checkpoint** What is a gizzard?

Crop
The crop stores food before it enters the stomach.

Gizzard
The gizzard is a thick-walled muscular part of the stomach that squeezes and grinds the food.

FIGURE 3
Digestive System of a Hawk
Some birds like this hawk have a crop and a gizzard. The crop stores food, and the gizzard crushes food. **Interpreting Diagrams** *Does food reach the crop or the gizzard first?*

FIGURE 4
Keeping Warm
A pine grosbeak puffs out its chest
to trap air in the layer of down
feathers next to its skin.

Keeping Conditions Stable Like all animals, birds use their food for energy. You know that birds need energy for flight. Because birds are endotherms, they also need a lot of energy to maintain their body temperature. Each day, an average bird eats food equal to about a quarter of its body weight. When people say, "You're eating like a bird," they usually mean that you're eating very little. But if you were actually eating as much as a bird does, you would be eating huge meals. You might be eating as many as 100 hamburger patties in one day!

To maintain their body temperature birds use feathers as well as energy from food. As you read earlier, down feathers are specialized to trap heat. They are found right next to a bird's skin. In Figure 4, you can see what a down feather looks like. Unlike contour feathers, down feathers are soft and flexible. So, they mingle and overlap, trapping air. Air is a good insulator—a material that does not conduct heat well and therefore helps prevent heat from escaping. By trapping a blanket of warm air next to the bird's skin, down feathers slow the rate at which the skin loses heat. In effect, down feathers cover a bird in lightweight long underwear. Humans use down feathers from the eider duck to insulate jackets, sleeping bags, and bedding.

FIGURE 5
A Down-Filled Jacket
Wearing a jacket stuffed with down feathers helps this boy stay warm.
Applying Concepts *Why is his down jacket so puffy?*

Reproduction and Caring for Young Like reptiles, birds have internal fertilization and lay eggs. Bird eggs are similar to reptile eggs except that their shells are harder. In most bird species, the female lays the eggs in a nest that has been prepared by one or both parents.

Bird eggs will only develop at a temperature close to the body temperature of the parent bird. Thus, a parent bird usually incubates the eggs by sitting on them to keep them warm. In some species, incubating the eggs is the job of just one parent. For example, female robins incubate their eggs. In other species, such as pigeons, the parents take turns incubating the eggs. Chicks may take from 12 to 80 days to develop, depending on the species.

When it is ready to hatch, a chick pecks its way out of the eggshell. Some newly hatched chicks, such as ducks, chickens, and partridges are covered with down and can run about soon after they have hatched. Other chicks, such as baby blue jays and robins, are featherless, blind, and so weak they can barely lift their heads to beg for food. Most parent birds feed and protect their young at least until they are able to fly.

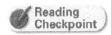

Reading Checkpoint **How is a bird egg different from a reptile egg?**

Lab zone Try This Activity

"Eggs-amination"

1. Observe the surface of a chicken egg with a hand lens. Then gently crack the egg into a bowl. Do not break the yolk.
2. Note the membrane attached to the inside of the shell. Then look at the blunt end of the egg. What do you see?
3. Fill one part of the egg-shell with water. What do you observe?
4. Find the egg yolk. What is its function?
5. Look for a small white spot on the yolk. This marks the spot where the embryo would have developed if the egg had been fertilized.
6. Wash your hands with soap.

Observing Draw a labeled diagram of the egg that names each structure and describes its function.

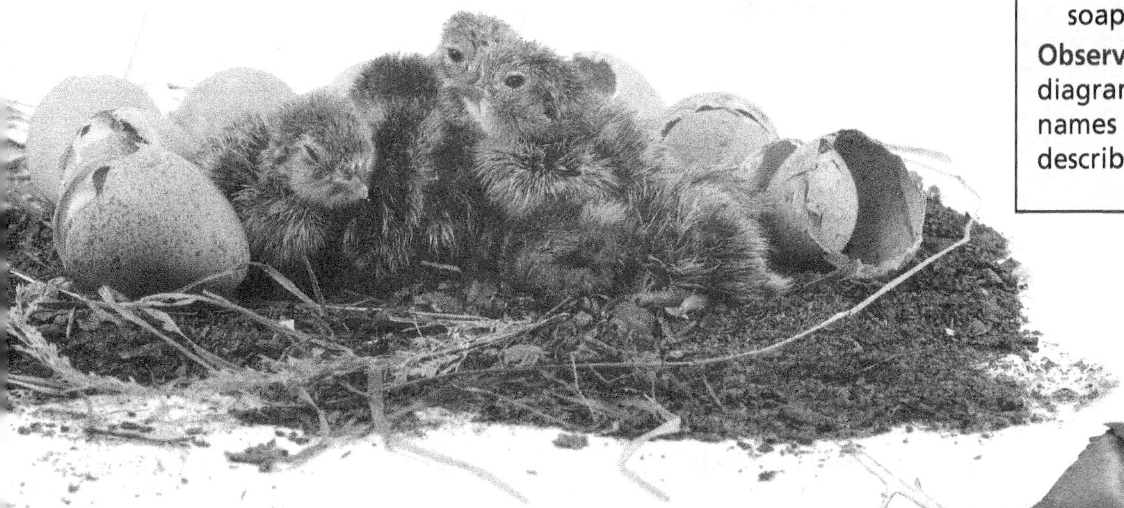

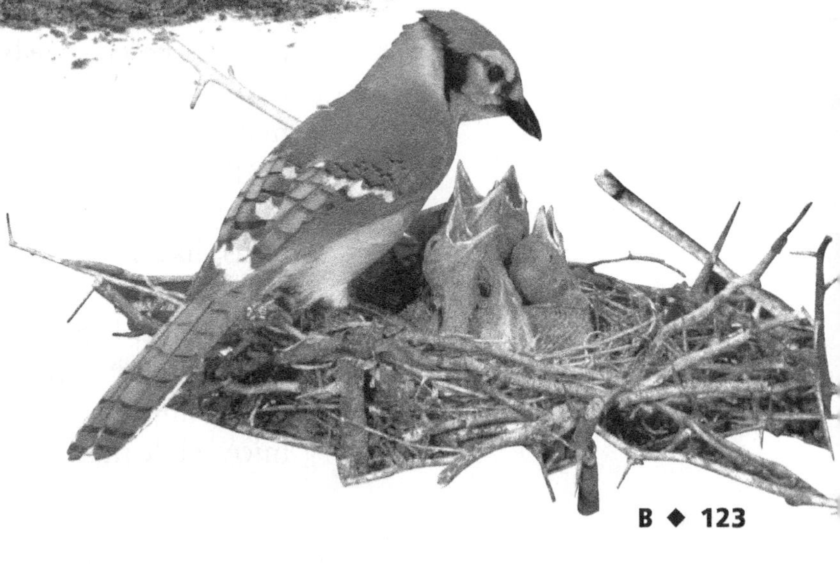

FIGURE 6
Parental Care
The partridge chicks (above) find their own food from the day they hatch. In contrast, the blue jay chicks (right) are featherless, blind, and totally dependent on their parents for food for several weeks.

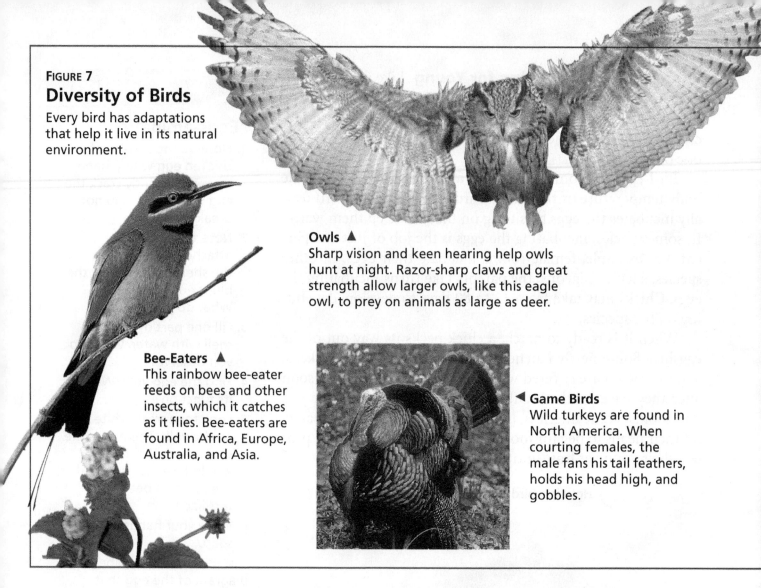

FIGURE 7

Diversity of Birds

Every bird has adaptations that help it live in its natural environment.

Owls ▲

Sharp vision and keen hearing help owls hunt at night. Razor-sharp claws and great strength allow larger owls, like this eagle owl, to prey on animals as large as deer.

Bee-Eaters ▲

This rainbow bee-eater feeds on bees and other insects, which it catches as it flies. Bee-eaters are found in Africa, Europe, Australia, and Asia.

◄ **Game Birds**

Wild turkeys are found in North America. When courting females, the male fans his tail feathers, holds his head high, and gobbles.

Birds in the Environment

With almost 10,000 species, birds are the most diverse land-dwelling vertebrates. **Birds are adapted for living in diverse environments. You can see some of these adaptations in the shapes of their legs, claws, and bills.** For example, the long legs and toes of wading birds, such as herons, cranes, and spoonbills, make wading easy. The claws of perching birds, such as goldfinches and mockingbirds, can lock onto a branch or other perch. The bills of woodpeckers are tools for chipping into the wood of trees. Birds also have adaptations for finding mates and caring for their young.

Birds play an important role in the environment. Nectar-eating birds, like hummingbirds, are pollinators. Seed-eating birds, like sparrows, carry the seeds of plants to new places. This happens when the birds eat the fruits or seeds of a plant, fly to a new location, and then eliminate some of the seeds in digestive wastes. In addition, birds are some of the chief predators of animals that may be pests. Hawks and owls eat rats and mice, while many perching birds feed on insect pests.

Ostriches ▼
The ostrich, found in Africa, is the largest living bird. It cannot fly, but it can run at speeds greater than 60 kilometers per hour. Its speed helps it escape from predators.

◄ Long-Legged Waders
The roseate spoonbill is found in the southern United States and throughout much of South America. The spoonbill catches small animals by sweeping its long, flattened bill back and forth under water.

Perching Birds ▶
Perching birds represent more than half of all the bird species in the world. The painted bunting, a seed-eating bird, lives in the southern United States and northern Mexico.

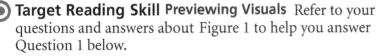

Section 1 Assessment

Target Reading Skill Previewing Visuals Refer to your questions and answers about Figure 1 to help you answer Question 1 below.

Reviewing Key Concepts

1. a. **Identifying** What characteristics do birds share?
   b. **Explaining** How is a bird's body adapted for flight?
   c. **Relating Cause and Effect** Why do birds need so much oxygen? What adaptation helps them obtain oxygen?
2. a. **Listing** What are three types of adaptations that allow birds to survive in diverse environments?
   b. **Summarizing** What are three roles birds play in the environment?
   c. **Comparing and Contrasting** Look at Figure 7. Compare and contrast the adaptations of an eagle owl and a roseate spoonbill for obtaining food.

At-Home Activity

Count Down With the help of a family member, look for products in your home that contain down feathers. (*Hint:* Don't forget to check closets!) What kinds of items contain down feathers? What common purpose do these items have? Explain to your family member what down feathers look like and where they are found on a bird.

Looking at an Owl's Leftovers

Problem

What can you learn about owls' diets from studying the pellets that they cough up?

Skills Focus

observing, drawing conclusions

Materials

- owl pellet
- hand lens
- dissecting needle
- metric ruler
- forceps

Procedure

1. An owl pellet is a collection of undigested materials that an owl coughs up after a meal. Write a hypothesis describing what items you expect an owl pellet to contain. List the reasons for your hypothesis.

2. Use a hand lens to observe the outside of an owl pellet. Record your observations.

3. Use one hand to grasp the owl pellet with forceps. Hold a dissecting needle in your other hand, and use it to gently separate the pellet into pieces. **CAUTION:** *Dissecting needles are sharp. Never cut material toward you; always cut away from your body.*

4. Using the forceps and dissecting needle, carefully separate the bones from the rest of the pellet. Remove any fur that might be attached to bones.

5. Group similar bones together in separate piles. Observe the skulls, and draw them. Record the number of skulls, their length, and the number, shape, and color of the teeth.

6. Use the chart on the right to determine what kinds of skulls you found. If any skulls do not match the chart exactly, record which animal skulls they resemble most.

Skull Identification Key	
Shrew 	Upper jaw has at least 18 teeth; tips of the teeth are reddish brown. Skull length is 23 mm or less.
House mouse 	Upper jaw has two biting teeth and extends past lower jaw. Skull length is 22 mm or less.
Meadow vole 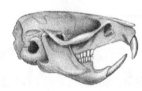	Upper jaw has two biting teeth that are smooth, not grooved. Skull length is 23 mm or more.
Mole 	Upper jaw has at least 18 teeth. Skull length is 23 mm or more.
Rat 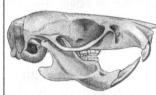	Upper jaw has two biting teeth. Upper jaw extends past lower jaw. Skull length is 22 mm or more.

7. Try to fit together any of the remaining bones to form complete or partial skeletons. Sketch your results.

8. Wash your hands thoroughly with soap when you are finished.

Analyze and Conclude

1. **Observing** How many animals' remains were in the pellet? What observations led you to that conclusion?

2. **Drawing Conclusions** Combine your results with the results of your classmates. Based on your class's data, which three animals were eaten most frequently? How do these results compare to your hypothesis?

3. **Calculating** Owls cough up about two pellets a day. Based on your class's data, what can you conclude about the number of animals an owl might eat in one month?

4. **Communicating** In this lab, you were able to examine only the part of the owl's diet that it did not digest. In a paragraph, explain how this fact might affect your confidence in the conclusions you reached.

Design an Experiment

Design an experiment to determine how an owl's diet varies at different times of the year. Give an example of a hypothesis you could test with such an experiment. What variables would you control? Before carrying out your experiment, obtain your teacher's approval of your plan.

The Physics of Bird Flight

Reading Preview

Key Concepts
- What causes a bird to rise in the air?
- How may birds fly?

Key Term
- lift

Target Reading Skill
Relating Cause and Effect A cause makes something happen. An effect is what happens. As you read, identify the physical properties of a bird's wing that cause lift. Write them in a graphic organizer like the one below.

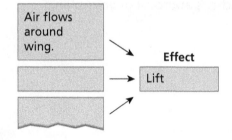

Causes

Air flows around wing.

Effect

Lift

Discover **Activity**

What Lifts Airplanes and Birds Into the Air?

1. Cut a strip of notebook paper 5 centimeters wide and 28 centimeters long. Insert about 5 centimeters of the paper strip into the middle of a book. The rest of the paper strip should hang over the edge.
2. Hold the book up so that the paper is below your mouth.
3. Blow gently across the top of the paper and watch what happens to the paper. Then blow harder.

Think It Over
Predicting If a strong current of air flowed across the top of a bird's outstretched wing, what might happen to the bird?

From ancient times, people have dreamed of soaring into the air like birds. When people first started experimenting with flying machines, they tried to glue feathers to their arms or to strap on feathered wings. Many failures, crash-landings, and broken bones later, these people had learned that feathers by themselves weren't the secret of flight.

Staying in the Air

All objects on land are surrounded by an invisible ocean of air. Air is a mixture of gas molecules that exert pressure on the objects they surround. Although you cannot see air pressure, you can see the results of air pressure. For example, when you blow into a balloon, it gets larger. The pressure of the air molecules pushing on the sides of the balloon makes it expand.

FIGURE 8
Bird Feather
Contour feathers give a smooth shape to a bird's body and wings. This smooth shape is helpful for flight.

Faster-moving air above wing exerts less pressure.

Air flow

Slower-moving air below wing exerts more pressure.

Lift

FIGURE 9
Wing Shape and Lift
The air pressure pushing up on the lower surface of this pelican's wing is greater than the pressure pushing down on its upper surface.
Relating Cause and Effect
How does the difference in pressure help a bird fly?

Movement and Air Pressure Air does not have to be inside a balloon to exert pressure. Moving air exerts pressure, too. The faster air moves, the less pressure it exerts. You saw this in the Discover Activity. The air blowing across the top of the paper was in motion. This moving air exerted less pressure on the paper than the air beneath it, so the paper rose.

Air Movement Around a Wing Like the paper, a flying bird's wing is surrounded by air molecules that exert pressure on the wing's surfaces. The wing allows air to flow smoothly over and under it. When a bird is between wing beats, the angle and shape of the wing cause the air to move faster above the wing than below it, as shown in Figure 9. The faster-moving air above the bird's wing exerts less pressure than the slower-moving air below it. **The difference in pressure above and below the wings as a bird moves through the air produces an upward force that causes the bird to rise.** That upward force is called **lift**.

DISCOVERY
CHANNEL
SCHOOL

Birds and Mammals

Video Preview
▶ Video Field Trip
Video Assessment

Reading Checkpoint — As air moves faster, what happens to the pressure it exerts?

Flapping allows these macaws to lift off and move forward through the air.

FIGURE 10
Types of Flight

Flapping, soaring and gliding, and diving are three types of flight. **Applying Concepts** *Which type of flight requires the most energy? Explain.*

It's Plane to See

1. Work with a partner to design a paper airplane with wings shaped like those of a bird. You can use any of these materials: paper, tape, glue, paper clips, string, rubber bands, and staples. Draw a sketch of your design.
2. Construct your "birdplane" and make one or two trial flights. If necessary, modify your design and try again.
3. Compare your design with those of other groups. Which designs were most successful?

Making Models In what ways was the flight of your airplane like the flight of a bird? In what ways was it different?

Birds in Flight

Before a bird can use lift to fly, it must have some way of getting off the ground. To get into the air, a bird pushes off with its legs and moves forward at the same time. The bird must move forward to make air move over its wings. Sharply pulling down its wings provides the power that pushes the bird forward. The forward motion creates lift. When birds are in the air, they fly in a variety of ways. **Three types of bird flight are flapping, soaring and gliding, and diving.**

Flapping Once in flight, all birds continue to flap their wings at least part of the time. To flap, a bird must sharply pull down its wings as it did when it pushed off the ground. Most small birds, such as sparrows, depend heavily on flapping flight. Canada geese and many other birds that travel long distances also use flapping flight. Flapping requires a lot of energy.

Soaring and Gliding Unlike flapping flight, soaring and gliding flight involve little wing movement. Birds soar and glide with their wings extended. When soaring, birds use rising currents of warm air to move upward. In contrast, when gliding, birds use falling currents of cool air to move downward. Soaring and gliding use less energy than flapping because they require less wing movement.

Sometimes birds fly using a combination of soaring and gliding. They "take the elevator up" by flying into a current of warm, rising air. The birds stretch their wings out and circle round and round, moving upward within the current of rising air. As the warm air rises it starts to cool. Finally, the air stops rising. At this point the bird begins gliding downward until it reaches another "up elevator" of rising air.

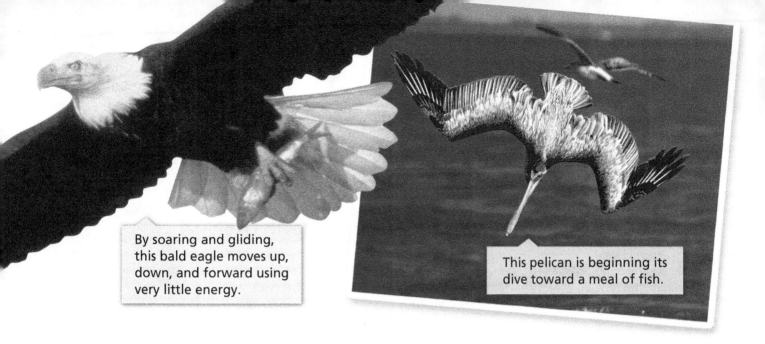

By soaring and gliding, this bald eagle moves up, down, and forward using very little energy.

This pelican is beginning its dive toward a meal of fish.

Diving A type of flight that doesn't use lift is diving. Birds that hunt their prey from the sky may use diving flight. For example, a brown pelican flies above the ocean, looking for schools of fish under the water's surface. Once it spots the fish, the pelican dives with great speed. As it dives, the pelican pulls its wings in close to its body. Pulling in the wings changes the pelican's body shape. The new body shape produces no lift at all. Without lift, the pelican falls from the sky headfirst into the ocean and hits the fish with enough force to stun them.

Some hawks and falcons dive from high in the sky towards their prey, too. Peregrine falcons can clock speeds up to 300 kilometers per hour while diving for pigeons or other prey.

For: More on bird adaptations
Visit: PHSchool.com
Web Code: ced-2042

 **Reading Checkpoint** **Which type of bird flight is the fastest?**

Section 2 Assessment

Target Reading Skill Relating Cause and Effect Refer to your graphic organizer about lift to help you answer Question 1 below.

Reviewing Key Concepts

1. a. **Defining** What is lift?
   b. **Explaining** What effect does lift have on a flying bird?
   c. **Applying Concepts** What causes lift in an airplane?
2. a. **Identifying** What are three types of bird flight?
   b. **Summarizing** How does a bird take off from the ground to fly?
   c. **Comparing and Contrasting** How are soaring and gliding alike? How are they different?

Writing in Science

Advertisement You have been hired by an outdoor adventure company to write an exciting ad for one of their birdwatching hikes. In the ad, describe several interesting birds and types of bird flight that people will see on the hike.

Mammals

Reading Preview

Key Concepts
- What characteristics do all mammals share?
- What are the main groups of mammals and how do they differ?

Key Terms
- mammal • mammary gland
- diaphragm • monotreme
- marsupial • gestation period
- placental mammal • placenta

Target Reading Skill
Building Vocabulary A definition states the meaning of a word or phrase by telling about its most important feature or function. After you read the section, reread the paragraphs that contain definitions of Key Terms. Use all the information you have learned to write a definition of each Key Term in your own words.

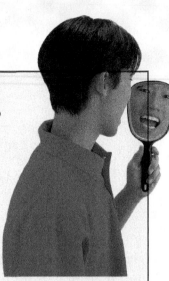

Discover Activity

What Are Mammals' Teeth Like?

1. Wash your hands before you begin. Then, with a small mirror, examine the shapes of your teeth. Observe the incisors (the front teeth); the pointed canine teeth; the premolars behind the canine teeth; and the molars, which are the large teeth in the very back.
2. Compare and contrast the structures of the different kinds of teeth.
3. Use your tongue to feel the cutting surfaces of the different kinds of teeth in your mouth.
4. Bite off a piece of cracker and chew it. Observe the teeth that you use to bite and chew. Wash your hands when you are finished.

Think It Over
Inferring What is the advantage of having teeth with different shapes?

High in the Himalaya Mountains of Tibet, several yaks inch their way, single file, along a narrow cliff path. The cliff plunges thousands of meters to the valley below, so one false step can mean disaster. But the sure-footed yaks, carrying heavy loads of grain, slowly but steadily cross the cliff and make their way through the mountains.

People who live in the mountains of central Asia have depended on yaks for thousands of years. Not only do yaks carry materials for trade, they also pull plows and provide milk. Mountain villagers weave blankets from yak hair and make shoes and ropes from yak hides.

The yak is a member of the group of vertebrates called **mammals.** Today about 4,000 different species of mammals exist. Some, like the yak and wildebeest, you may never have seen. But others, such as dogs, cats, and mice are very familiar to you. What characteristics do mammals share?

▲ Himalayan yak

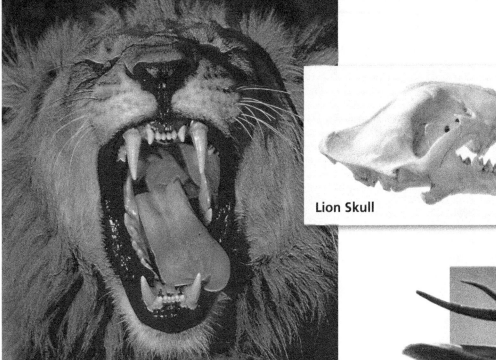

Lion Skull

Springbok Skull

Characteristics of Mammals

All mammals are endothermic vertebrates that have a four-chambered heart and skin covered with fur or hair. Most mammals are born alive, and every young mammal is fed with milk produced by organs in its mother's body. These organs are called **mammary glands.** The word *mammal,* in fact, comes from the term *mammary.*

Obtaining Food In addition to their other characteristics, most mammals have teeth. Their teeth are adapted to chew their food, breaking it into small bits that make digestion easier. Most mammals have teeth with four different shapes. If you did the Discover Activity, you observed these shapes. Incisors are flat-edged teeth used to bite off and cut food. Canines are pointed teeth that stab food and tear into it. Premolars and molars have broad, flat upper surfaces for grinding and shredding food.

The size, shape, and hardness of a mammal's teeth reflect its diet. For example, the canines of carnivores are especially large and sharp. Large carnivores, such as the lion in Figure 11, use their canines to hold their prey while they kill it. In contrast, herbivores, such as a springbok, have molars for grinding and mashing plants.

FIGURE 11
Teeth of Different Shapes
Lions have sharp, pointed canines. Springboks have broad molars.
Inferring *What kind of diet does each of these mammals eat?*

 **Reading Checkpoint** Which teeth stab and tear into food?

FIGURE 12
Fur and Hair
A hippo has hardly any hair. In contrast, a wolf has a thick coat of fur. **Inferring** *What can you infer about the environment each animal lives in?*

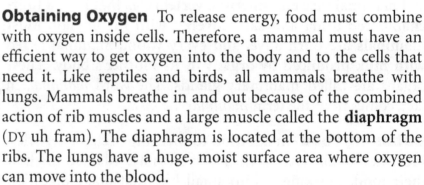

Obtaining Oxygen To release energy, food must combine with oxygen inside cells. Therefore, a mammal must have an efficient way to get oxygen into the body and to the cells that need it. Like reptiles and birds, all mammals breathe with lungs. Mammals breathe in and out because of the combined action of rib muscles and a large muscle called the **diaphragm** (DY uh fram). The diaphragm is located at the bottom of the ribs. The lungs have a huge, moist surface area where oxygen can move into the blood.

Like birds, mammals have a four-chambered heart and a two-loop circulatory system. This efficient system takes oxygen to the cells.

Keeping Conditions Stable Like birds, mammals are endotherms. They need the energy in food to keep a steady internal temperature. In addition, all mammals have fur or hair at some point in their lives that helps them keep their internal temperature stable. The amount of fur or hair that covers a mammal's skin varies greatly. Each strand of fur or hair is composed of dead cells strengthened with the same tough material that strengthens feathers. In general, animals that live in cold regions, like the wolf shown in Figure 12, have more fur than animals from warmer environments.

Fur is not the only adaptation that allows mammals to live in cold climates. Mammals also have a layer of fat beneath their skin. Like fur and feathers, fat is an insulator.

Try This Activity

Insulated Mammals
Discover whether or not fat is an effective insulator.

1. Put on a pair of rubber gloves.
2. Spread a thick coating of solid white shortening on the outside of one of the gloves. Leave the other glove uncoated.
3. Put both hands in a bucket or sink filled with cold water.

Inferring Which hand got cold faster? Explain how this activity relates to mammalian adaptations.

Movement In addition to adaptations for living in cold environments, mammals have adaptations that allow them to move in more ways than members of any other group of vertebrates. Most mammals walk or run on four limbs, but some have specialized ways of moving. For example, kangaroos hop, orangutans swing by their arms from branch to branch, and "flying" squirrels can spread their limbs and glide down from high perches. Bats have wings adapted from their front limbs. Whales, dolphins, and other sea mammals lack hind limbs, but their front limbs are adapted as flippers for swimming in water. These specialized ways of moving allow mammals to survive in many habitats.

Nervous System A mammal's nervous system coordinates its movements. In addition, the nervous system receives information about the environment. The brains of mammals enable them to learn, remember, and behave in complex ways. For example, in order for squirrels to eat nuts, they must crack the nutshell to get to the meat inside. Squirrels learn to use different methods to crack different kinds of nuts, depending on where the weak point in each kind of shell is located.

The senses of mammals are highly developed and adapted for the ways a species lives. Tarsiers, which are active at night, have huge eyes that enable them to see in the dark. Bats use a keen sense of hearing to navigate in the dark and catch prey. Dogs, cats, and bears often use smell to track their prey. Other mammals, such as antelopes, can smell approaching predators in time to flee.

 **Reading Checkpoint** What are three ways that mammals can move?

FIGURE 13
A Swinging Orangutan
This young orangutan can grasp branches with its limbs and swing from place to place.

FIGURE 14
The Senses of Seals
Seals can see under water in near darkness. Their long whiskers help them obtain food by detecting the movements of their prey.

Diversity of Mammals

Mammals are a very diverse group. Look at the spiny anteater and the kangaroo shown on this page. Both are mammals that feed their young milk. But, in other ways, they are different. **There are three main groups of mammals—monotremes, marsupials, and placental mammals. The groups differ in how their young develop.**

Monotremes Egg-laying mammals are called **monotremes.** There are just three species of monotremes—two species of spiny anteaters and the duck-billed platypus. A female spiny anteater lays one to three leathery-shelled eggs directly into a pouch on her belly. After the young hatch, they stay in the pouch for six to eight weeks. There they drink milk that seeps out of pores on the mother's skin. In contrast, the duck-billed platypus lays her eggs in an underground nest. The tiny young feed by lapping at the milk that oozes from slits onto the fur of their mother's belly.

Marsupials Koalas, kangaroos, and opossums are some of the better-known marsupials. **Marsupials** are mammals whose young are born at an early stage of development, and they usually continue to develop in a pouch on their mother's body.

Marsupials have a very short **gestation period,** the length of time between fertilization and birth. For example, opossums have a gestation period of about 13 days. Newborn marsupials are tiny—some opossums are less than 1 centimeter long at birth! When they are born, marsupials are blind, hairless, and pink. They crawl along the wet fur of their mother's belly until they reach her pouch. Once inside, they find one of her nipples and attach to it. They remain in the pouch until they have grown enough to peer out of the pouch opening.

FIGURE 15
A Spiny Anteater
The young of this spiny anteater, a monotreme, hatch from eggs.

FIGURE 16
Kangaroos
This gray kangaroo, a marsupial, carries her offspring in a pouch.
Classifying *How do marsupials differ from monotremes?*

Placental Mammals Unlike a monotreme or a marsupial, a **placental mammal** develops inside its mother's body until its body systems can function independently. The name of this group comes from the **placenta,** an organ in pregnant female mammals that passes materials between the mother and the developing embryo. Food and oxygen pass from the mother to her young. Wastes pass from the young to the mother, who eliminates them. An umbilical cord connects the young to the mother's placenta. Most mammals, including humans, are placental mammals. Gestation periods of placental mammals are generally longer than those of marsupials. Usually, the larger the placental mammal, the longer the gestation period. The gestation period for an elephant, for example, averages about 21 months, but for a mouse, it's only about 20 days.

Placental mammals are classified into groups on the basis of characteristics such as how they eat and how their bodies move. You can see the diversity of placental mammals in Figure 18 on the next page.

 **Reading Checkpoint** What is a placenta?

FIGURE 17 Mother and Baby Giraffe
This baby giraffe, a placental mammal, feeds on milk produced by its mother.

Math Analyzing Data

Percentages of Mammal Species

Mammal Diversity

This circle graph shows the percentage of species of some types of mammals.

1. **Reading Graphs** What percentage of species are bats?

2. **Calculating** What percentage of species are not bats?

3. **Graphing** Suppose you used the data shown in the circle graph to make a bar graph. Which bar would be tallest?

4. **Predicting** What total should all the percentages in the pie chart add up to? Do you have to add the percentages to obtain your answer? Explain.

Even-toed hoofed mammals
Carnivores
5%
5.6%
Marsupials
6.5%
14 Other Types
6.9%
Rodents 38%
Primates
8%
Insect-eaters
8.2%
Bats 21.8%

FIGURE 18
Diversity of Placental Mammals

From tiny moles to huge elephants, placental mammals are diverse. They are grouped on the basis of how they eat and move as well as other characteristics.

Rabbits and Hares ▶
Leaping mammals like this black-tailed jack rabbit have long hind legs specialized for spectacular jumps. Rabbits and hares have long, curved incisors for gnawing.

Carnivores ▶
This river otter belongs to the group known as carnivores. Dogs, raccoons, and seals are other members of this group. Most carnivores have large canine teeth and clawed toes that help them catch and eat their prey.

Marine Mammals ▲
Whales, manatees, and these Atlantic spotted dolphins are ocean-dwelling mammals with a body shape adapted for swimming.

Rodents ▶
Rodents are gnawing mammals such as mice, rats, beavers, and the capybaras shown here. The incisor teeth of most rodents keep growing throughout their lives but are constantly worn down by gnawing.

Mammals With Trunks ▲
Elephants' noses are long trunks that they use for collecting food and water.

Insect-Eaters ▲

Moles and their relatives have sharp cutting surfaces on all of their teeth. This star-nosed mole spends much of its time searching for prey with its sensitive, tentacled snout.

◀ **Flying Mammals**
The wings of bats are made of a thin skin that stretches from their wrists to the tips of their long finger bones.

◀ **Toothless Mammals**
Armadillos, such as the one shown here, are toothless mammals. So are sloths. Although a few members of this group have small teeth, most have none.

Primates ▼
This group of mammals with large brains and eyes that face forward includes humans, monkeys, and apes such as this chimpanzee.

Hoofed Mammals ▲

Some mammals with hooves have an even number of toes and some have an odd number of toes. Cows, deer, and pigs all have an even number of toes. Horses and zebras have an odd number of toes.

FIGURE 19
Parental Care by Dall's Sheep
Young mammals usually require much parental care. On a rocky slope in Alaska, this Dall's sheep, a placental mammal, keeps a close watch on her lamb.

Caring for Young Whether a monotreme, a marsupial, or a placental mammal, young mammals are usually quite helpless for a long time after being born. Many are born without a coat of insulating fur. Their eyes are often sealed and may not open for weeks. For example, black bear cubs are surprisingly tiny when they are born. The blind, nearly hairless cubs have a mass of only 240 to 330 grams—about the same mass as a grapefruit. The mass of an adult black bear, in contrast, ranges from about 120 to 150 kilograms— about 500 times as much as a newborn cub!

Young mammals usually stay with their mother or both parents for an extended time. After black bear cubs learn to walk, they follow their mother about for the next year, learning how to be a bear. They learn things that are important to their survival, such as which mushrooms and berries are good to eat and how to rip apart a rotten log and find good-tasting grubs within it. During the winter, when black bears go through a period of inactivity, the young bears stay with their mother. The following spring, she will usually force them to live independently.

Reading Checkpoint Why are most young mammals dependent on one or both parents after they are born?

Section 3 Assessment

Target Reading Skill Building Vocabulary Use your definitions to help answer the questions below.

Reviewing Key Concepts

1. a. **Defining** What characteristics do mammals share?
   b. **Describing** Describe the adaptation that most mammals have for obtaining food.
   c. **Relating Cause and Effect** What enables mammals to live in colder environments than reptiles? Explain.
2. a. **Reviewing** What are the three main groups of mammals?
   b. **Explaining** How do monotremes, marsupials, and placental mammals differ?
   c. **Interpreting Photographs** Look at Figure 18. Describe the adaptations for movement of marine mammals and flying mammals.

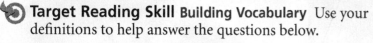

At-Home Activity

Mammals' Milk With a family member, examine the nutrition label on a container of whole milk. What types of nutrients does whole milk contain? Discuss why milk is an ideal source of food for young, growing mammals.

Keeping Warm

Problem

Do wool products provide insulation from the cold? How well does wool insulate when it is wet?

Skills Focus

graphing, interpreting data

Materials

- tap water, hot • scissors • beaker, 1-L
- 3 thermometers • clock or watch
- graph paper • a pair of wool socks
- tap water, room temperature
- 3 containers, 250-mL, with lids

Procedure

1. Put one container into a dry woolen sock. Soak a second sock with water at room temperature, wring it out so it's not dripping, and then slide the second container into the wet sock. Both containers should stand upright. Leave the third container uncovered.

2. Create a data table in your notebook, listing the containers in the first column. Provide four more columns in which to record the water temperatures during the experiment.

3. Use scissors to carefully cut a small "X" in the center of each lid. Make the X just large enough for a thermometer to pass through.

4. Fill a beaker with about 800 mL of hot tap water. Then pour hot water nearly to the top of each of the three containers. **CAUTION:** *Avoid spilling hot water on yourself or others.*

5. Place a lid on each of the containers, and insert a thermometer into the water through the hole in each lid. Gather the socks around the thermometers above the first two containers so that the containers are completely covered.

6. Immediately measure the temperature of the water in each container, and record it in your data table. Take temperature readings every 5 minutes for at least 15 minutes.

Analyze and Conclude

1. **Graphing** Graph your results using a different color to represent each container. Graph time in minutes on the horizontal axis and temperature on the vertical axis.

2. **Interpreting Data** Compare the temperature changes in the three containers. Relate your findings to the insulation characteristics of mammal skin coverings.

3. **Communicating** Suppose a company claims that its wool socks keep you warm even if they get wet. Do your findings support this claim? Write a letter to the company explaining why or why not.

Design an Experiment

Design an experiment to compare how wool's insulating properties compare with those of other natural materials (such as cotton) or manufactured materials (such as acrylic). Obtain your teacher's permission before carrying out your investigation.

For: Data sharing
Visit: PHSchool.com
Web Code: ced-2043

Study Guide

1 Birds

Key Concepts

- A bird is an endothermic vertebrate that has feathers and a four-chambered heart. A bird also lays eggs.

- Birds are adapted for living in diverse environments. You can see some of these adaptations in the shapes of their legs, claws, and bills.

Key Terms

bird
contour feather
down feather
crop
gizzard

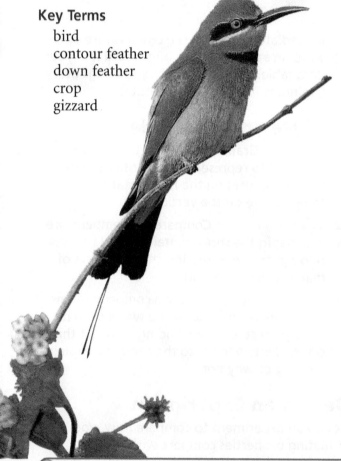

2 The Physics of Bird Flight

Key Concepts

- The difference in pressure above and below the wings as the bird moves through the air produces an upward force that causes the bird to rise.

- Three types of bird flight are flapping, soaring and gliding, and diving.

Key Term

lift

3 Mammals

Key Concepts

- All mammals are endothermic vertebrates that have a four-chambered heart and skin covered with fur or hair. Most mammals are born alive, and every young mammal is fed with milk produced by organs in its mother's body.

- There are three main groups of mammals—monotremes, marsupials, and placental mammals. The groups differ in how their young develop.

Key Terms

mammal
mammary gland
diaphragm
monotreme
marsupial
gestation period
placental mammal
placenta

Review and Assessment

Organizing Information

Comparing and Contrasting Copy the table comparing mammal groups onto a sheet of paper. Then fill in the empty spaces and add a title.

Characteristic	Monotremes	Marsupials	Placental Mammals
How Young Begin Life	a. ___?___	b. ___?___	c. ___?___
How Young Are Fed	milk from pores or slits on mother's skin	d. ___?___	e. ___?___
Example	f. ___?___	g. ___?___	h. ___?___

Reviewing Key Terms

Choose the letter of the best answer.

1. Birds are the only animals with
   a. scales.
   b. wings.
   c. feathers.
   d. a four-chambered heart.

2. The gizzard of a bird
   a. stores air.
   b. removes oxygen from air.
   c. helps a bird fly.
   d. grinds food.

3. An organ that produces milk to feed the young is called a
   a. mammary gland.
   b. placenta.
   c. pouch.
   d. egg.

4. Which muscle helps mammals move air into and out of their lungs?
   a. air muscle
   b. diaphragm
   c. placenta
   d. gestation

5. A monotreme differs from a placental mammal because it
   a. has fur.
   b. has a placenta.
   c. lays eggs.
   d. feeds its young milk.

If the statement is true, write *true*. If it is false, change the underlined word or words to make the statement true.

6. <u>Down feathers</u> give shape to a bird's body.

7. A bird's <u>crop</u> stores food.

8. The upward force on a bird's moving wing is called <u>lift</u>.

9. The function of <u>contour feathers</u> is similar to the function of fur.

10. A <u>diaphragm</u> is the length of time between fertilization and birth.

Writing in Science

Cause and Effect Paragraph Which adaptations improve a bird's ability to fly? Write a paragraph in which you describe the effects of adaptations you learned about on the ability of a bird to fly. Be sure to include a topic sentence.

Discovery CHANNEL SCHOOL™

Birds and Mammals
Video Preview
Video Field Trip
▶ Video Assessment

Review and Assessment

Checking Concepts

11. Explain how the skeleton of a bird is adapted for flight.

12. What adaptations help a bird obtain enough oxygen for flight? Explain.

13. Why is a bird's circulatory system efficient? Explain.

14. What causes lift?

15. Explain how soaring and gliding birds such as vultures use air currents in their flight.

16. How does the structure of an incisor relate to its function?

17. Identify and explain two ways in which mammals are adapted to live in climates that are very cold.

18. What is the function of a mammal's nervous system?

Thinking Critically

19. **Making Generalizations** What is the general relationship between whether an animal is an endotherm and whether it has a four-chambered heart? Relate this to the animal's need for energy.

20. **Relating Cause and Effect** Look at the diagram below. Explain how lift occurs and what effect it has on the bird.

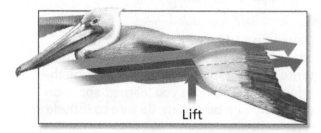

Lift

21. **Applying Concepts** Why do whales, polar bears, and seals have a thick layer of fat?

22. **Predicting** If a rodent were fed a diet consisting only of soft food that it did not need to gnaw, what might its front teeth look like after several months? Explain.

Applying Skills

Use the information in the table to answer Questions 23–25.

The data table below shows the approximate gestation period of several mammals and the approximate length of time that those mammals care for their young after birth.

Mammal	Gestation Period	Time Spent Caring for Young After Birth
Deer mouse	0.75 month	1 month
Chimpanzee	8 months	24 months
Harp seal	11 months	0.75 month
Elephant	21 months	24 months
Bobcat	2 months	8 months

23. **Graphing** Decide which kind of graph would be best for showing the data in the table. Then construct two graphs—one for gestation period and the other for time spent caring for young.

24. **Interpreting Data** Which mammals listed in the table care for their young for the longest time? The shortest time?

25. **Drawing Conclusions** How are the size of the mammal and the length of time it cares for its young related? Which animal is the exception to this pattern?

Chapter **Project**

Performance Assessment When you present your bird-watch project, display your graphs, charts, and pictures. Describe the ways in which birds eat and the interesting examples of bird behavior you observed. Then, analyze how successful the project was. Was the bird feeder located in a good place for attracting and observing birds? Did many birds come to the feeder? If not, why might this have happened? What are the advantages and limitations of using field guides for identifying birds?

Standardized Test Prep

Choose the letter of the best answer.

1. Of the following structures found in a bird, which one's main function is to store food?
   A stomach
   B gizzard
   C crop
   D bill

2. Which characteristics do birds and mammals share?
   F Both are endothermic vertebrates.
   G Both have fur or hair.
   H Both have a three-chambered heart.
   J Both are vertebrates that produce milk.

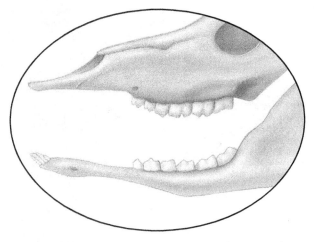

3. The diagram above shows the jawbone and teeth of an animal. The front of the mouth faces left. Which of the following best describes the teeth?
   A many sharp canines
   B broad molars at the back of the mouth
   C molars at the front of the mouth
   D flat incisors at the back of the mouth

4. Based on the kinds of teeth you observe in the diagram above, make your best inference about what this animal might be.
   F bird
   G cow
   H rabbit
   J bear

5. Which of the following best describes the function of the placenta?
   A to deliver oxygen to the body's cells
   B to store food inside the body before swallowing and digesting it
   C to direct and coordinate a mammal's complex movements
   D to pass materials between a mother and her offspring before it is born

Constructed Response

6. Describe how birds care for their eggs and newly hatched young. Your answer should include information about why this care is necessary.

Chapter
5

Animal Behavior

This pair of Sarus cranes is engaged in an elaborate courtship dance. ▶

 Chapter Project

Learning New Tricks

As you learn about animal behavior in this chapter, you will have a chance to study an animal on your own. Your challenge will be to teach the animal a new behavior.

Your Goal To monitor an animal's learning process as you teach it a new skill

To complete this project, you must

- observe an animal to learn about its behavior patterns
- choose a new skill for the animal to learn, and develop a plan that uses rewards to teach it the skill
- monitor the animal's learning over a specific period of time
- follow the safety guidelines in Appendix A

Plan It! Choose an animal to train. The animal could be a family pet, a neighbor's pet, or another animal approved by your teacher. Begin by observing the animal carefully to learn about its natural behaviors. Then think about an appropriate new skill to teach the animal. Write up a training plan to teach it the new skill. Be sure to have your teacher approve your training plan before you begin.

What Is Behavior?

Reading Preview

Key Concepts
- What causes animal behavior?
- What are instincts?
- What are four types of learned behaviors?

Key Terms
- behavior • stimulus
- response • instinct
- learning • imprinting
- conditioning
- trial-and-error learning
- insight learning

Target Reading Skill
Outlining As you read, make an outline about behavior. Use the red headings for the main topics and the blue headings for the subtopics.

Understanding Behavior
I. Behavior of animals
A. Behavior as response
B.
II. Behavior by instinct
III.
A.
B.
C.
D.

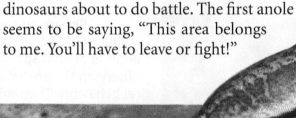

Discover Activity

What Behaviors Can You Observe?

1. Observe the behavior of a small vertebrate, such as a gerbil or a goldfish, for a few minutes. Write down your observations.
2. Place some food near the animal and observe the animal's behavior.
3. If there are other animals in the cage or aquarium, observe how the animals interact—for example, do they groom each other or ignore each other?
4. Note any other events that seem to make the animal change its behavior.

Think It Over
Predicting What are some circumstances under which you would expect an animal's behavior to change suddenly?

A male anole—a kind of lizard—stands in a patch of sun. As another male approaches, the first anole begins to lower and raise its head and chest in a series of quick push-ups. From beneath its neck a dewlap, a bright red flap of skin, flares out and then collapses, over and over. The anoles stare at one another, looking like miniature dinosaurs about to do battle. The first anole seems to be saying, "This area belongs to me. You'll have to leave or fight!"

FIGURE 1
Dewlap Display
These two anoles are displaying their dewlaps in a dispute over space.

The Behavior of Animals

The dewlap display by anole lizards is one example of behavior. An animal's **behavior** consists of all the actions it performs. For example, behaviors include actions an animal takes to obtain food, avoid predators, and find a mate. Like body structures, the behaviors of animals are adaptations that have evolved over long periods of time.

Most behavior is a complex process in which different parts of an animal's body work together. Consider what happens when a water current carries a small animal to a hydra's tentacles. After stinging cells on the tentacles catch the prey, the tentacles bend toward the hydra's mouth. At the same time, the hydra's mouth opens to receive the food.

Behavior as Response In the previous situation, the touch of the prey on the tentacles acts as a stimulus to the hydra. A **stimulus** (plural *stimuli*) is a signal that causes an organism to react in some way. The organism's reaction to the stimulus is called a **response.** The hydra's response to the prey is to sting it. **All animal behaviors are caused by stimuli.**

Some stimuli, such as prey brushing a hydra's tentacles, are outside the animal. Other stimuli, such as hunger, come from inside. An animal's response may include external actions or internal changes (such as a faster heartbeat), or both.

The Functions of Behavior Most behaviors help an animal survive or reproduce. When an animal looks for food or hides to avoid a predator, it is doing something that helps it stay alive. When animals search for mates and build nests for their young, they are behaving in ways that help them reproduce.

 **Reading Checkpoint** What is a stimulus?

FIGURE 2
A Moth's Startling "Eyes"
Certain moths have markings on their underwings that resemble eyes. When the moth is poked by a predator, it raises its forewings to reveal the "eyes." **Predicting** *How is this behavior important to the moth's survival?*

For: Links on animal behavior
Visit: www.SciLinks.org
Web Code: scn-0251

FIGURE 3
A Web Built by Instinct
Most spiders know by instinct how to build elaborate webs.

Predicting

Hawks, which have short necks, prey on gull chicks. Geese, which have long necks, do not prey on the chicks. When newly hatched gull chicks see any bird's shadow, they instinctively crouch down. As the chicks become older, they continue to crouch when they see the shadow of a hawk, but they learn not to crouch when they see a goose's shadow. Predict how older gull chicks will behave when they see bird shadows shaped like A, B, and C. Explain your prediction.

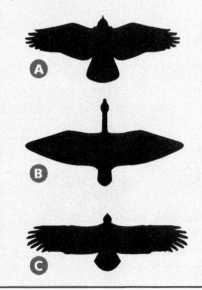

Behavior by Instinct

Animals perform some behaviors by **instinct,** without being taught. **An instinct is a response to a stimulus that is inborn and that an animal performs correctly the first time.** For example, a newborn kangaroo instinctively crawls into its mother's pouch and attaches itself to a nipple. Without this instinct, baby kangaroos could not obtain the milk they need to survive.

Some instincts are fairly simple. Earthworms, for example, crawl away from bright light. Other instincts are complex. Spiders spin complicated webs on their first try without making mistakes in the pattern. Most birds build their nests without ever being taught how.

 Reading Checkpoint) **What is an instinct?**

Learned Behavior

Recall the first time you rode a bicycle. It probably took a few tries before you did it well—you had to learn how. **Learning** is the process that leads to changes in behavior based on practice or experience. In general, the larger an animal's brain, the more the animal can learn. **Learned behaviors include imprinting, conditioning, trial-and-error learning, and insight learning.** Because learned behaviors result from an animal's experience, they are not usually done perfectly the first time.

All learned behaviors depend in part on inherited traits that have passed from parents to offspring. For example, lion cubs inherit physical features and instincts that are necessary for hunting. They are born with claws that help them capture prey. They also are born with the instinct to pounce on any object that attracts their attention. However, only through experience can they learn how to master hunting skills.

Imprinting Imprinting is a learned behavior. In **imprinting,** certain newly hatched birds and newborn mammals recognize and follow the first moving object they see. This object is usually the mother of the young animals. Imprinting involves a combination of instinct and learning. The young animal has an instinct to follow a moving object, but is not born knowing what its parent looks like. The young animal learns from experience what object to follow.

Once imprinting takes place, it cannot be changed. That is true even if the young animal has imprinted on something other than its mother. Young animals have imprinted on moving toys and even humans. Konrad Lorenz, an Austrian scientist, conducted experiments in which he, rather than the mother, was the first moving object that newly hatched birds saw. Figure 4 shows the result of one such experiment. Even as adults, the ducks followed Lorenz around.

Imprinting is valuable for two reasons. First, it keeps young animals close to their mothers, who know where to find food and how to avoid predators. Second, imprinting allows young animals to learn what other animals of their own species look like. This ability protects the animals while they are young. In later life, this ability is important when the animals search for mates.

FIGURE 4
Imprinting
Konrad Lorenz got these ducks to imprint on him by making himself the first moving object they ever saw.
Relating Cause and Effect *Why are the ducks following the swimmer?*

FIGURE 5
Conditioning

Pavlov followed specific steps to condition a dog to salivate at the sound of a bell.
Predicting *Predict what the dog would do if it heard a bell ringing in another part of the house.*

Normal Stimulus Alone

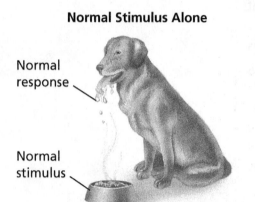

Normal response

Normal stimulus

❶ When a hungry dog sees or smells food, it produces saliva. Dogs do not usually salivate in response to other stimuli, such as the sound of a ringing bell.

Two Stimuli Together

❷ For many days, Pavlov rang a bell every time that he fed the dog. The dog learned to associate the ringing of the bell with the sight and smell of food.

New Stimulus Only

❸ Thus, when Pavlov rang a bell but did not give the dog food, the dog still produced saliva. The new stimulus produced the response that normally only food would produce.

Animal Behavior

Video Preview
▶ Video Field Trip
Video Assessment

Conditioning When a dog sees its owner approaching with a leash, the dog may jump up, eager to go for a walk. The dog has learned to associate the leash with a pleasant event—a brisk walk. Learning that a particular stimulus or response leads to a good or a bad outcome is called **conditioning.**

Pets are often trained using a form of conditioning. Suppose you want to train a puppy to come when you call it. The desired response is the puppy coming to you when it hears your call. The good outcome you will use is a food reward: a dog biscuit.

Here is how the conditioning works. At first, the puppy rarely comes when you call. But every now and then, the puppy runs to you in response to your call. Each time the puppy comes when you call, you give it a dog biscuit. Your puppy will soon learn to associate the desired response—coming when called—with the good outcome of a food reward. To get the reward, the puppy learns to come every time you call. After a while, the puppy will come to you even if you don't give it a dog biscuit.

During the early 1900s, the Russian scientist Ivan Pavlov performed experiments involving one kind of conditioning. Figure 5 shows the steps that Pavlov followed in his experiments.

"A-maze-ing" Mice

A scientist conducted an experiment to find out whether mice would learn to run a maze more quickly if they were given rewards. She set up two identical mazes. In one maze, cheese was placed at the end of the correct route through the maze. No cheese was placed in the second maze. Use the graph below to answer the questions.

1. **Reading Graphs** On Day 1, what was the average time it took mice with a cheese reward to complete the maze?

2. **Calculating** On Day 6, how much faster did mice with a reward complete the maze than mice without a reward?

3. **Interpreting Data** What was the manipulated variable in this experiment? Explain.

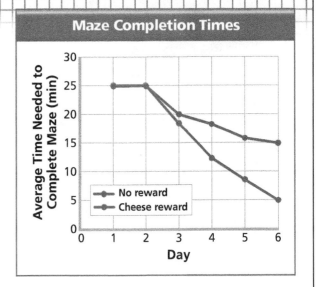

4. **Drawing Conclusions** Was the rate of learning faster for mice with the cheese reward or without the cheese reward? Explain.

Trial-and-Error Learning One form of conditioning is trial-and-error learning. In **trial-and-error learning,** an animal learns to perform a behavior more and more skillfully. Through repeated practice, an animal learns to repeat behaviors that result in rewards and avoid behaviors that result in punishment. When you learned to ride a bicycle, you did it by trial-and-error. You may have wobbled at first, but eventually you got better. You learned to move in ways that adjusted your balance and kept you from falling over.

Many animals learn by trial-and-error which methods are best for obtaining food. They also learn which methods to avoid. Think of what happens when a predator tries to attack a skunk. The skunk sprays the predator with a substance that stings and smells awful. In the future, the predator is likely to avoid skunks. The predator has learned to associate the sight of a skunk with its terrible spray.

FIGURE 6
Trial-and-Error Learning
After several failed attempts, this squirrel has finally figured out how to jump onto a hummingbird feeder, balance itself, and drink the water.

FIGURE 7
Insight Learning
Using insight, this raven has figured out how to bring meat hanging from a string close enough to eat.

Insight Learning The first time you try out a new video game, you may not need someone to explain how to play it. Instead, you may use what you already know about other video games to figure out how the new one works. When you solve a problem or learn how to do something new by applying what you already know, without a period of trial-and-error, you are using **insight learning.**

Insight learning is most common in primates, such as gorillas, chimpanzees, and humans. For example, chimpanzees use twigs to probe into the nests of termites and other insects that they eat. The chimps use insight to bend or chew their twig "tools" into a shape that will best fit the holes.

In addition to primates, other kinds of animals have also shown insight learning. For example, you may be surprised to learn that the raven shown in Figure 7 is using insight learning to obtain food. The raven uses its beak to draw up a loop of string. Then, it holds the loop under its foot and draws up a second loop, and so on. Soon the food is within reach.

 **Reading Checkpoint** Give two examples of animals showing insight learning.

Section 1 Assessment

 Target Reading Skill Outlining Use the information in your outline about behavior to help you answer the questions below.

Reviewing Key Concepts

1. **a. Defining** What are signals that cause behavior called?
   b. Describing What is meant by *response*? Describe an example of a response.
   c. Relating Cause and Effect What are the functions of behavior? Think about the response you described. What function did that response serve?
2. **a. Listing** What are instincts? List two examples.
   b. Inferring Would instincts get better with practice? Explain.
   c. Developing Hypotheses Why do you think instincts are particularly important for newborn animals?

3. **a. Identifying** Identify the types of learned behaviors.
   b. Reviewing Describe what happens during imprinting.
   c. Predicting Right after hatching, before seeing anything else, a duckling sees a child riding a tricycle. What will probably happen the next time the child rides the tricycle in front of the duckling? Explain.

Writing in Science

List of Questions Suppose you could travel back in time and interview Dr. Pavlov and Dr. Lorenz. Formulate a list of five questions you would ask each scientist about his research on animal learning.

Become a Learning Detective

Problem

What are some factors that make it easier for people to learn new things?

Skills Focus

calculating, posing questions, designing experiments

Materials

- paper
- pencil

Design a Plan

1. Look over the two lists of words shown in the diagram on this page. Researchers use groups of words like these to investigate how people learn. Notice the way the two groups differ. The words in List A have no meanings in ordinary English. List B contains familiar but unrelated words.

2. What do you think will happen if people try to learn the words in each list? Write a hypothesis about which list will be easier to learn. How much easier will it be to learn that list?

3. With a partner, design an experiment to test your hypothesis. Brainstorm a list of the variables you will need to control in order to make the results of your experiment reliable. Then write out your plan and present it to your teacher.

4. If necessary, revise your plan according to your teacher's instructions. Then perform your experiment using people your teacher has approved as test subjects. Keep careful records of your results.

List A	List B
zop	bug
rud	rag
tig	den
wab	hot
hev	fur
paf	wax
mel	beg
kib	cut
col	sip
nug	job

Analyze and Conclude

1. **Calculating** Find the average (mean) number of words people learned from each list. How do the results compare with your hypothesis?

2. **Posing Questions** What factors may have made one list easier to learn than the other? What other questions can you ask about your data?

3. **Designing Experiments** Look back at your experimental plan. Think about how well you were able to carry it out in the actual experiment. What difficulties did you encounter? What improvements could you make, either in your plan or in the way you carried it out?

4. **Communicating** Share your results with the rest of the class. How do the results of the different experiments in your class compare? What factors might explain the similarities or differences?

More to Explore

Plan an experiment to investigate how long people remember what they learn. Develop a hypothesis, and design an experiment to test your hypothesis.

Patterns of Behavior

Reading Preview

Key Concepts
- What are three main ways animals communicate?
- What are some examples of competitive behaviors and cooperative behaviors?
- What is a cyclic behavior?

Key Terms
- pheromone • aggression
- territory • courtship behavior
- society • circadian rhythm
- hibernation • migration

Target Reading Skill

Using Prior Knowledge Your prior knowledge is what you already know before you read about a topic. Before you read, write what you know about the different ways animals communicate in a graphic organizer like the one below. As you read, write what you learn.

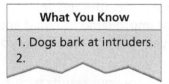

What You Know

1. Dogs bark at intruders.
2.

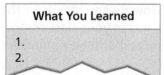

What You Learned

1.
2.

Discover **Activity**

What Can You Express Without Words?

1. Use facial expressions and body movements, but no words, to show surprise or another emotion to your partner.
2. By observing your behavior, your partner should infer what you are communicating. Your partner should also note the behavior clues that led to this inference.
3. Now your partner should try to communicate a feeling or situation to you without words. Infer what your partner is trying to communicate, and note the behavior clues that led to your inference.

Think It Over
Forming Operational Definitions Write your own definition of *communication*. How did this activity change your idea of communication?

Oh no—ants have gotten into the sugar! As you watch in dismay, a stream of ants moves along the kitchen counter. They are heading right for the sugar bowl. Using their sense of smell, the ants follow a chemical trail that was first laid down by the ant that discovered the sugar. Each ant adds to the trail by depositing a tiny droplet of scent onto the counter. The droplet quickly evaporates, making an invisible cloud of scent above the path of the ants. The ants hold their antennae forward and use them to sniff their way to the sugar bowl. Then they turn around and follow the same chemical signal back to their nest.

Communication

You've just read that ants can communicate the location of foods using scent. Animal communication comes in many forms. Perhaps you've seen a cat hissing and arching its back. It is using sound and body posture to communicate a message that seems to say, "Back off!" **Animals use mostly sounds, scents, and body movements to communicate with one another.** An animal's ability to communicate helps it interact with other animals.

Animals communicate many kinds of messages using sound. Some animals use sound to attract mates. Female crickets, for example, are attracted to the sound of a male's chirping. Animals may also communicate warnings with sound. When it sees a coyote or other predator approaching, a prairie dog makes a yipping sound that warns other prairie dogs to take cover in their burrows. The wolf in Figure 8 is warning wolves outside its pack to keep away.

Animals also communicate with chemical scents. A chemical released by one animal that affects the behavior of another animal of the same species is called a **pheromone** (FEHR uh mohn). For example, perhaps you have seen a male house cat spraying a tree. The musky scent he leaves contains pheromones that advertise his presence to other cats in the neighborhood. The scent trail that leads the ants to the sugar bowl in Figure 9 is also made of pheromones.

 **Reading Checkpoint** What is a pheromone?

FIGURE 8
Howling Wolf
Wolves in a pack may howl all together to warn other packs to stay away.

Go Online
active art

For: Pheromones activity
Visit: PHSchool.com
Web Code: cep-2052

FIGURE 9
Follow the Pheromone Trail
These ants are finding their way to the sugar by following a pheromone trail. The first ant to find the sugar began the trail, and each ant added to its strength. **Applying Concepts** *What form of communication is a pheromone trail?*

FIGURE 10
Boxing Hares
These Arctic hares are resolving their conflict by boxing. **Inferring** *What event might have led to this behavior?*

FIGURE 11
Aggressive Gorilla
This lowland gorilla needs no words to say, "Stay away!"

Competitive Behavior

Have you ever fed ducks in the park or pigeons on the street? Then you have probably seen how they fight over every crumb. These animals compete because there usually isn't enough food to go around. **Animals compete with one another for limited resources, such as food, water, space, shelter, and mates.**

Competition can occur among different species of animals. For example, a pride of lions may try to steal a prey from a troop of hyenas that has just killed the prey. Competition can also occur between members of the same species. A female aphid, a type of insect, kicks and shoves another female aphid while competing for the best leaf on which to lay eggs.

Showing Aggression When they compete, animals may display aggression. **Aggression** is a threatening behavior that one animal uses to gain control over another. Before a pride of lions settles down to eat its prey, individual lions show aggression by snapping, clawing, and snarling. First, the most aggressive members of the pride eat their fill. Then, the less aggressive and younger members of the pride get a chance to feed on the leftovers.

Aggression between members of the same species hardly ever results in the injury or death of any of the competitors. Typically, the loser communicates, "I give up" with its behavior. For example, to protect themselves from the aggressive attacks of older dogs, puppies often roll over on their backs, showing their bellies. This signal calms the older dog. The puppy can then creep away.

Establishing a Territory On an early spring day, a male oriole fills the warm air with song. You may think the bird is singing just because it is a nice day. But in fact, he is alerting other orioles that he is the "owner" of a particular territory. A **territory** is an area that is occupied and defended by an animal or group of animals. If another animal of the same species enters the territory, the owner will attack the newcomer and try to drive it away. Birds use songs and aggressive behaviors to maintain their territories. Other animals may use calls, scratches, droppings, or pheromones.

By establishing a territory, an animal protects its access to resources such as food and possible mates. A territory also provides a safe area. Within it, animals can raise their young without competition from other members of their species. In most songbird species, and in many other animal species, a male cannot attract a mate unless he has a territory.

Attracting a Mate A male and female salamander swim gracefully in the water, moving around one another. They are engaging in **courtship behavior,** which is behavior in which males and females of the same species prepare for mating. Courtship behavior ensures that the males and females of the same species recognize one another, so that mating and reproduction can take place. Courtship behavior is typically also competitive. For example, in some species, several males may perform courtship behaviors for a single female. She then chooses one of them to mate with.

 **Reading Checkpoint** How does having a territory help an animal survive?

zone Skills Activity

Developing Hypotheses

The three-spined stickleback is a kind of fish in which the males' undersides turn red during the mating season. The males readily attack other male sticklebacks that enter their territory. In the laboratory, a biologist notices that males also show aggressive behavior whenever a red object passes their tank. What do you think is the stimulus for the stickleback's aggressive display in the wild? How could you test your hypothesis? Explain.

FIGURE 12
Kingfisher Courtship
These common kingfishers are engaged in courtship. The male on the left is offering the female a gift of food—a freshly caught fish.

Group Behavior

Not all animal behaviors are competitive. **Living in groups enables animals to cooperate.** Although many animals live alone and only rarely meet one of their own kind, other animals live in groups. Some fishes form schools, and some insects live in large groups. Hoofed mammals, such as bison and wild horses, often form herds. Living in a group usually helps animals survive. For example, group members may protect one another or work together to find food.

How can group members help one another? If an elephant gets stuck in a mudhole, for example, other members of its herd will dig it out. When animals such as lions hunt in a group, they usually can kill larger prey than a single hunter can.

Safety in Groups Living in groups often protects animals against predators. Fishes that swim in schools are often safer than fishes that swim alone. It is harder for predators to see and select an individual fish in a group. In a herd, some animals may watch for danger while others feed.

Animals in a group sometimes cooperate in fighting off a predator. For example, the North American musk oxen shown in Figure 13 make a defensive circle against a predator, such as a wolf. Their young calves are sheltered in the middle of the circle. The adult musk oxen stand with their horns lowered, ready to charge. The predator often gives up rather than face a whole herd of angry musk oxen.

Animal Societies Some animals, including ants, termites, honeybees, naked mole rats, and pistol shrimp, live in groups called societies. A **society** is a group of closely related animals of the same species that work together in a highly organized way. In a society, there is a division of labor—different individuals perform different tasks. In a honeybee society, for example, there are thousands of worker bees that take on different tasks in the beehive. Some workers feed larvae. Some bring back nectar and pollen from flowers as food for the hive. Other worker bees guard the entrance to the hive.

 **Reading Checkpoint** What is a society?

Lab zone **Try This Activity**

Worker Bees

1. Make a paper chain by cutting paper strips for loops and gluing or taping the loops together. After 5 minutes, count the loops in the chain.

2. Now work in a small group to make a paper chain. Decide how to divide up the work before beginning. After 5 minutes, count the loops in the chain.

Calculating Find the difference between the number of loops in your individual and group chains. For Step 2, calculate the number of loops made per person by dividing the total number of loops by the number of people in your group. Was it more productive to work individually or as a group?

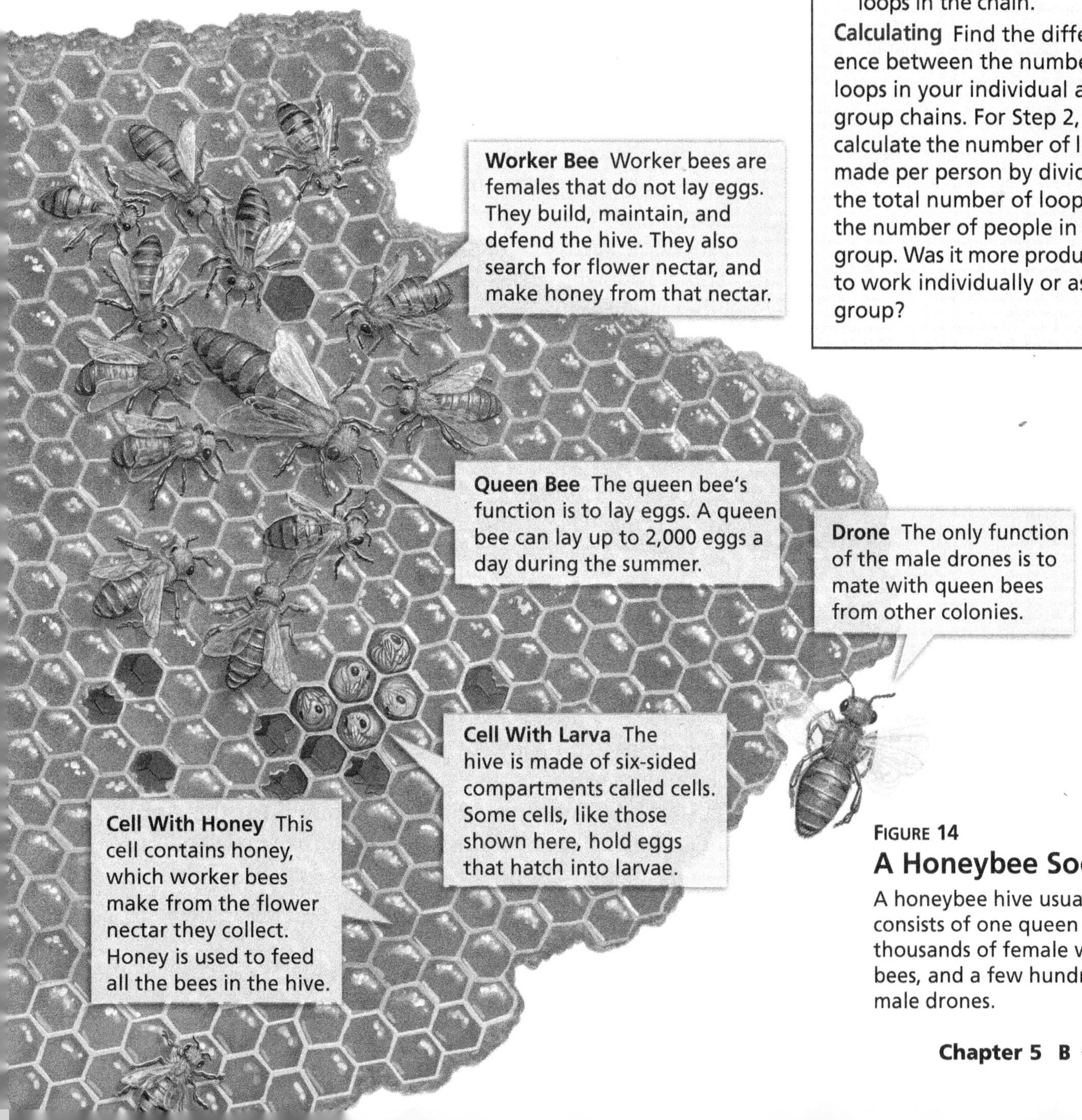

Worker Bee Worker bees are females that do not lay eggs. They build, maintain, and defend the hive. They also search for flower nectar, and make honey from that nectar.

Queen Bee The queen bee's function is to lay eggs. A queen bee can lay up to 2,000 eggs a day during the summer.

Drone The only function of the male drones is to mate with queen bees from other colonies.

Cell With Larva The hive is made of six-sided compartments called cells. Some cells, like those shown here, hold eggs that hatch into larvae.

Cell With Honey This cell contains honey, which worker bees make from the flower nectar they collect. Honey is used to feed all the bees in the hive.

FIGURE 14

A Honeybee Society

A honeybee hive usually consists of one queen bee, thousands of female worker bees, and a few hundred male drones.

Behavior Cycles

Some animal behaviors, called cyclic behaviors, occur in regular, predictable patterns. **Cyclic behaviors usually change over the course of a day or a season.**

Daily Cycles Behavior cycles that occur over a period of approximately one day are called **circadian rhythms** (sur KAY dee un). For example, blowflies search for food during the day and rest at night. In contrast, field mice are active during the night and rest by day. Animals that are active during the day can take advantage of sunlight, which makes food easy to see. On the other hand, animals that are active at night do not encounter predators that are active during the day.

Hibernation Other behavior cycles are related to seasons. For example, some animals, such as woodchucks and chipmunks, are active during warm seasons but hibernate during the cold winter. **Hibernation** is a state of greatly reduced body activity that occurs during the winter when food is scarce. During hibernation, all of an animal's body processes, such as breathing and heartbeat, slow down. This slowdown reduces the animal's need for food. In fact, hibernating animals do not eat. Their bodies use stored fat to meet their reduced nutrition needs.

Migration While many animals live their lives in one area, others migrate. **Migration** is the regular, seasonal journey of an animal from one place to another and back again. Some animals migrate short distances. Dall's sheep, for example, spend summers near the tops of mountains and move lower down for the winters. Other animals migrate thousands of kilometers. The record-holder for distance migrated is the Arctic tern. This bird flies more than 17,000 kilometers between the North and South poles.

Animals usually migrate to an area that provides a lot of food or a good environment for reproduction. Most migrations are related to the changing seasons and take place twice a year, in the spring and in the fall. American redstarts, for example, are insect-eating birds that spend the summer in North America. There, they mate and raise young. In the fall, insects become scarce. Then the redstarts migrate south to areas where they can again find plenty of food.

FIGURE 15
Hibernation
This common dormouse is hibernating for the winter.
Inferring Why is hibernation during the winter a useful adaptation for animals?

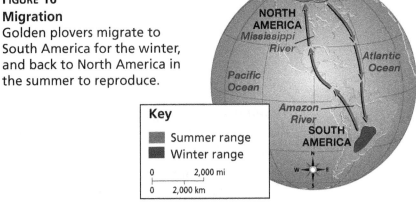

FIGURE 16
Migration
Golden plovers migrate to South America for the winter, and back to North America in the summer to reproduce.

Key

Summer range

Winter range

0   2,000 mi

0   2,000 km

NORTH AMERICA
Mississippi River
Pacific Ocean
Atlantic Ocean
Amazon River
SOUTH AMERICA

Scientists are still learning about how migrating animals find their way. But they have discovered that animals use sight, taste, and other senses, including some that humans do not have. Some birds and sea turtles, for example, have a magnetic sense that acts something like a compass needle. Migrating birds also seem to navigate by using the positions of the sun, moon, and stars, as sailors have always done. Salmon use scent and taste to locate the streams where they were born, and return there to mate.

 **Reading Checkpoint** **What happens to an animal during hibernation?**

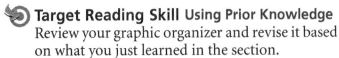

Section 2 Assessment

Target Reading Skill Using Prior Knowledge
Review your graphic organizer and revise it based on what you just learned in the section.

Reviewing Key Concepts

1. a. **Reviewing** What are three main ways animals communicate?
   b. **Explaining** When house cats spray a tree with their scent, are they communicating? Explain.
   c. **Developing Hypotheses** What are some advantages of using pheromones to communicate instead of using sound?

2. a. **Listing** List examples of competitive behavior and cooperative behavior.
   b. **Explaining** Explain how competition is involved in establishing a territory.
   c. **Predicting** What might happen when a male mockingbird flies into the territory of another male mockingbird?

3. a. **Reviewing** What are behaviors that change over the course of a day or a season called?
   b. **Comparing and Contrasting** How are circadian rhythm and hibernation the same? How are they different?

At-Home Activity

Animal Signs With a family member, spend some time making detailed observations of the behavior of an animal—a pet, an insect, a bird, or another animal. Watch the animal for signs of aggressive behavior or other communication. Try to figure out why the animal is behaving aggressively or what it is trying to communicate.

One for All

Problem

How does an ant society show organization and cooperative behavior?

Skills Focus

observing, inferring

Materials

- large glass jar • sandy soil • shallow pan
- water • wire screen • sponge • 20–30 ants
- hand lens • bread crumbs • sugar
- black paper • tape • glass-marking pencil
- forceps • large, thick rubber band

Procedure

1. Read over the entire lab to preview the kinds of observations you will be making. Copy the data table into your notebook. You may also want to leave space for sketches.

2. Mark the outside of a large jar with four evenly spaced vertical lines, as shown in the photograph on the next page. Label the sections with the letters A, B, C, and D. You can use these labels to identify the sections of soil on and below the surface.

3. Fill the jar about three-fourths full with soil. Place the jar in a shallow pan of water to prevent any ants from escaping. Place a wet sponge on the surface of the soil as a water source for the ants.

4. Observe the condition of the soil, both on the surface and along the sides of the jar. Record your observations.

5. Add the ants to the jar. Immediately cover the jar with the wire screen, using the rubber band to hold the screen firmly in place.

6. Observe the ants for at least 10 minutes. Look for differences in the appearance of adult ants, and look for eggs, larvae, and pupae. Examine both individual behavior and interactions between the ants.

7. Remove the screen cover and add small amounts of bread crumbs and sugar to the soil surface. Close the cover. Observe the ants for at least 10 more minutes.

8. Create dark conditions for the ants by covering the jar with black paper above the water line. Remove the paper only when you are making your observations.

9. Observe the ant colony every day for two weeks. Remove the dark paper, and make and record your observations. Look at the soil as well as the ants, and always examine the food. If any food has started to mold, use forceps to remove it. Place the moldy food in a plastic bag, seal the bag, and throw it away. Add more food as necessary, and keep the sponge moist. When you finish your observations, replace the dark paper.

10. At the end of the lab, follow your teacher's directions for returning the ants.

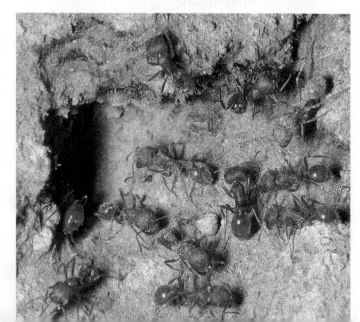

Data Table				
Date	Section A	Section B	Section C	Section D

Analyze and Conclude

1. **Observing** Describe the various types of ants you observed. What differences, if any, did you observe in their behavior? What evidence did you see of different kinds of ants performing different tasks?

2. **Inferring** How do the different behaviors you observed contribute to the survival of the colony?

3. **Inferring** How did the soil change over the period of your observations? What caused those changes? How do you know?

4. **Communicating** What kinds of environmental conditions do you think ant colonies need to thrive outdoors? Use the evidence you obtained in this lab to write a paragraph that supports your answer.

Design an Experiment

Design an experiment to investigate how an ant colony responds when there is a change in the ants' environment, such as the introduction of a new type of food. *Obtain your teacher's permission before carrying out your investigation.*

Tracking Migrations

Reading Preview

Key Concepts
- How do electronic technologies help scientists track animals?
- What are the benefits of tracking animal migrations?

Key Terms
- transmitter • receiver
- satellite

Target Reading Skill

Comparing and Contrasting As you read, compare and contrast three types of animal tags by completing a table like the one below.

Animal Tags

Feature	Simple Banding	Radio	Satellite
Kind of Signal	None		
Cost			
Weight			

Discover Activity

How Can You Track Animals?

1. On a sheet of graph paper, sketch a map of your classroom.
2. Your teacher will produce a set of "signals" from a tracking device on an animal. Record the location of each signal on your map. Sketch the path of the animal you just tracked.
3. Your teacher will produce a second set of tracking signals. Record the location of each signal, then draw the animal's path. Compare the two pathways.

Think It Over
Inferring What does this activity show about actual animal tracking?

Have you ever changed your mind because of new information? Scientists who study manatees have done just that. The information came from a signaling device on a manatee.

Florida manatees are marine mammals that spend their winters in Florida and migrate north for the summer. Scientists once thought that the manatees didn't go any farther north than Virginia. Then they attached signaling devices to manatees to track their migration. They were quite surprised when they picked up a signal from a manatee swimming off the coast of Rhode Island, which is far north of Virginia.

FIGURE 17
Florida Manatee Migration

This map shows the long distance that at least one Florida manatee migrated one summer. Electronic tags like the one shown at the far right are used to track migrating manatees.

Manatee Migration

Rhode Island

Florida

Key
- Typical summer range of manatee
- --▶ Unusually long summer migration

Technologies for Tracking

In the fall of 1803, American naturalist John James Audubon wondered whether migrating birds returned to the same place each year. So he tied a string around the leg of a bird before it flew south. The following spring, Audubon saw the bird with the string. He learned that the bird had indeed come back.

Scientists today still attach tags, such as metal bands, to track the movement of animals. But metal bands are not always useful tags. That is because the tagged animals have to be caught again for the scientists to get any data. Unfortunately, most tagged animals are never seen again.

Recent technologies have helped solve this problem. **Electronic tags give off repeating signals that are picked up by radio devices or satellites. Scientists can track the locations and movements of the tagged animals without recapturing them.** These electronic tags can provide a great deal of data. However, they are much more expensive than the "low-tech" tags that aren't electronic. Also, because of their weight, electronic tags may harm some animals by slowing them down.

Radio Tracking Tracking an animal by radio involves two devices. A **transmitter** attached to the animal sends out a signal in the form of radio waves, just as a radio station does. A scientist might place the transmitter around an animal's ankle, neck, wing, or fin. A **receiver** picks up the signal, just like your radio at home picks up a station's signal. The receiver is usually in a truck or an airplane. To keep track of the signal, the scientist follows the animal in the truck or plane.

FIGURE **18**
Banded Puffin
Bands like the ones around the ankles of this Atlantic puffin are low-tech tags. **Inferring** *Why is a metal band tag useful?*

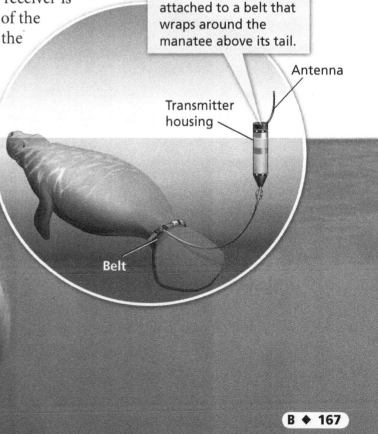

A radio transmitter is attached to a belt that wraps around the manatee above its tail.

Antenna

Transmitter housing

Belt

FIGURE 19
Tracking Caribou
Scientists are fitting this caribou with a collar containing a satellite transmitter. **Inferring** *Why would it be difficult to track caribou without a satellite receiver?*

Satellite Tracking Receivers can be placed in satellites as well as in airplanes and trucks. A **satellite** is an instrument in orbit thousands of kilometers above Earth. Networks, or groups, of satellites are used to track animals. Each satellite in a network picks up electronic signals from a transmitter on an animal. Together, the signals from all the satellites determine the precise location of the animal.

Satellites can also track an animal's path as it moves. Satellite tracking is especially useful because the scientists do not have to follow after the animal. Satellite networks have tracked the migrations of many types of animals, including caribou, sea turtles, whales, seals, elephants, bald eagles, and ospreys.

Why Tracking Is Important

Electronic tracking tags are giving scientists a complete, accurate picture of migration patterns. For example, when scientists used radio transmitters to track one herd of caribou, they learned two important things. First, they learned that the herd moves over a larger area than previously thought. Second, they learned that each year the herd returns to about the same place to give birth to its young. This information would have been difficult to obtain with "low tech" tags.

Tracking migrations is an important tool to better understand and protect species. For example, Florida manatees are an endangered species, and therefore they need protection. Radio tracking showed that Florida manatees may travel as far north as Rhode Island when they migrate. This information suggests that the manatees may need protection along much of the Atlantic Coast of the United States. Previously, protection efforts focused mainly in the Florida area.

For: Links on migration
Visit: www.SciLinks.com
Web Code: scn-0253

Technologies for tracking animals may also help people whose work or recreation affects animals. For example, suppose officials at a state park want to protect a group of migrating animals during the spring. The officials plan to ban fishing or boating for the entire spring season. Detailed migration information, however, might give the officials a better choice. They might be able to decrease the length of time the ban is in effect, or ban fishing and boating only in those few areas visited by the animals.

FIGURE 20
Caribou Migration
These caribou are migrating across Alaska on the same path used by caribou for thousands of years.

 Reading Checkpoint **What information did tracking provide biologists about a caribou herd?**

Section 3 Assessment

Target Reading Skill
Comparing and Contrasting Use the information in your table about animal tags to help you answer Question 1 below.

Reviewing Key Concepts

1. a. **Identifying** What are two methods of electronic animal tracking?
   b. **Comparing and Contrasting** How are electronic tracking methods similar? How are they different?
   c. **Making Judgments** Are electronic tags better than traditional tags?
2. a. **Reviewing** What are the benefits of tracking migrations?

   b. **Applying Concepts** Migrating birds are sometimes killed by crashing into cellular telephone towers. How could tracking bird migrations help people protect the birds?
   c. **Making Judgments** Should governments spend more money tracking migrations? Defend your position.

Writing in Science

Persuasive Letter Suppose you are a scientist who needs money to study the migrations of an endangered sea turtle species. Write a letter justifying why you need money for electronic tags.

① What Is Behavior?

Key Concepts

- All animal behaviors are caused by stimuli.
- An instinct is a response to a stimulus that is inborn and that an animal performs correctly the first time.
- Learned behaviors include imprinting, conditioning, trial-and-error learning, and insight learning.

Key Terms

behavior
stimulus
response
instinct
learning
imprinting
conditioning
trial-and-error learning
insight learning

② Patterns of Behavior

Key Concepts

- Animals use mostly sounds, scents, and body movements to communicate with one another.
- Animals compete with one another for limited resources, such as food, water, space, shelter, and mates.
- Living in groups enables animals to cooperate.
- Cyclic behaviors usually change over the course of a day or a season.

Key Terms

pheromone
aggression
territory
courtship behavior
society
circadian rhythm
hibernation
migration

③ Tracking Migrations

Key Concepts

- Electronic tags give off repeating signals that are picked up by radio devices or satellites. Scientists can track the locations and movements of the tagged animals without recapturing them.
- Tracking migrations is an important tool to better understand and protect species.

Key Terms

transmitter
receiver
satellite

Review and Assessment

Organizing Information

Concept Mapping Copy the concept map about behavior onto a separate sheet of paper. Then complete the map and add a title. (For more on Concept Mapping, see the Skills Handbook.)

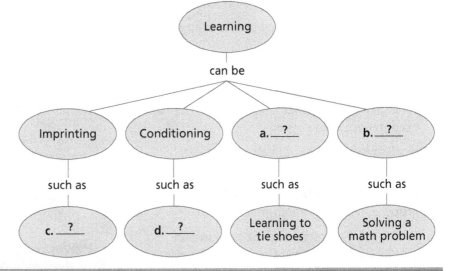

Reviewing Key Terms

Choose the letter of the best answer.

1. An organism's reaction to a signal is called
   a. a response.
   b. a stimulus.
   c. aggression.
   d. learning.

2. A process that leads to a change in behavior based on practice is called
   a. instinct.
   b. response.
   c. learning.
   d. behavior.

3. Learning that a particular stimulus or response leads to a good or a bad outcome is called
   a. instinct.
   b. imprinting.
   c. conditioning.
   d. insight learning.

4. A chemical released by one animal that affects the behavior of another animal of the same species is called a(n)
   a. stimulus.
   b. instinct.
   c. pheromone.
   d. circadian rhythm.

5. A threatening behavior that one animal uses to gain control over another is called
   a. courtship behavior.
   b. aggression.
   c. conditioning.
   d. cyclic behavior.

6. When a bird travels from its winter home in South America to its nesting area in New York, this is called
   a. learning.
   b. conditioning.
   c. migration.
   d. territorial behavior.

7. An instrument in orbit thousands of kilometers above Earth is called a
   a. pheromone.
   b. transmitter.
   c. receiver.
   d. satellite.

Writing in Science

Health Article Write a magazine article describing how dogs can be trained. Explain how trained dogs might assist people with special needs.

Animal Behavior
Video Preview
Video Field Trip
▶ Video Assessment

Review and Assessment

Checking Concepts

8. What are the functions of behavior?

9. Explain how both instinct and learning are involved in imprinting.

10. Explain what trial-and-error learning is. Describe an example.

11. What are pheromones? Explain how they are used in communication.

12. Explain how territorial behavior and courtship behavior are related.

13. Describe two examples of how living in a group can benefit an animal.

14. What is one disadvantage of tracking an animal by radio rather than by satellite?

Thinking Critically

15. **Inferring** Look at the photograph below. On its first try, this weaver bird is building a nest of grass with a hole at the bottom just the right size for the bird to enter. What kind of behavior is this? Explain.

16. **Applying Concepts** Explain how a racehorse's ability to win races is a combination of inherited and learned characteristics.

17. **Problem Solving** A dog keeps jumping onto a sofa. Describe how the owner might train the dog not to do this. The procedure must not involve any pain or harm to the dog.

18. **Applying Concepts** Give an example of something that you have learned by insight learning. Explain how you made use of your past knowledge and experience in learning it.

19. **Drawing Conclusions** How can hibernation help an animal survive the winter?

20. **Applying Concepts** Because a highway has been constructed through a forest, many animals have had to move to a different wooded area. Is their move an example of migration? Explain.

21. **Making Judgments** Is satellite tracking a good way to track the migration of monarch butterflies? Explain.

Applying Skills

Use the diagrams below, showing (A) a toad catching a bee and (B) the toad's reaction, to answer Questions 22–24.

A   **B**

22. **Inferring** Explain why the toad probably behaves as it does in diagram B.

23. **Predicting** If another bee flies by, how will the toad probably behave? Explain.

24. **Classifying** What type of learning might result from the toad's experience? Explain.

Lab zone Chapter **Project**

Performance Assessment Obtain your teacher's permission before bringing an animal to class. You can also show photographs or illustrations of the animal's training. Describe your training plan. What did you discover about the animal's learning process? How could you have improved your plan?

Standardized Test Prep

Choose the letter of the best answer.

1. An enclosed cage at a university laboratory holds dozens of birds. When a biologist adjusts the light schedule and temperature in the cage to match fall conditions, she observes that the birds spend most of their time at the south end of the cage. What is the most likely explanation for the behavior?
   A The birds are forming a society.
   B There is more food at the south end of the cage.
   C The birds are exhibiting migratory behavior.
   D The scientist has conditioned the birds to prefer the south end of the cage.

2. The chimpanzee in the diagram below has learned a way to reach the bananas. What type of learning most likely applies to this situation?
   F instinct
   G conditioning
   H insight
   J imprinting

3. Ants have laid a pheromone trail to a food source. While the ants are in their nest at night, a researcher pours gasoline over the entire trail. Which of the following will probably happen the next morning?
   A The gasoline will have no effect on the ants.
   B The ants will find the food more rapidly.
   C The ants will eat the gasoline.
   D The ants will be unable to find the food.

4. You are awake during the day and asleep at night. This behavior is an example of
   F circadian rhythm.
   G aggression.
   H trail-and-error learning.
   J hibernation.

Constructed Response

5. Describe the organization of a honeybee society, including daily tasks.

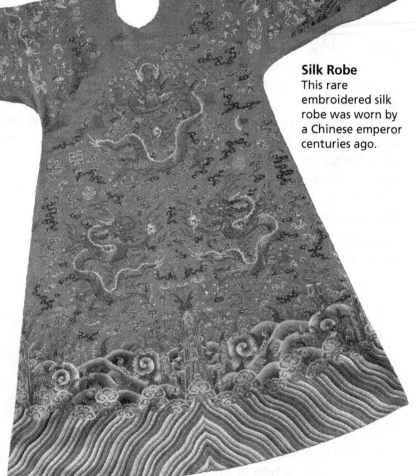

Silk Robe
This rare embroidered silk robe was worn by a Chinese emperor centuries ago.

The Secret of Silk

What animal—

- was a secret for thousands of years?
- was smuggled across mountains in a hollow cane?
- is not really what its name says it is?

Modern Robe
This Chinese silk robe is embroidered with dragons from Chinese legends.

If you guessed that this amazing animal is the silkworm, you are right. The silk thread that this caterpillar spins is woven into silk cloth. For at least 4,000 years, people have treasured silk.

Chinese legends say that in 2640 B.C., a Chinese empress accidentally dropped a silkworm cocoon in warm water and watched the thread unravel. She had discovered silk. But for thousands of years, the Chinese people kept the work of silkworms a secret. Death was the penalty for telling the secret.

Then, it is said, in A.D. 552, two travelers from Persia visited China and returned to the West carrying silkworm eggs hidden in their hollow canes. Ever since then, the world has enjoyed the beauty of silk—its warmth, strength, softness, and shimmer.

Metamorphosis of the Silkworm

The silkworm is not really a worm; it's the larva of an insect—a moth named *Bombyx mori.* In its entire feeding period, this larva consumes about 20 times its own weight in mulberry leaves. The silkworm undergoes complete metamorphosis during its life.

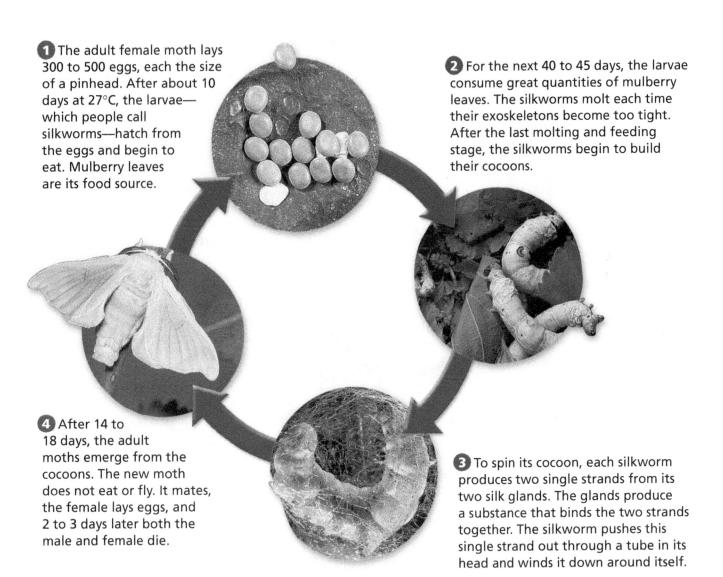

❶ The adult female moth lays 300 to 500 eggs, each the size of a pinhead. After about 10 days at 27°C, the larvae— which people call silkworms—hatch from the eggs and begin to eat. Mulberry leaves are its food source.

❷ For the next 40 to 45 days, the larvae consume great quantities of mulberry leaves. The silkworms molt each time their exoskeletons become too tight. After the last molting and feeding stage, the silkworms begin to build their cocoons.

❹ After 14 to 18 days, the adult moths emerge from the cocoons. The new moth does not eat or fly. It mates, the female lays eggs, and 2 to 3 days later both the male and female die.

❸ To spin its cocoon, each silkworm produces two single strands from its two silk glands. The glands produce a substance that binds the two strands together. The silkworm pushes this single strand out through a tube in its head and winds it down around itself.

Science Activity

Examine a silkworm cocoon. After softening the cocoon in water, find the end of the strand of silk. Pull this strand, wind it onto an index card, and measure its length.

With a partner, design an experiment to compare the strength of the silk thread you just collected to that of cotton and/or nylon thread of the same weight or thickness.

- Develop a hypothesis about the strength of the threads.

- Decide on the setup you will use to test the threads.

- Check your safety plan with your teacher.

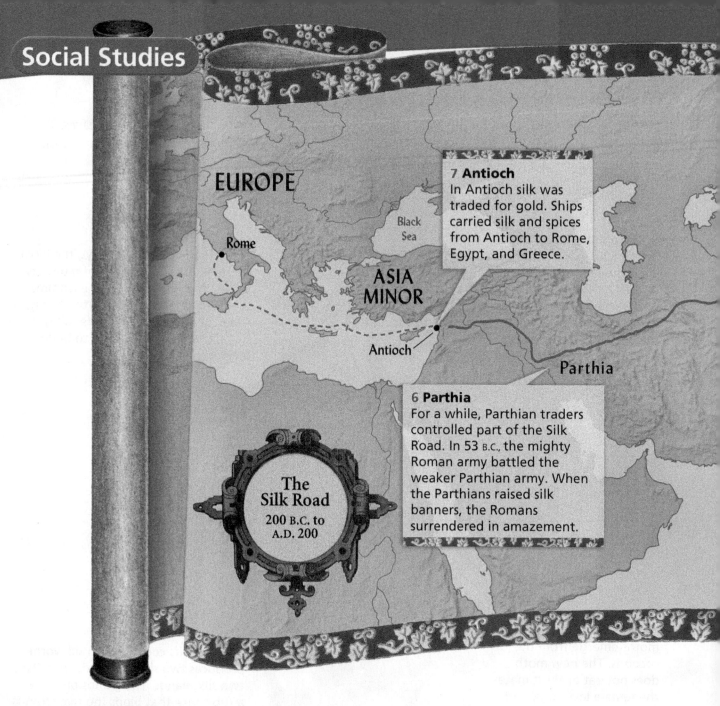

EUROPE

Rome

Black
Sea

ASIA
MINOR

Antioch

Parthia

The
Silk Road
200 B.C. to
A.D. 200

7 Antioch
In Antioch silk was traded for gold. Ships carried silk and spices from Antioch to Rome, Egypt, and Greece.

6 Parthia
For a while, Parthian traders controlled part of the Silk Road. In 53 B.C., the mighty Roman army battled the weaker Parthian army. When the Parthians raised silk banners, the Romans surrendered in amazement.

The Silk Road

Long before the rest of the world learned how silk was made, the Chinese were trading this treasured fabric with people west of China. Merchants who bought and sold silk traveled along a system of hazardous routes that came to be known as the Silk Road. The Silk Road stretched 6,400 kilometers from Ch'ang-an in China to the Mediterranean Sea. Silk, furs, and spices traveled west toward Rome along the road. Gold, wool, glass, grapes, garlic, and walnuts moved east toward China.

Travel along the Silk Road was treacherous and difficult. For safety, traders traveled in caravans of many people and animals. Some kinds of pack animals were better equipped to handle certain parts of the journey than others. Camels, for instance, were well suited to the desert; they could go without drinking for several days and withstand most sandstorms. Yaks were often used in the high mountains.

The entire journey along the Silk Road could take years. Many people and animals died along the way. Very few individuals or caravans traveled the length of the Silk Road.

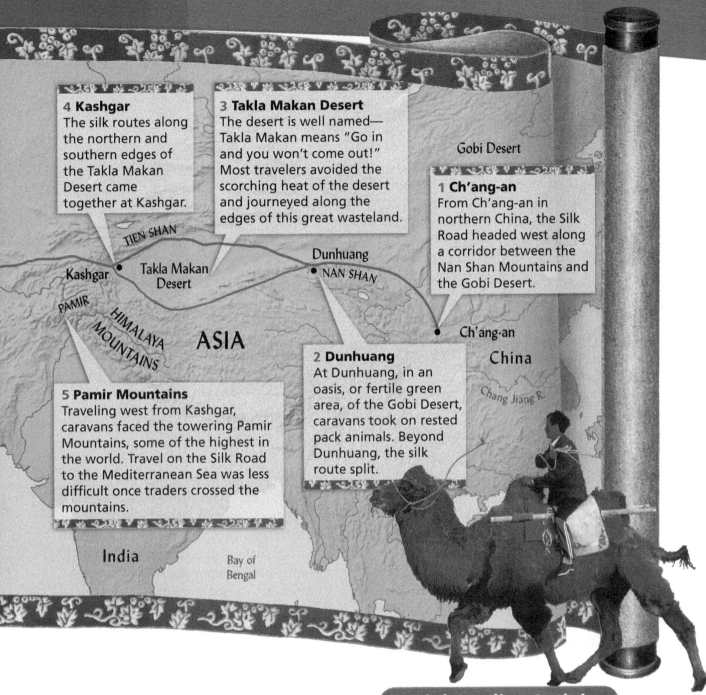

4 Kashgar
The silk routes along the northern and southern edges of the Takla Makan Desert came together at Kashgar.

3 Takla Makan Desert
The desert is well named—Takla Makan means "Go in and you won't come out!" Most travelers avoided the scorching heat of the desert and journeyed along the edges of this great wasteland.

Gobi Desert

1 Ch'ang-an
From Ch'ang-an in northern China, the Silk Road headed west along a corridor between the Nan Shan Mountains and the Gobi Desert.

TIEN SHAN

Kashgar   Takla Makan Desert

Dunhuang

NAN SHAN

PAMIR

HIMALAYA MOUNTAINS

ASIA

Ch'ang-an

China

Chang Jiang R.

5 Pamir Mountains
Traveling west from Kashgar, caravans faced the towering Pamir Mountains, some of the highest in the world. Travel on the Silk Road to the Mediterranean Sea was less difficult once traders crossed the mountains.

2 Dunhuang
At Dunhuang, in an oasis, or fertile green area, of the Gobi Desert, caravans took on rested pack animals. Beyond Dunhuang, the silk route split.

India

Bay of Bengal

Silk fabric became highly prized in Rome. In fact, it was said that the first silk products to reach Rome after 50 B.C. were worth their weight in gold. The Chinese, of course, kept the secret of the silkworm and controlled silk production. They were pleased that the Romans thought that silk grew on trees. It was not until about A.D. 550 that the Roman Empire learned the secret of silk.

In time, silk production spread around the world. The Silk Road, though, opened forever the exchange of goods and ideas between China and the West.

Social Studies Activity

You are a merchant traveling from Dunhuang to Kashgar and back. You will carry silk, furs, and cinnamon to Kashgar where you'll trade for gold, garlic, and glass. Plan your route and hire a guide.

- Look at the map to find the distances and the physical features you will see.
- Explain why you chose the route you did.
- List the animals and supplies you will take.
- Write a help-wanted ad for a guide to lead your caravan.

The Gift of Silk

A myth is a story handed down from past cultures—often to explain an event or natural phenomenon. Myths may be about gods and goddesses or about heroes.

The Yellow Emperor, Huang Di, who is mentioned in this Chinese myth, was a real person. Some stories say that he was the founder of the Chinese nation. He was thought to be a god who came to rule on Earth. Here the silkworm goddess appears to him at a victory celebration.

The Goddess of the Silkworm

A goddess descended from the heavens with a gift for the Yellow Emperor. Her body was covered with a horse's hide, and she presented two shining rolls of silk to the god. She was the "goddess of the silkworm", sometimes called the "lady with a horse's head". Long, long ago she had been a beautiful girl, but now a horse's skin grew over her body. If she pulled the two sides of the skin close to her body she became a silkworm with a horse's head, spinning a long, glittering thread of silk from her mouth. It is said she lived in a mulberry tree, producing silk day and night in the wild northern plain. This is her story.

Once in ancient times there lived a man, his daughter and their horse. Often the man had to travel, leaving his daughter alone at home to take care of the beast. And often the girl was lonely. One day, because she missed her father she teased the horse: "Dear long-nosed one, if you could bring my father home right how, I'd marry you and be your wife." At that the horse broke out of his harness. He galloped away and came quickly to the place where the master was doing business.

The master, surprised to see his beast, grasped his mane and jumped up on his back. The horse stood mournfully staring in the direction he had come from, so the man decided there must be something amiss at home and hurried back.

When they arrived home, the daughter explained that she had only remarked that she missed her father and the horse had dashed off wildly. The man said nothing but was secretly pleased to own such a remarkable animal and fed him special sweet hay. But the horse would not touch it and whinnied and reared each time he saw the girl.

The man began to worry about the horse's strange behavior, and one day he said to the girl, "Why is it that our horse behaves so strangely whenever you are about?"

So the young girl confessed the teasing remark she had made.

When he heard this the father was enraged, "For shame to say such a thing to an animal! No one must know of this! You will stay locked in the house!"

Bronze Horse
This galloping horse was crafted in the second century.

Now the man had always liked this horse, but he would not hear of its becoming his son-in-law. That night, to prevent any more trouble, he crept quietly into the stable with his bow and arrow and shot the horse through the heart. Then he skinned it and hung up the hide in the courtyard.

Next day, when the father was away, the girl ran out of the house to join some other children playing in the courtyard near the horse hide. When she saw it she kicked it angrily and said, "Dirty horse hide! What made you think such an ugly long-snouted creature as you could become my . . . ."

But before she could finish, the hide suddenly flew up and wrapped itself around her, swift as the wind, and carried her away out of sight. The other children watched dumbfounded; there was nothing they could do but wait to tell the old man when he arrived home.

Her father set out immediately in search of his daughter, but in vain. Some days later a neighbouring family found the girl wrapped up in the hide in the branches of a mulberry tree. She had turned into a wormlike creature spinning a long thread of shining silk from her horse-shaped head, spinning it round and round her in a soft cocoon.

Such is the story of the goddess of the silkworm. The Yellow Emperor was delighted to receive her exquisite gift of silk . . . . He ordered his official tailor, Bo Yu, to create new ceremonial robes and hats. And Lei Zu, the revered queen mother of gods and people, wife of the Emperor, began then to collect silkworms and grow them. And so it was that the Chinese people learned of silk.

—————Yuan Ke, *Dragons and Dynasties*, translated by Kim Echlin and Nie Zhixiong

Language Arts Activity

What two details in the myth tell you that silkworms were important to the Chinese people?

The girl in the myth gets into trouble because she breaks her promise. Write a story of your own using the idea of a broken promise.

- Decide on the place, time, and main characters.

- Think about the events that will happen and how your story will conclude.

Counting on Caterpillars

Lai opened the door to the silkworm room. She was greeted by the loud sound of thousands of silkworms crunching on fresh leaves from mulberry trees. Lai enjoyed raising silkworms, but it was hard work. Over its lifetime, each silkworm eats about twenty times its own weight.

Lai had a chance to care for more silkworms. But first she had to figure out how many more she could raise. She now had 6,000 silkworms that ate the leaves from 125 mulberry trees. Should she have her parents buy another piece of land with another 100 mulberry trees? If she had 100 more trees, how many more silkworms could she feed?

Silkworms
Silkworms are fed fresh mulberry leaves every four hours, around the clock.

❶ Analyze.

You know that 125 trees can feed 6,000 silkworms. You want to know the number of silkworms 100 trees will feed. Write a proportion, using n to represent the number of silkworms.

❷ Write the proportion.

$$\frac{\text{Trees} \rightarrow}{\text{Silkworms} \rightarrow} \frac{125}{6,000} = \frac{100}{n} \frac{\leftarrow \text{Trees}}{\leftarrow \text{Silkworms}}$$

❸ Cross multiply.

$125 \times n = 6,000 \times 100$

❹ Simplify.

$125n = 600,000$

❺ Solve.

$n = \dfrac{600,000}{125}$ $n = 4,800$

❻ Think about it.

"Yes," she decided. She could raise 4,800 more silkworms!

Math Activity

Solve the following problems.

1. Lai's friend Cheng also raises silkworms. He buys mulberry leaves. If 20 sacks of leaves feed 12,000 silkworms a day, how many sacks of leaves will 9,600 silkworms eat per day?

2. When Lai's silkworms are ready to spin, she places them in trays. If 3 trays can hold 150 silkworms, how many trays does Lai use for her 6,000 silkworms?

3. A silkworm spins silk at a rate of about 30.4 centimeters per minute. (a) How many centimeters can it spin in an hour? (b) It takes a silkworm 60 hours to spin the entire cocoon. How many centimeters is that?

4. Lai's silk thread contributes to the creation of beautiful silk clothes. It takes the thread of 630 cocoons to make a blouse and the thread of 110 cocoons to make a tie.
(a) If each of Lai's 6,000 silkworms produces a cocoon, how many blouses can be made from the thread? (b) How many ties can be made?

Chinese Silk Umbrellas

Tie It Together

Plan a Silk Celebration

People use silk in many ways other than just to make fine clothing. Did you know that silk was used for parachutes during World War II? Or that some bicycle racers choose tires containing silk because they provide good traction? Today, silk is used for a variety of purposes:

- recreation—fishing lines and nets, bicycle tires
- business—electrical insulations, typewriter and computer ribbons, surgical sutures
- decoration—some silkscreen printing, artificial flowers

Work in small groups to learn about one of the ways that people have used silk in the past or are using it today. Devise an interesting way to share your project with the class. Here are some ideas.

- a booth to display or advertise a silk product
- a skit in which you wear silk
- a historical presentation on the uses of silk in other countries
- a presentation about a process, such as silkscreen painting or silk flowers

Ask volunteers to bring pictures or silk products to class. After rehearsing or reviewing your presentation, work with other groups to decide how to organize your Silk Festival.

Tires of Silk
Professional bicycle racers such as Lance Armstrong often rely on tires containing silk. Silk gives the tires better traction, or grip, on the road.

Think Like a Scientist

Scientists have a particular way of looking at the world, or scientific habits of mind. Whenever you ask a question and explore possible answers, you use many of the same skills that scientists do. Some of these skills are described on this page.

Observing

When you use one or more of your five senses to gather information about the world, you are **observing.** Hearing a dog bark, counting twelve green seeds, and smelling smoke are all observations. To increase the power of their senses, scientists sometimes use microscopes, telescopes, or other instruments that help them make more detailed observations.

An observation must be an accurate report of what your senses detect. It is important to keep careful records of your observations in science class by writing or drawing in a notebook. The information collected through observations is called evidence, or data.

Inferring

When you interpret an observation, you are **inferring,** or making an inference. For example, if you hear your dog barking, you may infer that someone is at your front door. To make this inference, you combine the evidence—the barking dog—and your experience or knowledge—you know that your dog barks when strangers approach—to reach a logical conclusion.

Notice that an inference is not a fact; it is only one of many possible interpretations for an observation. For example, your dog may be barking because it wants to go for a walk. An inference may turn out to be incorrect even if it is based on accurate observations and logical reasoning. The only way to find out if an inference is correct is to investigate further.

Predicting

When you listen to the weather forecast, you hear many predictions about the next day's weather—what the temperature will be, whether it will rain, and how windy it will be. Weather forecasters use observations and knowledge of weather patterns to predict the weather. The skill of **predicting** involves making an inference about a future event based on current evidence or past experience.

Because a prediction is an inference, it may prove to be false. In science class, you can test some of your predictions by doing experiments. For example, suppose you predict that larger paper airplanes can fly farther than smaller airplanes. How could you test your prediction?

Activity

Use the photograph to answer the questions below.

Observing Look closely at the photograph. List at least three observations.

Inferring Use your observations to make an inference about what has happened. What experience or knowledge did you use to make the inference?

Predicting Predict what will happen next. On what evidence or experience do you base your prediction?

Classifying

Could you imagine searching for a book in the library if the books were shelved in no particular order? Your trip to the library would be an all-day event! Luckily, librarians group together books on similar topics or by the same author. Grouping together items that are alike in some way is called **classifying.** You can classify items in many ways: by size, by shape, by use, and by other important characteristics.

Like librarians, scientists use the skill of classifying to organize information and objects. When things are sorted into groups, the relationships among them become easier to understand.

Activity

Classify the objects in the photograph into two groups based on any characteristic you choose. Then use another characteristic to classify the objects into three groups.

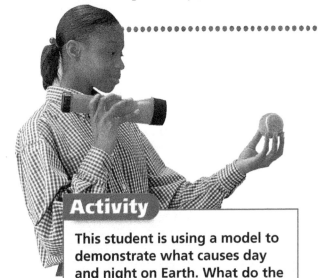

Activity

This student is using a model to demonstrate what causes day and night on Earth. What do the flashlight and the tennis ball in the model represent?

Making Models

Have you ever drawn a picture to help someone understand what you were saying? Such a drawing is one type of model. A model is a picture, diagram, computer image, or other representation of a complex object or process. **Making models** helps people understand things that they cannot observe directly.

Scientists often use models to represent things that are either very large or very small, such as the planets in the solar system, or the parts of a cell. Such models are physical models—drawings or three-dimensional structures that look like the real thing. Other models are mental models—mathematical equations or words that describe how something works.

Communicating

Whenever you talk on the phone, write a report, or listen to your teacher at school, you are communicating. **Communicating** is the process of sharing ideas and information with other people. Communicating effectively requires many skills, including writing, reading, speaking, listening, and making models.

Scientists communicate to share results, information, and opinions. Scientists often communicate about their work in journals, over the telephone, in letters, and on the Internet.

They also attend scientific meetings where they share their ideas with one another in person.

Activity

On a sheet of paper, write out clear, detailed directions for tying your shoe. Then exchange directions with a partner. Follow your partner's directions exactly. How successful were you at tying your shoe? How could your partner have communicated more clearly?

Making Measurements

By measuring, scientists can express their observations more precisely and communicate more information about what they observe.

Measuring in SI

The standard system of measurement used by scientists around the world is known as the International System of Units, which is abbreviated as SI (**Système International d'Unités,** in French). SI units are easy to use because they are based on multiples of 10. Each unit is ten times larger than the next smallest unit and one tenth the size of the next largest unit. The table lists the prefixes used to name the most common SI units.

Common SI Prefixes		
Prefix	Symbol	Meaning
kilo-	k	1,000
hecto-	h	100
deka-	da	10
deci-	d	0.1 (one tenth)
centi-	c	0.01 (one hundredth)
milli-	m	0.001 (one thousandth)

Length To measure length, or the distance between two points, the unit of measure is the **meter (m).** The distance from the floor to a doorknob is approximately one meter. Long distances, such as the distance between two cities, are measured in kilometers (km). Small lengths are measured in centimeters (cm) or millimeters (mm). Scientists use metric rulers and meter sticks to measure length.

Common Conversions	
1 km	= 1,000 m
1 m	= 100 cm
1 m	= 1,000 mm
1 cm	= 10 mm

Liquid Volume To measure the volume of a liquid, or the amount of space it takes up, you will use a unit of measure known as the **liter (L).** One liter is the approximate volume of a medium-size carton of milk. Smaller volumes are measured in milliliters (mL). Scientists use graduated cylinders to measure liquid volume.

Common Conversion
1 L = 1,000 mL

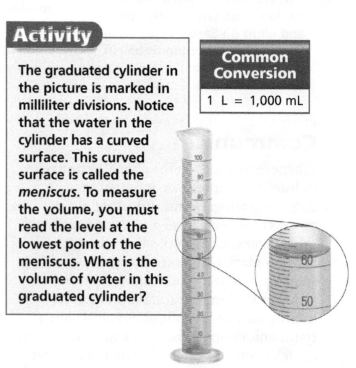

Mass To measure mass, or the amount of matter in an object, you will use a unit of measure known as the **gram (g).** One gram is approximately the mass of a paper clip. Larger masses are measured in kilograms (kg). Scientists use a balance to find the mass of an object.

Common Conversion
1 kg = 1,000 g

Activity

The mass of the potato in the picture is measured in kilograms. What is the mass of the potato? Suppose a recipe for potato salad called for one kilogram of potatoes. About how many potatoes would you need?

Temperature To measure the temperature of a substance, you will use the **Celsius scale.** Temperature is measured in degrees Celsius (°C) using a Celsius thermometer. Water freezes at 0°C and boils at 100°C.

Time The unit scientists use to measure time is the **second (s).**

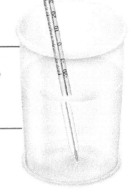

Activity

What is the temperature of the liquid in degrees Celsius?

Converting SI Units

To use the SI system, you must know how to convert between units. Converting from one unit to another involves the skill of **calculating,** or using mathematical operations. Converting between SI units is similar to converting between dollars and dimes because both systems are based on multiples of ten.

Suppose you want to convert a length of 80 centimeters to meters. Follow these steps to convert between units.

1. Begin by writing down the measurement you want to convert—in this example, 80 centimeters.

2. Write a conversion factor that represents the relationship between the two units you are converting. In this example, the relationship is 1 meter = 100 centimeters. Write this conversion factor as a fraction, making sure to place the units you are converting from (centimeters, in this example) in the denominator.

3. Multiply the measurement you want to convert by the fraction. When you do this, the units in the first measurement will cancel out with the units in the denominator. Your answer will be in the units you are converting to (meters, in this example).

Example

80 centimeters = ▊ meters

$$80 \text{ centimeters} \times \frac{1 \text{ meter}}{100 \text{ centimeters}} = \frac{80 \text{ meters}}{100}$$
$$= 0.8 \text{ meters}$$

Activity

Convert between the following units.
1. 600 millimeters = ▊ meters
2. 0.35 liters = ▊ milliliters
3. 1,050 grams = ▊ kilograms

Conducting a Scientific Investigation

In some ways, scientists are like detectives, piecing together clues to learn about a process or event. One way that scientists gather clues is by carrying out experiments. An experiment tests an idea in a careful, orderly manner. Although experiments do not all follow the same steps in the same order, many follow a pattern similar to the one described here.

Posing Questions

Experiments begin by asking a scientific question. A scientific question is one that can be answered by gathering evidence. For example, the question "Which freezes faster—fresh water or salt water?" is a scientific question because you can carry out an investigation and gather information to answer the question.

Developing a Hypothesis

The next step is to form a hypothesis. A **hypothesis** is a possible explanation for a set of observations or answer to a scientific question. In science, a hypothesis must be something that can be tested. A hypothesis can be worded as an *If . . . then . . .* statement. For example, a hypothesis might be *"If I add salt to fresh water, then the water will take longer to freeze."* A hypothesis worded this way serves as a rough outline of the experiment you should perform.

Designing an Experiment

Next you need to plan a way to test your hypothesis. Your plan should be written out as a step-by-step procedure and should describe the observations or measurements you will make.

Two important steps involved in designing an experiment are controlling variables and forming operational definitions.

Controlling Variables In a well-designed experiment, you need to keep all variables the same except for one. A **variable** is any factor that can change in an experiment. The factor that you change is called the **manipulated variable**. In this experiment, the manipulated variable is the amount of salt added to the water. Other factors, such as the amount of water or the starting temperature, are kept constant.

The factor that changes as a result of the manipulated variable is called the **responding variable.** The responding variable is what you measure or observe to obtain your results. In this experiment, the responding variable is how long the water takes to freeze.

An experiment in which all factors except one are kept constant is called a **controlled experiment.** Most controlled experiments include a test called the control. In this experiment, Container 3 is the control. Because no salt is added to Container 3, you can compare the results from the other containers to it. Any difference in results must be due to the addition of salt alone.

Forming Operational Definitions Another important aspect of a well-designed experiment is having clear operational definitions. An **operational definition** is a statement that describes how a particular variable is to be measured or how a term is to be defined. For example, in this experiment, how will you determine if the water has frozen? You might decide to insert a stick in each container at the start of the experiment. Your operational definition of "frozen" would be the time at which the stick can no longer move.

Experimental Procedure
1. Fill 3 containers with 300 milliliters of cold tap water.
2. Add 10 grams of salt to Container 1; stir. Add 20 grams of salt to Container 2; stir. Add no salt to Container 3.
3. Place the 3 containers in a freezer.
4. Check the containers every 15 minutes. Record your observations.

Interpreting Data

The observations and measurements you make in an experiment are called **data.** At the end of an experiment, you need to analyze the data to look for any patterns or trends. Patterns often become clear if you organize your data in a data table or graph. Then think through what the data reveal. Do they support your hypothesis? Do they point out a flaw in your experiment? Do you need to collect more data?

Drawing Conclusions

A **conclusion** is a statement that sums up what you have learned from an experiment. When you draw a conclusion, you need to decide whether the data you collected support your hypothesis or not. You may need to repeat an experiment several times before you can draw any conclusions from it. Conclusions often lead you to pose new questions and plan new experiments to answer them.

Activity

Is a ball's bounce affected by the height from which it is dropped? Using the steps just described, plan a controlled experiment to investigate this problem.

Technology Design Skills

Engineers are people who use scientific and technological knowledge to solve practical problems. To design new products, engineers usually follow the process described here, even though they may not follow these steps in the exact order. As you read the steps, think about how you might apply them in technology labs.

Identify a Need

Before engineers begin designing a new product, they must first identify the need they are trying to meet. For example, suppose you are a member of a design team in a company that makes toys. Your team has identified a need: a toy boat that is inexpensive and easy to assemble.

Research the Problem

Engineers often begin by gathering information that will help them with their new design. This research may include finding articles in books, magazines, or on the Internet. It may also include talking to other engineers who have solved similar problems. Engineers often perform experiments related to the product they want to design.

For your toy boat, you could look at toys that are similar to the one you want to design. You might do research on the Internet. You could also test some materials to see whether they will work well in a toy boat.

Drawing for a boat design ▼

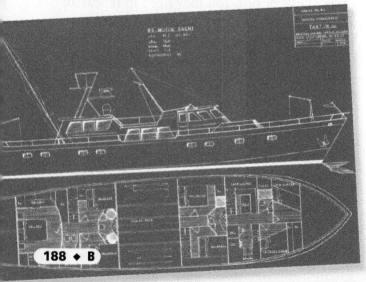

Design a Solution

Research gives engineers information that helps them design a product. When engineers design new products, they usually work in teams.

Generating Ideas Often design teams hold brainstorming meetings in which any team member can contribute ideas. **Brainstorming** is a creative process in which one team member's suggestions often spark ideas in other group members. Brainstorming can lead to new approaches to solving a design problem.

Evaluating Constraints During brainstorming, a design team will often come up with several possible designs. The team must then evaluate each one.

As part of their evaluation, engineers consider constraints. **Constraints** are factors that limit or restrict a product design. Physical characteristics, such as the properties of materials used to make your toy boat, are constraints. Money and time are also constraints. If the materials in a product cost a lot, or if the product takes a long time to make, the design may be impractical.

Making Trade-offs Design teams usually need to make trade-offs. In a **trade-off,** engineers give up one benefit of a proposed design in order to obtain another. In designing your toy boat, you will have to make trade-offs. For example, suppose one material is sturdy but not fully waterproof. Another material is more waterproof, but breakable. You may decide to give up the benefit of sturdiness in order to obtain the benefit of waterproofing.

Build and Evaluate a Prototype

Once the team has chosen a design plan, the engineers build a prototype of the product. A **prototype** is a working model used to test a design. Engineers evaluate the prototype to see whether it works well, is easy to operate, is safe to use, and holds up to repeated use.

Think of your toy boat. What would the prototype be like? Of what materials would it be made? How would you test it?

Troubleshoot and Redesign

Few prototypes work perfectly, which is why they need to be tested. Once a design team has tested a prototype, the members analyze the results and identify any problems. The team then tries to **troubleshoot,** or fix the design problems. For example, if your toy boat leaks or wobbles, the boat should be redesigned to eliminate those problems.

Communicate the Solution

A team needs to communicate the final design to the people who will manufacture and use the product. To do this, teams may use sketches, detailed drawings, computer simulations, and word descriptions.

Activity

You can use the technology design process to design and build a toy boat.

Research and Investigate

1. Visit the library or go online to research toy boats.
2. Investigate how a toy boat can be powered, including wind, rubber bands, or baking soda and vinegar.
3. Brainstorm materials, shapes, and steering for your boat.

Design and Build

4. Based on your research, design a toy boat that
   - is made of readily available materials
   - is no larger than 15 cm long and 10 cm wide
   - includes a power system, a rudder, and an area for cargo
   - travels 2 meters in a straight line carrying a load of 20 pennies
5. Sketch your design and write a step-by-step plan for building your boat. After your teacher approves your plan, build your boat.

Evaluate and Redesign

6. Test your boat, evaluate the results, and troubleshoot any problems.
7. Based on your evaluation, redesign your toy boat so it performs better.

Creating Data Tables and Graphs

**How can you make sense of the data in a science experiment?
The first step is to organize the data to help you understand them.
Data tables and graphs are helpful tools for organizing data.**

Data Tables

You have gathered your materials and set up your experiment. But before you start, you need to plan a way to record what happens during the experiment. By creating a data table, you can record your observations and measurements in an orderly way.

Suppose, for example, that a scientist conducted an experiment to find out how many Calories people of different body masses burn while doing various activities. The data table shows the results.

Notice in this data table that the manipulated variable (body mass) is the heading of one column. The responding variable (for

Calories Burned in 30 Minutes			
Body Mass	Experiment 1: Bicycling	Experiment 2: Playing Basketball	Experiment 3: Watching Television
30 kg	60 Calories	120 Calories	21 Calories
40 kg	77 Calories	164 Calories	27 Calories
50 kg	95 Calories	206 Calories	33 Calories
60 kg	114 Calories	248 Calories	38 Calories

Experiment 1, the number of Calories burned while bicycling) is the heading of the next column. Additional columns were added for related experiments.

Bar Graphs

To compare how many Calories a person burns doing various activities, you could create a bar graph. A bar graph is used to display data in a number of separate, or distinct, categories. In this example, bicycling, playing basketball, and watching television are the three categories.

To create a bar graph, follow these steps.

1. On graph paper, draw a horizontal, or *x*-, axis and a vertical, or *y*-, axis.

2. Write the names of the categories to be graphed along the horizontal axis. Include an overall label for the axis as well.

3. Label the vertical axis with the name of the responding variable. Include units of measurement. Then create a scale along the axis by marking off equally spaced numbers that cover the range of the data collected.

4. For each category, draw a solid bar using the scale on the vertical axis to determine the height. Make all the bars the same width.

5. Add a title that describes the graph.

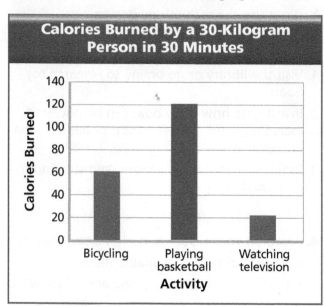

Line Graphs

To see whether a relationship exists between body mass and the number of Calories burned while bicycling, you could create a line graph. A line graph is used to display data that show how one variable (the responding variable) changes in response to another variable (the manipulated variable). You can use a line graph when your manipulated variable is **continuous,** that is, when there are other points between the ones that you tested. In this example, body mass is a continuous variable because there are other body masses between 30 and 40 kilograms (for example, 31 kilograms). Time is another example of a continuous variable.

Line graphs are powerful tools because they allow you to estimate values for conditions that you did not test in the experiment. For example, you can use the line graph to estimate that a 35-kilogram person would burn 68 Calories while bicycling.

To create a line graph, follow these steps.

1. On graph paper, draw a horizontal, or x-, axis and a vertical, or y-, axis.

2. Label the horizontal axis with the name of the manipulated variable. Label the vertical axis with the name of the responding variable. Include units of measurement.

3. Create a scale on each axis by marking off equally spaced numbers that cover the range of the data collected.

4. Plot a point on the graph for each piece of data. In the line graph above, the dotted lines show how to plot the first data point (30 kilograms and 60 Calories). Follow an imaginary vertical line extending up from the horizontal axis at the 30-kilogram mark. Then follow an imaginary horizontal line extending across from the vertical axis at the 60-Calorie mark. Plot the point where the two lines intersect.

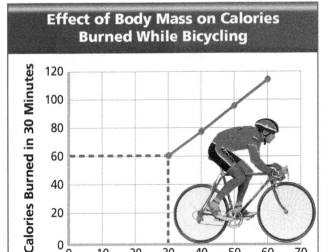

Effect of Body Mass on Calories Burned While Bicycling

5. Connect the plotted points with a solid line. (In some cases, it may be more appropriate to draw a line that shows the general trend of the plotted points. In those cases, some of the points may fall above or below the line. Also, not all graphs are linear. It may be more appropriate to draw a curve to connect the points.)

6. Add a title that identifies the variables or relationship in the graph.

Activity

Create line graphs to display the data from Experiment 2 and Experiment 3 in the data table.

Activity

You read in the newspaper that a total of 4 centimeters of rain fell in your area in June, 2.5 centimeters fell in July, and 1.5 centimeters fell in August. What type of graph would you use to display these data? Use graph paper to create the graph.

Circle Graphs

Like bar graphs, circle graphs can be used to display data in a number of separate categories. Unlike bar graphs, however, circle graphs can only be used when you have data for *all* the categories that make up a given topic. A circle graph is sometimes called a pie chart. The pie represents the entire topic, while the slices represent the individual categories. The size of a slice indicates what percentage of the whole a particular category makes up.

The data table below shows the results of a survey in which 24 teenagers were asked to identify their favorite sport. The data were then used to create the circle graph at the right.

Favorite Sports	
Sport	Students
Soccer	8
Basketball	6
Bicycling	6
Swimming	4

To create a circle graph, follow these steps.

1. Use a compass to draw a circle. Mark the center with a point. Then draw a line from the center point to the top of the circle.

2. Determine the size of each "slice" by setting up a proportion where x equals the number of degrees in a slice. (*Note:* A circle contains 360 degrees.) For example, to find the number of degrees in the "soccer" slice, set up the following proportion:

$$\frac{\text{Students who prefer soccer}}{\text{Total number of students}} = \frac{x}{\text{Total number of degrees in a circle}}$$

$$\frac{8}{24} = \frac{x}{360}$$

Cross-multiply and solve for x.

$$24x = 8 \times 360$$
$$x = 120$$

The "soccer" slice should contain 120 degrees.

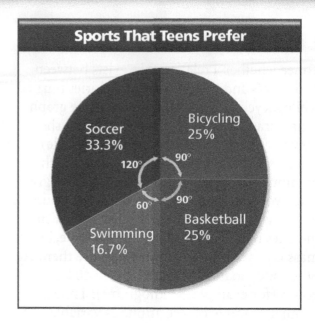

Sports That Teens Prefer

3. Use a protractor to measure the angle of the first slice, using the line you drew to the top of the circle as the 0° line. Draw a line from the center of the circle to the edge for the angle you measured.

4. Continue around the circle by measuring the size of each slice with the protractor. Start measuring from the edge of the previous slice so the wedges do not overlap. When you are done, the entire circle should be filled in.

5. Determine the percentage of the whole circle that each slice represents. To do this, divide the number of degrees in a slice by the total number of degrees in a circle (360), and multiply by 100%. For the "soccer" slice, you can find the percentage as follows:

$$\frac{120}{360} \times 100\% = 33.3\%$$

6. Use a different color for each slice. Label each slice with the category and with the percentage of the whole it represents.

7. Add a title to the circle graph.

Activity

In a class of 28 students, 12 students take the bus to school, 10 students walk, and 6 students ride their bicycles. Create a circle graph to display these data.

Math Review

Scientists use math to organize, analyze, and present data. This appendix will help you review some basic math skills.

Mean, Median, and Mode

The **mean** is the average, or the sum of the data divided by the number of data items. The middle number in a set of ordered data is called the **median**. The **mode** is the number that appears most often in a set of data.

Example

A scientist counted the number of distinct songs sung by seven different male birds and collected the data shown below.

Male Bird Songs							
Bird	A	B	C	D	E	F	G
Number of Songs	36	29	40	35	28	36	27

To determine the mean number of songs, add the total number of songs and divide by the number of data items—in this case, the number of male birds.

Mean $= \frac{231}{7} = 33$ songs

To find the median number of songs, arrange the data in numerical order and find the number in the middle of the series.

27 28 29 35 36 36 40

The number in the middle is 35, so the median number of songs is 35.

The mode is the value that appears most frequently. In the data, 36 appears twice, while each other item appears only once. Therefore, 36 songs is the mode.

Practice

Find out how many minutes it takes each student in your class to get to school. Then find the mean, median, and mode for the data.

Probability

Probability is the chance that an event will occur. Probability can be expressed as a ratio, a fraction, or a percentage. For example, when you flip a coin, the probability that the coin will land heads up is 1 in 2, or $\frac{1}{2}$, or 50 percent.

The probability that an event will happen can be expressed in the following formula.

$$P(\text{event}) = \frac{\text{Number of times the event can occur}}{\text{Total number of possible events}}$$

Example

A paper bag contains 25 blue marbles, 5 green marbles, 5 orange marbles, and 15 yellow marbles. If you close your eyes and pick a marble from the bag, what is the probability that it will be yellow?

$$P(\text{yellow marbles}) = \frac{15 \text{ yellow marbles}}{50 \text{ marbles total}}$$

$$P = \frac{15}{50}, \text{ or } \frac{3}{10}, \text{ or } 30\%$$

Practice

Each side of a cube has a letter on it. Two sides have *A*, three sides have *B*, and one side has *C*. If you roll the cube, what is the probability that *A* will land on top?

Area

The **area** of a surface is the number of square units that cover it. The front cover of your text-book has an area of about 600 cm².

Area of a Rectangle and a Square To find the area of a rectangle, multiply its length times its width. The formula for the area of a rectangle is

$$A = \ell \times w, \text{ or } A = \ell w$$

Since all four sides of a square have the same length, the area of a square is the length of one side multiplied by itself, or squared.

$$A = s \times s, \text{ or } A = s^2$$

Example

A scientist is studying the plants in a field that measures 75 m × 45 m. What is the area of the field?

$$A = \ell \times w$$
$$A = 75 \text{ m} \times 45 \text{ m}$$
$$A = 3{,}375 \text{ m}^2$$

Area of a Circle The formula for the area of a circle is

$$A = \pi \times r \times r, \text{ or } A = \pi r^2$$

The length of the radius is represented by r, and the value of π is approximately $\frac{22}{7}$.

Example

Find the area of a circle with a radius of 14 cm.

$$A = \pi r^2$$
$$A = 14 \times 14 \times \frac{22}{7}$$
$$A = 616 \text{ cm}^2$$

Practice

Find the area of a circle that has a radius of 21 m.

Circumference

The distance around a circle is called the circumference. The formula for finding the circumference of a circle is

$$C = 2 \times \pi \times r, \text{ or } C = 2\pi r$$

Example

The radius of a circle is 35 cm. What is its circumference?

$$C = 2\pi r$$
$$C = 2 \times 35 \times \frac{22}{7}$$
$$C = 220 \text{ cm}$$

Practice

What is the circumference of a circle with a radius of 28 m?

Volume

The volume of an object is the number of cubic units it contains. The volume of a wastebasket, for example, might be about 26,000 cm³.

Volume of a Rectangular Object To find the volume of a rectangular object, multiply the object's length times its width times its height.

$$V = \ell \times w \times h, \text{ or } V = \ell w h$$

Example

Find the volume of a box with length 24 cm, width 12 cm, and height 9 cm.

$$V = \ell w h$$
$$V = 24 \text{ cm} \times 12 \text{ cm} \times 9 \text{ cm}$$
$$V = 2{,}592 \text{ cm}^3$$

Practice

What is the volume of a rectangular object with length 17 cm, width 11 cm, and height 6 cm?

Fractions

A **fraction** is a way to express a part of a whole. In the fraction $\frac{4}{7}$, 4 is the numerator and 7 is the denominator.

Adding and Subtracting Fractions To add or subtract two or more fractions that have a common denominator, first add or subtract the numerators. Then write the sum or difference over the common denominator.

To find the sum or difference of fractions with different denominators, first find the least common multiple of the denominators. This is known as the least common denominator. Then convert each fraction to equivalent fractions with the least common denominator. Add or subtract the numerators. Then write the sum or difference over the common denominator.

> **Example**
>
> $$\frac{5}{6} - \frac{3}{4} = \frac{10}{12} - \frac{9}{12} = \frac{10 - 9}{12} = \frac{1}{12}$$

Multiplying Fractions To multiply two fractions, first multiply the two numerators, then multiply the two denominators.

> **Example**
>
> $$\frac{5}{6} \times \frac{2}{3} = \frac{5 \times 2}{6 \times 3} = \frac{10}{18} = \frac{5}{9}$$

Dividing Fractions Dividing by a fraction is the same as multiplying by its reciprocal. Reciprocals are numbers whose numerators and denominators have been switched. To divide one fraction by another, first invert the fraction you are dividing by—in other words, turn it upside down. Then multiply the two fractions.

> **Example**
>
> $$\frac{2}{5} \div \frac{7}{8} = \frac{2}{5} \times \frac{8}{7} = \frac{2 \times 8}{5 \times 7} = \frac{16}{35}$$

> **Practice**
>
> Solve the following: $\frac{3}{7} \div \frac{4}{5}$.

Decimals

Fractions whose denominators are 10, 100, or some other power of 10 are often expressed as decimals. For example, the fraction $\frac{9}{10}$ can be expressed as the decimal 0.9, and the fraction $\frac{7}{100}$ can be written as 0.07.

Adding and Subtracting With Decimals To add or subtract decimals, line up the decimal points before you carry out the operation.

> **Example**
>
> ```
>   27.4        278.635
> + 6.19       - 191.4
> ------       --------
>  33.59         87.235
> ```

Multiplying With Decimals When you multiply two numbers with decimals, the number of decimal places in the product is equal to the total number of decimal places in each number being multiplied.

> **Example**
>
> ```
>    46.2  (one decimal place)
>  × 2.37  (two decimal places)
>  ------
> 109.494  (three decimal places)
> ```

Dividing With Decimals To divide a decimal by a whole number, put the decimal point in the quotient above the decimal point in the dividend.

> **Example**
>
> $$15.5 \div 5$$
>
> $$5\overline{)15.5} = 3.1$$

To divide a decimal by a decimal, you need to rewrite the divisor as a whole number. Do this by multiplying both the divisor and dividend by the same multiple of 10.

> **Example**
>
> $$1.68 \div 4.2 = 16.8 \div 42$$
>
> $$42\overline{)16.8} = 0.4$$

> **Practice**
>
> Multiply 6.21 by 8.5.

Ratio and Proportion

A **ratio** compares two numbers by division. For example, suppose a scientist counts 800 wolves and 1,200 moose on an island. The ratio of wolves to moose can be written as a fraction, $\frac{800}{1,200}$, which can be reduced to $\frac{2}{3}$. The same ratio can also be expressed as 2 to 3 or 2 : 3.

A **proportion** is a mathematical sentence saying that two ratios are equivalent. For example, a proportion could state that $\frac{800\ \text{wolves}}{1,200\ \text{moose}} = \frac{2\ \text{wolves}}{3\ \text{moose}}$. You can sometimes set up a proportion to determine or estimate an unknown quantity. For example, suppose a scientist counts 25 beetles in an area of 10 square meters. The scientist wants to estimate the number of beetles in 100 square meters.

Example

1. Express the relationship between beetles and area as a ratio: $\frac{25}{10}$, simplified to $\frac{5}{2}$.

2. Set up a proportion, with x representing the number of beetles. The proportion can be stated as $\frac{5}{2} = \frac{x}{100}$.

3. Begin by cross-multiplying. In other words, multiply each fraction's numerator by the other fraction's denominator.

   $5 \times 100 = 2 \times x$, or $500 = 2x$

4. To find the value of x, divide both sides by 2. The result is 250, or 250 beetles in 100 square meters.

Practice

Find the value of x in the following proportion: $\frac{6}{7} = \frac{x}{49}$.

Percentage

A **percentage** is a ratio that compares a number to 100. For example, there are 37 granite rocks in a collection that consists of 100 rocks. The ratio $\frac{37}{100}$ can be written as 37%. Granite rocks make up 37% of the rock collection.

You can calculate percentages of numbers other than 100 by setting up a proportion.

Example

Rain falls on 9 days out of 30 in June. What percentage of the days in June were rainy?

$$\frac{9\ \text{days}}{30\ \text{days}} = \frac{d\%}{100\%}$$

To find the value of d, begin by cross-multiplying, as for any proportion:

$9 \times 100 = 30 \times d \qquad d = \frac{900}{30} \qquad d = 30$

Practice

There are 300 marbles in a jar, and 42 of those marbles are blue. What percentage of the marbles are blue?

Significant Figures

The **precision** of a measurement depends on the instrument you use to take the measurement. For example, if the smallest unit on the ruler is millimeters, then the most precise measurement you can make will be in millimeters.

The sum or difference of measurements can only be as precise as the least precise measurement being added or subtracted. Round your answer so that it has the same number of digits after the decimal as the least precise measurement. Round up if the last digit is 5 or more, and round down if the last digit is 4 or less.

> **Example**
>
> Subtract a temperature of 5.2°C from the temperature 75.46°C.
>
> **75.46 − 5.2 = 70.26**
>
> 5.2 has the fewest digits after the decimal, so it is the least precise measurement. Since the last digit of the answer is 6, round up to 3. The most precise difference between the measurements is 70.3°C.

> **Practice**
>
> Add 26.4 m to 8.37 m. Round your answer according to the precision of the measurements.

Significant figures are the number of nonzero digits in a measurement. Zeroes between nonzero digits are also significant. For example, the measurements 12,500 L, 0.125 cm, and 2.05 kg all have three significant figures. When you multiply and divide measurements, the one with the fewest significant figures determines the number of significant figures in your answer.

> **Example**
>
> Multiply 110 g by 5.75 g.
>
> **110 × 5.75 = 632.5**
>
> Because 110 has only two significant figures, round the answer to 630 g.

Scientific Notation

A **factor** is a number that divides into another number with no remainder. In the example, the number 3 is used as a factor four times.

An **exponent** tells how many times a number is used as a factor. For example, $3 \times 3 \times 3 \times 3$ can be written as 3^4. The exponent 4 indicates that the number 3 is used as a factor four times. Another way of expressing this is to say that 81 is equal to 3 to the fourth power.

> **Example**
>
> $3^4 = 3 \times 3 \times 3 \times 3 = 81$

Scientific notation uses exponents and powers of ten to write very large or very small numbers in shorter form. When you write a number in scientific notation, you write the number as two factors. The first factor is any number between 1 and 10. The second factor is a power of 10, such as 10^3 or 10^6.

> **Example**
>
> The average distance between the planet Mercury and the sun is 58,000,000 km. To write the first factor in scientific notation, insert a decimal point in the original number so that you have a number between 1 and 10. In the case of 58,000,000, the number is 5.8.
>
> To determine the power of 10, count the number of places that the decimal point moved. In this case, it moved 7 places.
>
> **58,000,000 km = 5.8 × 10^7 km**

> **Practice**
>
> Express 6,590,000 in scientific notation.

Reading Comprehension Skills

Each section in your textbook introduces a Target Reading Skill. You will improve your reading comprehension by using the Target Reading Skills described below.

Using Prior Knowledge

Your prior knowledge is what you already know before you begin to read about a topic. Building on what you already know gives you a head start on learning new information. Before you begin a new assignment, think about what you know. You might look at the headings and the visuals to spark your memory. You can list what you know. Then, as you read, consider questions like these.

- How does what you learn relate to what you know?
- How did something you already know help you learn something new?
- Did your original ideas agree with what you have just learned?

Asking Questions

Asking yourself questions is an excellent way to focus on and remember new information in your textbook. For example, you can turn the text headings into questions. Then your questions can guide you to identify the important information as you read. Look at these examples:

Heading: Using Seismographic Data

Question: How are seismographic data used?

Heading: Kinds of Faults

Question: What are the kinds of faults?

You do not have to limit your questions to text headings. Ask questions about anything that you need to clarify or that will help you understand the content. *What* and *how* are probably the most common question words, but you may also ask *why, who, when,* or *where* questions.

Previewing Visuals

Visuals are photographs, graphs, tables, diagrams, and illustrations. Visuals contain important information. Before you read, look at visuals and their labels and captions. This preview will help you prepare for what you will be reading.

Often you will be asked what you want to learn about a visual. For example, after you look at the normal fault diagram below, you might ask: What is the movement along a normal fault? Questions about visuals give you a purpose for reading—to answer your questions.

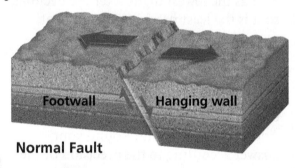

Footwall   Hanging wall

Normal Fault

Outlining

An outline shows the relationship between main ideas and supporting ideas. An outline has a formal structure. You write the main ideas, called topics, next to Roman numerals. The supporting ideas, called subtopics, are written under the main ideas and labeled A, B, C, and so on. An outline looks like this:

Technology and Society
I. Technology through history
II. The impact of technology on society
A.
B.

Identifying Main Ideas

When you are reading science material, it is important to try to understand the ideas and concepts that are in a passage. Each paragraph has a lot of information and detail. Good readers try to identify the most important—or biggest—idea in every paragraph or section. That's the main idea. The other information in the paragraph supports or further explains the main idea.

Sometimes main ideas are stated directly. In this book, some main ideas are identified for you as key concepts. These are printed in bold-face type. However, you must identify other main ideas yourself. In order to do this, you must identify all the ideas within a paragraph or section. Then ask yourself which idea is big enough to include all the other ideas.

Comparing and Contrasting

When you compare and contrast, you examine the similarities and differences between things. You can compare and contrast in a Venn diagram or in a table.

Venn Diagram A Venn diagram consists of two overlapping circles. In the space where the circles overlap, you write the characteristics that the two items have in common. In one of the circles outside the area of overlap, you write the differing features or characteristics of one of the items. In the other circle outside the area of overlap, you write the differing characteristics of the other item.

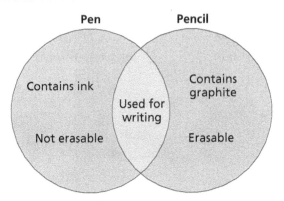

Table In a compare/contrast table, you list the characteristics or features to be compared across the top of the table. Then list the items to be compared in the left column. Complete the table by filling in information about each characteristic or feature.

Blood Vessel	Function	Structure of Wall
Artery	Carries blood away from heart	
Capillary		
Vein		

Identifying Supporting Evidence

A hypothesis is a possible explanation for observations made by scientists or an answer to a scientific question. Scientists must carry out investigations and gather evidence that either supports or disproves the hypothesis.

Identifying the supporting evidence for a hypothesis or theory can help you understand the hypothesis or theory. Evidence consists of facts—information whose accuracy can be confirmed by testing or observation.

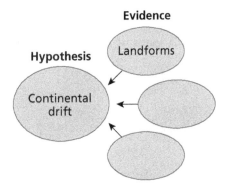

Sequencing

A sequence is the order in which a series of events occurs. A flowchart or a cycle diagram can help you visualize a sequence.

Flowchart To make a flowchart, write a brief description of each step or event in a box. Place the boxes in order, with the first event at the top of the page. Then draw an arrow to connect each step or event to the next.

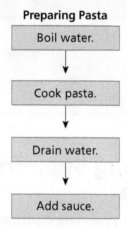

Preparing Pasta

Boil water.

Cook pasta.

Drain water.

Add sauce.

Cycle Diagram A cycle diagram shows a sequence that is continuous, or cyclical. A continuous sequence does not have an end because when the final event is over, the first event begins again. To create a cycle diagram, write the starting event in a box placed at the top of a page in the center. Then, moving in a clockwise direction, write each event in a box in its proper sequence. Draw arrows that connect each event to the one that occurs next.

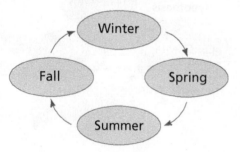

Seasons of the Year

Winter

Spring

Summer

Fall

Relating Cause and Effect

Science involves many cause-and-effect relationships. A cause makes something happen. An effect is what happens. When you recognize that one event causes another, you are relating cause and effect.

Words like *cause, because, effect, affect,* and *result* often signal a cause or an effect. Sometimes an effect can have more than one cause, or a cause can produce several effects.

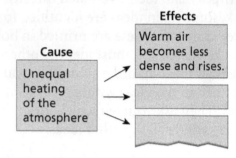

Cause

Unequal heating of the atmosphere

Effects

Warm air becomes less dense and rises.

Concept Mapping

Concept maps are useful tools for organizing information on any topic. A concept map begins with a main idea or core concept and shows how the idea can be subdivided into related subconcepts or smaller ideas.

You construct a concept map by placing concepts (usually nouns) in ovals and connecting them with linking words (usually verbs). The biggest concept or idea is placed in an oval at the top of the map. Related concepts are arranged in ovals below the big idea. The linking words connect the ovals.

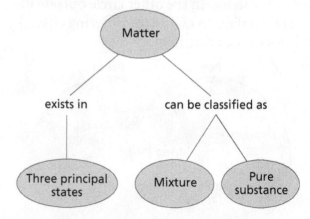

Matter

exists in

can be classified as

Three principal states

Mixture

Pure substance

Building Vocabulary

**Knowing the meaning of these prefixes, suffixes, and roots will
help you understand the meaning of words you do not recognize.**

Word Origins Many science words come to English from other languages, such as Greek and Latin. By learning the meaning of a few common Greek and Latin roots, you can determine the meaning of unfamiliar science words.

Prefixes A prefix is a word part that is added at the beginning of a root or base word to change its meaning.

Suffixes A suffix is a word part that is added at the end of a root word to change the meaning.

Greek and Latin Roots

Greek Roots	Meaning	Example
ast-	star	astronaut
geo-	Earth	geology
metron-	measure	kilometer
opt-	eye	optician
photo-	light	photograph
scop-	see	microscope
therm-	heat	thermostat

Latin Roots	Meaning	Example
aqua-	water	aquarium
aud-	hear	auditorium
duc-, duct-	lead	conduct
flect-	bend	reflect
fract-, frag-	break	fracture
ject-	throw	reject
luc-	light	lucid
spec-	see	inspect

Prefixes and Suffixes

Prefix	Meaning	Example
com-, con-	with	communicate, concert
de-	from; down	decay
di-	two	divide
ex-, exo-	out	exhaust
in-, im-	in, into; not	inject, impossible
re-	again; back	reflect, recall
trans-	across	transfer

Suffix	Meaning	Example
-al	relating to	natural
-er, -or	one who	teacher, doctor
-ist	one who practices	scientist
-ity	state of	equality
-ology	study of	biology
-tion, -sion	state or quality of	reaction, tension

Safety Symbols

These symbols warn of possible dangers in the laboratory and remind you to work carefully.

 Safety Goggles Wear safety goggles to protect your eyes in any activity involving chemicals, flames or heating, or glassware.

 Lab Apron Wear a laboratory apron to protect your skin and clothing from damage.

 Breakage Handle breakable materials, such as glassware, with care. Do not touch broken glassware.

 Heat-Resistant Gloves Use an oven mitt or other hand protection when handling hot materials such as hot plates or hot glassware.

 Plastic Gloves Wear disposable plastic gloves when working with harmful chemicals and organisms. Keep your hands away from your face, and dispose of the gloves according to your teacher's instructions.

 Heating Use a clamp or tongs to pick up hot glassware. Do not touch hot objects with your bare hands.

 Flames Before you work with flames, tie back loose hair and clothing. Follow instructions from your teacher about lighting and extinguishing flames.

 No Flames When using flammable materials, make sure there are no flames, sparks, or other exposed heat sources present.

 Corrosive Chemical Avoid getting acid or other corrosive chemicals on your skin or clothing or in your eyes. Do not inhale the vapors. Wash your hands after the activity.

 Poison Do not let any poisonous chemical come into contact with your skin, and do not inhale its vapors. Wash your hands when you are finished with the activity.

 Fumes Work in a ventilated area when harmful vapors may be involved. Avoid inhaling vapors directly. Only test an odor when directed to do so by your teacher, and use a wafting motion to direct the vapor toward your nose.

 Sharp Object Scissors, scalpels, knives, needles, pins, and tacks can cut your skin. Always direct a sharp edge or point away from yourself and others.

 Animal Safety Treat live or preserved animals or animal parts with care to avoid harming the animals or yourself. Wash your hands when you are finished with the activity.

 Plant Safety Handle plants only as directed by your teacher. If you are allergic to certain plants, tell your teacher; do not do an activity involving those plants. Avoid touching harmful plants such as poison ivy. Wash your hands when you are finished with the activity.

 Electric Shock To avoid electric shock, never use electrical equipment around water, or when the equipment is wet or your hands are wet. Be sure cords are untangled and cannot trip anyone. Unplug equipment not in use.

 Physical Safety When an experiment involves physical activity, avoid injuring yourself or others. Alert your teacher if there is any reason you should not participate.

 Disposal Dispose of chemicals and other laboratory materials safely. Follow the instructions from your teacher.

 Hand Washing Wash your hands thoroughly when finished with the activity. Use antibacterial soap and warm water. Rinse well.

 General Safety Awareness When this symbol appears, follow the instructions provided. When you are asked to develop your own procedure in a lab, have your teacher approve your plan before you go further.

Science Safety Rules

General Precautions

Follow all instructions. Never perform activities without the approval and supervision of your teacher. Do not engage in horseplay. Never eat or drink in the laboratory. Keep work areas clean and uncluttered.

Dress Code

Wear safety goggles whenever you work with chemicals, glassware, heat sources such as burners, or any substance that might get into your eyes. If you wear contact lenses, notify your teacher.

Wear a lab apron or coat whenever you work with corrosive chemicals or substances that can stain. Wear disposable plastic gloves when working with organisms and harmful chemicals. Tie back long hair. Remove or tie back any article of clothing or jewelry that can hang down and touch chemicals, flames, or equipment. Roll up long sleeves. Never wear open shoes or sandals.

First Aid

Report all accidents, injuries, or fires to your teacher, no matter how minor. Be aware of the location of the first-aid kit, emergency equipment such as the fire extinguisher and fire blanket, and the nearest telephone. Know whom to contact in an emergency.

Heating and Fire Safety

Keep all combustible materials away from flames. When heating a substance in a test tube, make sure that the mouth of the tube is not pointed at you or anyone else. Never heat a liquid in a closed container. Use an oven mitt to pick up a container that has been heated.

Using Chemicals Safely

Never put your face near the mouth of a container that holds chemicals. Never touch, taste, or smell a chemical unless your teacher tells you to.

Use only those chemicals needed in the activity. Keep all containers closed when chemicals are not being used. Pour all chemicals over the sink or a container, not over your work surface. Dispose of excess chemicals as instructed by your teacher.

Be extra careful when working with acids or bases. When mixing an acid and water, always pour the water into the container first and then add the acid to the water. Never pour water into an acid. Wash chemical spills and splashes immediately with plenty of water.

Using Glassware Safely

If glassware is broken or chipped, notify your teacher immediately. Never handle broken or chipped glass with your bare hands.

Never force glass tubing or thermometers into a rubber stopper or rubber tubing. Have your teacher insert the glass tubing or thermometer if required for an activity.

Using Sharp Instruments

Handle sharp instruments with extreme care. Never cut material toward you; cut away from you.

Animal and Plant Safety

Never perform experiments that cause pain, discomfort, or harm to animals. Only handle animals if absolutely necessary. If you know that you are allergic to certain plants, molds, or animals, tell your teacher before doing an activity in which these are used. Wash your hands thoroughly after any activity involving animals, animal parts, plants, plant parts, or soil.

During field work, wear long pants, long sleeves, socks, and closed shoes. Avoid poisonous plants and fungi as well as plants with thorns.

End-of-Experiment Rules

Unplug all electrical equipment. Clean up your work area. Dispose of waste materials as instructed by your teacher. Wash your hands after every experiment.

English and Spanish Glossary

A

abdomen The hind section of an arthropod's body that contains its reproductive organs and part of its digestive tract. (p. 52)
abdomen Sección posterior del cuerpo de un artrópodo que contiene sus órganos reproductores y parte de su aparato digestivo.

adaptation A characteristic that helps an organism survive or reproduce in its environment. (p. 8)
adaptación Característica que ayuda a un organismo a sobrevivir o a reproducirse en su medio ambiente.

aggression A threatening behavior that one animal uses to gain control over another. (p. 158)
agresión Comportamiento amenazante que usa un animal para ganar el control sobre otro.

amniotic egg An egg with a shell and internal membranes that keep the embryo moist; a major adaptation to life on land characteristic of reptiles, birds, and egg-laying mammals. (p. 101)
huevo amniótico Huevo con cáscara y membranas internas que mantiene al embrión húmedo; adaptación principal a la vida en la tierra característica de los reptiles, las aves y los mamíferos que ponen huevos.

amphibian An ectothermic vertebrate that spends its early life in water and its adult life on land. (p. 94)
anfibio Vertebrado ectotérmico que pasa la primera etapa de su vida en el agua y la madurez en la tierra.

antenna An appendage on the head of an animal that contains sense organs. (p. 49)
antena Apéndice en la cabeza de un animal que contiene órganos sensoriales.

anus The opening at the end of an organism's digestive system through which wastes exit. (p. 30)
ano Abertura al final del sistema digestivo de un organismo a través del cual se eliminan los desechos.

arachnid An arthropod with two body sections, four pairs of legs, and no antennae. (p. 52)
arácnido Artrópodo con dos secciones corporales, cuatro pares de patas y sin antenas.

arthropod An invertebrate that has an external skeleton, a segmented body, and jointed appendages. (p. 47)
artrópodo Invertebrado que tiene esqueleto externo, cuerpo segmentado y apéndices anexos.

asexual reproduction The process by which a single organism produces a new organism identical to itself. (p. 9)
reproducción asexual Proceso por el cual un solo organismo produce un nuevo organismo idéntico a él.

atrium An upper chamber of the heart that receives blood. (p. 96)
aurícula Cámara superior del corazón que recibe la sangre.

B

behavior All the actions an animal performs. (p. 149)
comportamiento Todas las acciones que realiza un animal.

bilateral symmetry Line symmetry; the quality of being divisible into halves that are mirror images. (p. 13)
simetría bilateral Simetría lineal; la cualidad de ser divisible en mitades que son imágenes reflejas.

biological control A natural predator or disease released into an area to combat a pest insect. (p. 67)
control biológico Depredador o enfermedad natural liberada en un área para combatir una plaga de insectos.

bird An endothermic vertebrate that lays eggs and has feathers and a four-chambered heart. (p. 119)
ave Vertebrado endotérmico que pone huevos y tiene plumas y un corazón de cuatro cámaras.

bivalve A mollusk that has two shells held together by hinges and strong muscles. (p. 43)
bivalvo Molusco que tiene dos conchas unidas por charnelas y fuertes músculos.

C

carnivore An animal that eats only other animals. (p. 42)
carnívoro Animal que sólo come otros animales.

cartilage A tissue that is more flexible than bone. (p. 89)
cartílago Tejido que es más flexible que un hueso.

cell The basic unit of structure and function in living things. (p. 7)
célula Unidad básica de estructura y función en los seres vivos.

cephalopod An ocean-dwelling mollusk whose foot is adapted as tentacles that surround its mouth. (p. 44)
cefalópodo Molusco que vive en el océano, cuyas extremidades se adaptaron a la forma de tentáculos alrededor de su boca.

chordate The phylum whose members have a notochord, a nerve cord, and slits in their throat area at some point in their lives. (p. 80)
cordado Fílum cuyos miembros poseen un notocordio, un cordón nervioso y aberturas en el área de la garganta en alguna etapa de su vida.

circadian rhythm A behavior cycle that occurs over a period of about one day. (p. 162)
ritmo circadiano Ciclo de comportamiento que ocurre en un período de aproximadamente un día.

closed circulatory system A circulatory system in which blood moves only within a connected network of tubes called blood vessels. (p. 31)
sistema circulatorio cerrado Sistema circulatorio en el cual la sangre se mueve sólo dentro de una red conectada de conductos llamados vasos sanguíneos.

cnidarian An invertebrate animal that uses stinging cells to capture food and defend itself. (p. 19)
cnidario Animal invertebrado que usa células punzantes para capturar alimento y defenderse.

colony A group of many individual animals. (p. 22)
colonia Grupo de muchos animales individuales.

complete metamorphosis A type of metamorphosis characterized by four dramatically different stages. (p. 58)
metamorfosis completa Tipo de metamorfosis caracterizada por cuatro etapas muy diferentes.

conditioning The process of learning to connect a stimulus or a response with a good or bad event. (p. 152)
condicionamiento Proceso de aprendizaje que relaciona un estímulo o una respuesta con un suceso bueno o malo.

consumer An organism that obtains energy by feeding on other organisms. (p. 62)
consumidor Organismo que obtiene la energía alimentándose de otros organismos.

contour feather A large feather that helps give shape to a bird's body. (p. 119)
pluma remera Pluma grande que ayuda a dar forma al cuerpo del ave.

coral reef A diverse environment named for the coral animals that make up its stony structure. (p. 22)
arrecife de coral Medio ambiente diverso nombrado así por los animales coralinos que forman la estructura rocosa.

courtship behavior The behavior that animals of the same species engage in to prepare for mating. (p. 159)
comportamiento de cortejo Comportamiento en el que participan los animales de la misma especie en preparación para el apareamiento.

crop An internal organ of many birds that stores food. (p. 121)
buche Órgano interno de muchas aves, donde se almacena alimento.

crustacean An arthropod that has two or three body sections, five or more pairs of legs, and two pairs of antennae. (p. 50)
crustáceo Artrópodo que tiene dos o tres secciones corporales, cinco o más pares de patas y dos pares de antenas.

decomposer An organism that breaks down wastes and dead organisms. (p. 62)
descomponedor Organismo que degrada los desechos y organismos muertos.

diaphragm A large muscle located at the bottom of a mammal's rib cage that functions in breathing. (p. 134)
diafragma Músculo grande ubicado en la parte inferior de la caja torácica de un mamífero que participa en la respiración.

down feather A short, fluffy feather that traps heat and keeps a bird warm. (p. 119)
plumones Plumas cortas y mullidas que atrapan el calor y mantienen al ave abrigada.

echinoderm A radially symmetrical invertebrate that lives on the ocean floor and has an internal skeleton. (p. 70)
equinodermo Invertebrado con simetría radial que vive en el suelo oceánico y tienen esqueleto interno.

ecology The study of how organisms interact with their environment. (p. 62)
ecología El estudio de cómo interactúan los organismos con su medio ambiente.

ectotherm An animal whose body does not produce much internal heat. (p. 82)
ectotermo Animal cuyo cuerpo no produce mucho calor interno.

endoskeleton An internal skeleton. (p. 70)
endoesqueleto Esqueleto interno.

English and Spanish Glossary

endotherm An animal whose body regulates its own temperature by controlling the internal heat it produces. (p. 83)
endotermo Animal cuyo cuerpo regula su propia temperatura controlando el calor interno que produce.

exoskeleton A waxy, waterproof outer shell or outer skeleton that protects the animal and helps prevent evaporation of water. (p. 48)
exoesqueleto Concha externa cerosa e impermeable o esqueleto externo que protege al animal y ayuda a evitar la evaporación del agua.

fertilization The joining of an egg cell and a sperm cell. (p. 9)
fecundación Unión de un espermatozoide y un óvulo.

fish An ectothermic vertebrate that lives in the water and has fins. (p. 87)
pez Vertebrado ectotérmico que vive en el agua y tiene branquias.

food chain A series of events in which one organism eats another and obtains energy. (p. 62)
cadena alimentaria Serie de sucesos en los que un organismo se come a otro y obtiene energía.

fossil The hardened remains or other evidence of a living thing that existed a long time ago. (p. 108)
fósil Restos endurecidos u otro vestigio de un ser vivo que existió hace mucho tiempo.

free-living organism An organism that does not live in or on other organisms. (p. 28)
organismo autónomo Organismo que no vive dentro o sobre otro organismo.

gastropod A mollusk with a single shell or no shell. (p. 42)
gasterópodo Molusco con una única concha o sin concha.

gestation period The length of time between fertilization and birth of a mammal. (p. 136)
período de gestación Tiempo entre la fecundación y el nacimiento del mamífero.

gill An organ that removes oxygen from water. (p. 41)
branquia Órgano que extrae el oxígeno del agua.

gizzard A muscular, thick-walled part of a bird's stomach that squeezes and grinds partially digested food.
molleja Parte muscular, de paredes gruesas del estómago del ave que exprime y muele parcialmente el alimento digerido. (p. 121)

gradual metamorphosis A type of metamorphosis in which an egg hatches into a nymph that resembles an adult, and which has no distinct larval stage. (p. 58)
metamorfosis gradual Tipo de metamorfosis en la que un huevo incubado pasa a la etapa de ninfa con aspecto de adulto, y no tiene una etapa de larva diferenciada.

habitat The specific environment in which an animal lives. (p. 98)
hábitat Medio ambiente específico en el que vive un animal.

herbivore An animal that eats only plants. (p. 42)
herbívoro Animal que sólo come plantas.

hibernation A state of greatly reduced body activity that occurs during the winter. (p. 162)
hibernación Estado de gran disminución de la actividad corporal que ocurre durante el invierno.

host An organism that provides food to a parasite that lives on or inside it. (p. 28)
huésped Organismo que proporciona alimento a un parásito que vive sobre o dentro de él.

imprinting A process in which newly hatched birds or newborn mammals learn to follow the first object they see. (p. 151)
impronta Proceso por el cual las aves o mamíferos recién nacidos aprenden a seguir al primero objeto que ven.

insect An arthropod with three body sections, six legs, one pair of antennae, and usually one or two pairs of wings. (p. 56)
insecto Artrópodo con tres secciones corporales, seis patas, un par de antenas y normalmente uno o dos pares de alas.

insight learning The process of learning how to solve a problem or do something new by applying what is already known. (p. 154)
aprendizaje por discernimiento Proceso de aprender cómo resolver un problema o hacer algo nuevo aplicando lo que ya se sabe.

instinct An inborn behavior pattern that an animal performs correctly the first time. (p. 150)
instinto Patrón innato de conducta que un animal ejecuta correctamente desde la primera vez.

invertebrate An animal that has no backbone. (p. 11)
invertebrado Animal que no posee columna vertebral.

kidney An organ that filters wastes from the blood. (p. 100)
riñón Órgano que filtra los desechos de la sangre.

larva The immature form of an animal that looks very different from the adult. (p. 17)
larva Forma inmadura de un animal que se ve muy diferente al adulto.

learning The process that leads to changes in behavior based on practice or experience. (p. 150)
aprendizaje Proceso que conduce a cambios en el comportamiento basados en la práctica o la experiencia.

lift The difference in pressure between the upper and lower surfaces of a bird's wings that produces an upward force that causes the bird to rise. (p. 129)
fuerza de elevación Diferencia de presión entre la superficie superior e inferior de las alas de un ave, que produce una fuerza ascendente que permite que el ave se eleve.

lung An organ found in air-breathing vertebrates that exchanges oxygen and carbon dioxide with the blood. (p. 96)
pulmón Órgano que se encuentra en los vertebrados que respiran aire, con el que intercambian oxígeno y dióxido de carbono con la sangre.

mammal An endothermic vertebrate with a four-chambered heart and skin covered with fur or hair, that feeds its young with milk from the mother's body. (p. 133)
mamífero Vertebrado endotérmico con un cora-zón de cuatro cámaras y piel cubierta de pelaje o pelo, que alimenta a sus crías con leche materna.

mammary gland An organ in female mammals that produces milk for the mammal's young. (p. 133)
glándula mamaria Órgano en los mamíferos hembra que produce leche para alimentar a las crías.

marsupial A mammal whose young are born at an early stage of development, and which usually continue to develop in a pouch on their mother's body. (p. 136)
marsupial Mamífero cuyas crías nacen en una etapa muy temprana del desarrollo, y que normalmente continúan el desarrollo en una bolsa del cuerpo de la madre.

medusa A cnidarian body plan characterized by a bowl shape and adapted for a free-swimming life.
medusa Cnidario cuyo cuerpo se caracteriza por tener forma de cuenco, y que está adaptado para nadar libremente en el agua. (p. 19)

metamorphosis A process in which an animal's body undergoes dramatic changes in form during its life cycle. (p. 51)
metamorfosis Proceso por el cual el cuerpo de un animal cambia de forma de manera drástica durante su ciclo de vida.

migration The regular, periodic journey of an animal from one place to another and back again for the purpose of feeding or reproduction. (p. 162)
migración Viaje regular y periódico de un animal de un lugar a otro y de regreso al mismo lugar con el propósito de alimentarse o reproducirse.

mollusk An invertebrate with a soft, unsegmented body; most are protected by a hard outer shell. (p. 41)
molusco Invertebrado con cuerpo blando y sin segmentos; la mayoría están protegidos por una concha exterior dura.

molting The process of shedding an outgrown exoskeleton. (p. 48)
muda Proceso de cambio de un exoesqueleto a otro.

monotreme A mammal that lays eggs. (p. 136)
monotrema Mamífero que pone huevos.

notochord A flexible rod that supports a chordate's back. (p. 80)
notocordio Bastoncillo flexible que sostiene el lomo de los cordados.

nymph A stage of gradual metamorphosis that usually resembles the adult insect. (p. 58)
ninfa Etapa de la metamorfosis gradual en la que normalmente el insecto se parece a un insecto adulto.

omnivore An animal that eats both plants and animals.
omnívoro Animal que come tanto plantas como animales. (p. 43)

open circulatory system A circulatory system in which the heart pumps blood into open spaces in the body and blood is not confined to blood vessels.
sistema circulatorio abierto Sistema circulatorio en el que el corazón bombea la sangre en espacios abiertos del cuerpo, y la sangre no se mantiene en vasos sanguíneos. (p. 41)

organ A structure that is composed of different kinds of tissue. (p. 7)
órgano Estructura compuesta de diferentes tipos de tejidos.

P

paleontologist A scientist who studies extinct organisms, examines fossil structure, and makes comparisons to present-day organisms. (p. 110)
paleontólogo Científico que estudia los organismos extintos, examina las estructuras de los fósiles y los compara con los organismos de la actualidad.

parasite An organism that lives inside or on another organism and takes food from the organism in or on which it lives. (p. 28)
parásito Organismo que vive dentro o sobre otro organismo y que se alimenta de él.

pesticide A chemical designed to kill a pest animal. (p. 67)
pesticida Sustancia química diseñada para matar una plaga animal.

pheromone A chemical released by one animal that affects the behavior of another animal of the same species. (p. 157)
feromona Sustancia química liberada por un animal que afecta el comportamiento de otro animal de la misma especie.

phylum One of about 35 major groups into which biologists classify members of the animal kingdom. (p. 10)
fílum Uno de alrededor de 35 grupos principales en los que los biólogos clasifican los miembros del reino animal.

placenta An organ in pregnant placental mammals that passes materials between the mother and the developing embryo. (p. 137)
placenta Órgano de la hembra embarazada del mamífero placentario que permite el paso de sustancias entre la madre y embrión en desarrollo.

placental mammal A mammal that develops inside its mother's body until its body systems can function independently. (p. 137)
mamífero placentario Mamífero que se desarrolla dentro del cuerpo de la madre hasta que sus sistemas corporales pueden funcionar por sí solos.

pollinator An animal that carries pollen from one plant to another of the same species, enabling plants to reproduce. (p. 66)
polinizador Animal que lleva polen de una planta a otra de la misma especie, permitiendo que las plantas se reproduzcan.

polyp A cnidarian body plan characterized by a vase-like shape and usually adapted for a life attached to an underwater surface. (p. 19)
pólipo Cnidario cuyo cuerpo se caracteriza por tener forma cilíndrica, y que generalmente está adaptado para vivir adherido a una superficie submarina.

producer An organism that can make its own food. (p. 62)
productor Organismo que puede producir su propio alimento.

pupa The third stage of complete metamorphosis, in which an insect changes from a larva to an adult. (p. 58)
pupa Tercera etapa de la metamorfosis completa, en la cual un insecto cambia de larva a adulto.

R

radial symmetry The quality of having many lines of symmetry that all pass through a central point. (p. 13)
simetría radial Cualidad de tener muchos ejes de simetría que pasan por un punto central.

radula A flexible ribbon of tiny teeth in mollusks. (p. 42)
rádula Hilera flexible de minúsculos dientes en los moluscos.

receiver A device that receives radio waves and converts them into a sound or light signal. (p. 167)
receptor Aparato que recibe las ondas de radio y las convierte en señales de sonido o de luz.

reptile An ectothermic vertebrate that lays eggs and has lungs and scaly skin. (p. 100)
reptil Vertebrado ectotérmico que pone huevos, y que tiene pulmones y piel con escamas.

response An organism's reaction to a stimulus. (p. 149)
respuesta Lo que un organismo hace como reacción a un estímulo.

S

satellite An instrument that orbits a celestial body, such as Earth. (p. 168)
satélite Instrumento que orbita un cuerpo celeste, como la Tierra.

scavenger An organism that feeds on dead or decaying material. (p. 28)
carroñero Organismo que se alimenta de materia muerta o en descomposición.

sedimentary rock Rock formed of hardened layers of sediments. (p. 108)
roca sedimentaria Roca formada por las capas endurecidas de sedimentos.

sexual reproduction The process by which a new organism develops from the joining of two sex cells. (p. 9)
reproducción sexual Proceso por el cual se forma un nuevo organismo a partir de la unión de dos células sexuales.

society A group of closely related animals of the same species that divide up the labor and work together in a highly organized way. (p. 161)
sociedad Grupo de animales de la misma especie estrechamente relacionados que se dividen el trabajo y lo realizan juntos de una manera altamente organizada.

stimulus A signal that causes an organism to react in some way. (p. 149)
estímulo Señal que hace que un organismo reaccione de alguna manera.

swim bladder An internal gas-filled organ that helps a bony fish stabilize its body at different water depths. (p. 91)
vejiga natatoria Órgano interno lleno de gas que ayuda a un pez con esqueleto a estabilizar su cuerpo a diferentes profundidades.

tadpole The larval form of a frog or toad. (p. 95)
renacuajo Estado de larva de una rana o un sapo.

territory An area that is occupied and defended by an animal or group of animals. (p. 159)
territorio Área que ocupa y defiende un animal o grupo de animales.

thorax An insect's midsection, to which its wings and legs are attached. (p. 56)
tórax Sección media de un insecto, a la que están unidas las alas y las patas.

tissue A group of similar cells that perform a specific function. (p. 7)
tejido Grupo de células semejantes que realizan una función específica.

transmitter A device that sends out signals in the form of radio waves. (p. 167)
transmisor Aparato que envía señales en forma de ondas de radio.

trial-and-error learning A form of conditioning in which an animal learns to perform a behavior more and more skillfully. (p. 153)
aprendizaje por ensayo y error Forma de condicionamiento en el cual un animal aprende a ejecutar un comportamiento más y más hábilmente.

tube feet Extensions of an echinoderm's water vascular system that stick out from the body and function in movement and obtaining food. (p. 71)
pies ambulacrales Extensiones del sistema vascular de agua de un equinodermo que sobresalen del cuerpo y sirven para la locomoción y la obtención de alimento.

urine A watery fluid produced by the kidneys that contains wastes. (p.100)
orina Fluido acuoso producido por los riñones que contiene desechos.

ventricle A lower chamber of the heart that pumps blood out to the lungs and body. (p. 96)
ventrículo Cámara inferior del corazón que bombea la sangre hacia los pulmones y el cuerpo.

vertebrae The bones that make up the backbone of an animal. (p. 81)
vértebras Huesos que forman la columna vertebral de un animal.

vertebrate An animal that has a backbone. (p. 11)
vertebrado Animal que posee columna vertebral.

water vascular system A system of fluid-filled tubes in an echinoderm's body. (p. 71)
sistema vascular de agua Sistema de vasos llenos de líquidos en el cuerpo de un equinodermo.

Index

Page numbers for key terms are printed in **boldface** type.
Page numbers for illustrations, maps, and charts are printed in *italics*.

Index

Index

Page numbers for key terms are printed in **boldface** type.
Page numbers for illustrations, maps, and charts are printed in *italics*.

Acknowledgments

Acknowledgment for pages 178–179: Excerpt from *Dragons and Dynasties: An Introduction to Chinese Mythology* by Yuan Ke. Selected and translated by Kim Echlin and Nie Zhixiong and Penguin Books, 1993. First published in the People's Republic of China by Foreign Languages Press, Beijing 1991–1993. Copyright © Foreign Languages Press, 1991, 1992, 1993.

Staff Credits

Diane Alimena, Scott Andrews, Jennifer Angel, Michele Angelucci, Laura Baselice, Carolyn Belanger, Barbara A. Bertell, Suzanne Biron, Peggy Bliss, Stephanie Bradley, James Brady, Anne M. Bray, Sarah M. Carroll, Kerry Cashman, Jonathan Cheney, Joshua D. Clapper, Lisa J. Clark, Bob Craton, Patricia Cully, Patricia M. Dambry, Kathy Dempsey, Leanne Esterly, Emily Ellen, Thomas Ferreira, Jonathan Fisher, Patricia Fromkin, Paul Gagnon, Kathy Gavilanes, Holly Gordon, Robert Graham, Ellen Granter, Diane Grossman, Barbara Hollingdale, Linda Johnson, Anne Jones, John Judge, Kevin Keane, Kelly Kelliher, Toby Klang, Sue Langan, Russ Lappa, Carolyn Lock, Rebecca Loveys, Constance J. McCarty, Carolyn B. McGuire, Ranida Touranont McKneally, Anne McLaughlin, Eve Melnechuk, Natania Mlawer, Janet Morris, Karyl Murray, Francine Neumann, Baljit Nijjar, Marie Opera, Jill Ort, Kim Ortell, Joan Paley, Dorothy Preston, Maureen Raymond, Laura Ross, Rashid Ross, Siri Schwartzman, Melissa Shustyk, Laurel Smith, Emily Soltanoff, Jennifer A. Teece, Elizabeth Torjussen, Amanda M. Watters, Merce Wilczek, Amy Winchester, Char Lyn Yeakley. **Additional Credits** Tara Alamilla, Louise Gachet, Allen Gold, Andrea Golden, Terence Hegarty, Etta Jacobs, Meg Montgomery, Stephanie Rogers, Kim Schmidt, Adam Teller, Joan Tobin.

Illustration

Sally Bensusen: 56, 58–59; **Patrice Rossi Calkin:** 29, 145, 152; **Kerry Cashman:** 37, 184, 185; **Walter Cutler:** 95; **John Edwards and Associates:** 17, 20t, 21, 27, 36, 42, 43, 49, 76, 81, 101, 119, 120t, 121, 126, 129, 144, 167; **Foerster Interactive Arts:** 19; **Andrea Golden:** 33, 51; **Biruta Hansen:** 156–157; **Fran Milner:** 50, 91; **Karen Minot:** 41; **Paul Mirocha:** 173; **Morgan Cain & Associates:** 93, 141, 199; **Matthew Pippin:** 110; **Ortelius Design Inc.:** 163; **Walter Stuart:** 16, 46, 71, 106, 161; **J/B Woolsey Associates (Mark Desman):** 10, 80, 84–85, 172; **J/B Woolsey Associates:** 31, 150; **XNR Productions:** 166; **All charts and graphs by Matt Mayerchak**

Photography

Photo Research Sue McDermott
Cover Image top, Art Wolfe/Getty Images; bottom, Dale Wilson/Masterfile.
Page vi t, Douglas Faulkner/Corbis; **vi b,** Kim Taylor & Jane Burton/Dorling Kindersley; **vii,** Richard Haynes; **viii,** Richard Haynes; **x,** Claudio Vazquez; **1b,** Rob Walls/Alamy Images; **1t,** John Giustina/Getty Images, Inc.; **2 both,** Mary Ann McDonald/Corbis; **3,** Daniel Lyons/Bruce Coleman.
Chapter 1 Pages 4–5, Deep Sea Photos; **5 inset,** Richard Haynes; **6t,** Richard Haynes; **6bl,** Heather Angel/Natural Visions; **6br,** Heather Angel/Natural Visions; **7,** Neil Fletcher/Oxford University Museum; **8t,** Frank Greenaway/Dorling Kindersley; **8b,** Frank Oberle/Getty Images, Inc.; **9,** Michael Quinton/Minden Pictures; **11,** Wolfgang Bayer/Bruce Coleman, Inc.; **12,** Tom and Pat Leeson; **13tl,** Norbert Wu/Minden Pictures; **13tm,** Andrew J. Martinez/Photo Researchers, Inc.; **13tr,** James Watt/Visuals Unlimited; **13b,** Stuart Westmorland/Corbis; **14,** Tom Brakefield/Corbis; **15,** Michael DeFreitas/Bruce Coleman, Inc.; **19l,** Dale Sanders/Masterfile Corporation; **19r,** G. S. Grant/Photo Researchers, Inc.; **20tl,** Jeff Rotman/www.jeffrotman.com; **20b all,** Dorling Kindersley; **22,** Tim McKenna/Corbis; **22 inset,** Linda Pitkin/Masterfile Corporation; **23,** David B. Fleetham/Tom Stack & Associates, Inc.; **24t,** Richard Cummins/Corbis; **24–25,** Jeff Hunter/Getty Images, Inc.; **26t,** Richard Haynes; **26b,** Dr. Alan L. Yen; **28,** Hans Strand ; **28 inset,** David M. Dennis/Tom Stack & Associates, Inc.; **30,** Sinclair Stammers/Photo Researchers, Inc.; **32,** David Young-Wolff/PhotoEdit; **34t,** Dorling Kindersley; **34b,** Andrew J. Martinez/Photo Researchers, Inc.
Chapter 2 Pages 38–39, Barrett and MacKay; **39 inset,** Richard Haynes; **40b,** Richard Nowitz; **40t,** Corel Corp.; **42r,** Brandon Cole/Visuals Unlimited; **42l,** Digital Vision/Getty Images, Inc.; **44l,** Douglas Faulkner/Photo Researchers, Inc.; **44b,** Norbert Wu/Minden Pictures; **44t,** Ken Lucas/Visuals Unlimited; **45 both,** Dave Fleetham/Tom Stack & Associates; **46,** William Leonard/DRK Photo; **47b,** R.J. Erwin/Photo Researchers, Inc.; **47t,** Richard Haynes; **48b,** Robert A. Lubeck/Animals Animals; **48t,** John Gerlach/Tom Stack & Associates, Inc.; **51,** Dr. P. Wilson/FLAP/Bruce Coleman, Inc.; **52b,** Meckes/Ottawa/Eye of Science/Photo Researchers, Inc.; **52t,** Geoff Dann/Dorling Kindersley; **53b,** Robert Calentine/Visuals Unlimited; **53t,** Tim Flach/Getty Images, Inc.; **54l,** Marty Cordano/DRK Photo; **54r,** Simon D. Pollard/Photo Researchers, Inc.; **55b,** Valerie Hodgson/Visuals Unlimited; **55t,** Robert Calentine/Visuals Unlimited; **57l,** Dorling Kindersley; **57m,** Gregory G. Dimijian/Photo Researchers, Inc.; **57r,** Andrew Syred/SPL/Photo Researchers, Inc.; **60,** Robert A. Lubeck/Animals Animals; **61,** Richard Haynes; **62t,** Richard Haynes; **62–63b,** James P. Rowan/DRK Photo; **63l,** Bob Jensen/Bruce Coleman, Inc.; **63m,** Michael Edergerr/DRK Photo; **63r,** J. Fennell/Bruce Coleman, Inc.; **64l,** Bettmann/Corbis; **64r,** Aberdeen University Library, Scotland/Bridgeman Art Library; **65l,** Robert Frerck/Odyssey Productions; **65m,** Sergio Piumatti; **65r,** Darwin Dale/Photo Researchers, Inc.; **66b,** Geoff du Feu/Getty Images, Inc.; **66t,** John Trager/Visuals Unlimited; **67,** Anthony Bannister/Gallo Images/Corbis; **68–69,** Norm Thomas/Photo Researchers, Inc.; **69t,** Frank Whitney/Getty Images, Inc.; **70,** Richard Haynes; **72l,** Neil G. McDaniel/Photo Researchers, Inc.; **72r,** Brian Parker/Tom Stack & Associates, Inc.; **72–73t,** Kerrick James; **73l,** Brandon D. Cole/Corbis; **73r,** Ed Bravendam/Minden Pictures.
Chapter 3 Pages 78–79, Norbert Wu/Minden Pictures; **79 inset,** Richard Haynes; **80,** Russ Lappa; **81,** Tom Flach/Getty Images, Inc.; **82,** Dave King/Dorling Kindersley; **83l,** Michael Fogden/DRK Photo; **83r,** Frans Lanting/Minden Pictures; **86t,** Gerard Lacz/Animals Animals/Earth Scenes; **86b,** Brian Parker/Tom Stack & Associates; **87,** NHPA/Lutra; **88tl,** John D. Cunningham/Visuals Unlimited; **88tr,** Michael Patrick O'Neil/Photo Researchers, Inc.; **88b,** Animals Animals/Earth Scenes; **89t,** Bruce Coleman, Inc.; **89b,** Animals Animals/Earth Scenes; **89b inset,** Herve Berthoule Jacana/Photo Researchers, Inc.; **90t,** Frank Burek/Animals Animals/Earth Scenes; **90b,** Amos Nachoum/Corbis; **92tr,** Norbert Wu; **92m,** Stuart Westmorland/Getty Images, Inc.; **92bl,** Norbert Wu; **92br,** DRK Photo; **94,** Michael Fogden/Photo Researchers, Inc.; **96,** Gerry Ellis/Minden Pictures; **97l,** Visuals Unlimited; **97r,** Animals Animals/Earth Scenes; **98,** Michael Fogden/OSF/Animals Animals/Earth Scenes; **99t,** Richard Haynes; **99b,** Joe McDonald/Tom Stack & Associates, Inc.; **101,** Jay Ireland & Georgienne Bradley/Bradleyireland.com; **102,** Dorling Kindersley; **103t,** Kim Taylor & Jane Burton/Dorling Kindersley; **103b,** Art Wolfe/Getty Images, Inc.; **104l,** M.C. Chamberlain/DRK Photo; **104r,** Gerald & Buff Corsi/Tom Stack & Associates; **105,** T.A. Wiewandt/DRK Photo; **107t,** Richard Haynes; **107b,** Tom Bean/DRK Photo; **108t,** Ernst Mayr Library of the Museum of Comparative Zoology, Harvard University, ©President and Fellows of Harvard; **108m,** Natural History Museum, London; **108b,** Typ 605.77.700 F, Department of Printing and Graphic Arts, Houghton Library, Harvard College Library; **109t,** Louis Psihoyos/Matrix; **109b,** Andy Crawford/Dorling Kindersley; **112,** Stuart Westmorland/Getty Images, Inc.
Chapter 4 Pages 116–117, Barrett and MacKay; **117 inset,** Richard Haynes; **118t,** Richard Haynes; **118b,** John Downes/Dorling Kindersley; **119,** Russell & Martha Hansen; **121,** Geoff Higgins/PhotoLibrary.com; **122t,** Stephen J. Krasemann/DRK Photo; **122t inset,** Jerome Wexler/Photo Researchers, Inc.; **122b,** Nancy Sheehan/PhotoEdit; **123t,** Kim Taylor/Dorling Kindersley; **123b,** Richard Wagner; **124t,** NHPA/Manfred Danegger; **124bl,** Dave Watts/Tom Stack & Associates, Inc.; **124br,** Gary Griffen/Animals Animals/Earth Scenes; **125l,** D. Allen/Animals Animals/Earth Scenes; **125m,** Stephen J. Krasemann/DRK Photo; **125r,** Wayne Lankinen/DRK Photo; **127,** Richard Haynes; **128t,** Richard Haynes; **128b,** Darrell Gulin/DRK Photo; **129,** Thomas Mangelsen/Minden Pictures; **130,** Frans Lanting/Minden Pictures; **131l,** Michio Hoshino/Minden Pictures; **131r,** Arthur Morris/Visuals Unlimited; **132t,** Richard Haynes; **132b,** Eric Valli/Minden Pictures; **133t,** Hilary Pooley/Animals Animals/Earth Scenes; **133t inset,** Phillip Dowell/Dorling Kindersley; **133b,** Philip Dowell/Dorling Kindersley; **133b inset,** Dave King/Dorling Kindersley; **134l,** Daryl Balfour/Getty Images, Inc.; **134r,** Art Wolfe; **135 both,** Frans Lanting/Minden Pictures; **136t,** Tom McHugh/Photo Researchers; **136b,** Dave Watts/Tom Stack & Associates, Inc.; **137,** Joe McDonald/Visuals Unlimited; **138tr,** Roger Aitkenhead/Animals Animals/Earth Scenes; **138br,** Johnny Johnson/DRK Photo; **138tl,** Stephen J. Krasemann/DRK Photo; **138ml,** Chuck Davis/Getty Images, Inc.; **138bl,** Dave Welling; **139tl,** Dwight Kuhn; **139ml,** Charlie Heidecker/Visuals Unlimited; **139bl,** M.P. Kahl/DRK Photo; **139tr,** Art Wolfe/Getty Images, Inc.; **139br,** Renee Lynn/Getty Images, Inc.; **140,** Johnny Johnson/DRK Photo; **142l,** Dave Watts/Tom Stack & Associates, Inc.; **142r,** Joe McDonald/Visuals Unlimited.
Chapter 5 Pages 146—147, M. Philip Kahl Jr./Photo Researchers, Inc.; **147 inset,** Getty Images, Inc.; **148b,** Michael Fogden/DRK Photo; **148t,** Jerome Wexler/Photo Researchers, Inc.; **149 both,** Heather Angel/Natural Visions; **150,** Lawrence Stepanowicz/Alamy; **151,** Nina Leen/Time Life Pictures/Getty Images, Inc.; **153,** Steve Solum/Bruce Coleman Inc.; **154,** Bernd Heinrich; **156,** Richard Haynes; **157,** Natural Visions; **158b,** John Cancalosi/DRK Photo; **158t,** Art Wolfe; **159,** OSF/David Boag/Animals Animals; **160,** David E. Myers/Getty Images, Inc.; **162,** Kim Taylor/Bruce Coleman, Inc.; **163,** M.A. Chappell/Animals Animals; **164,** Doug Wechsler; **165,** Richard Haynes; **166–167b,** Douglas Faulkner/Corbis; **167t,** Arthur Morris/Visuals Unlimited; **168,** Natalie Fobes/Corbis; **169,** Michio Hoshino/Minden Pictures; **170l,** Steve Solum/Bruce Coleman Inc.; **170r,** Natural Visions; **172,** David Hosking/Getty Images. Inc. **174b,** Roy Parkes/Eye Ubiquitous/Corbis; **174t,** Christie's Images/Corbis; **175b,** Cary Wolinsky/Stock Boston; **175l,** Harry Rogers/Photo Researchers, Inc.; **175r,** Cary Wolinsky/Stock Boston; **175t,** E.R. Degginger/Animals Animals/Earth Scenes; **177,** Wolfgang Kaehler/Corbis; **178–179b,** Christie's Images, Inc./Christie's Images; **179r,** People's Republic of China Giraudon/Bridgeman Art Library; **180,** Xinhua/Liaison/Getty Images, Inc.; **181b,** Duomo/Corbis; **181t,** Keren Su/Corbis; **182,** Tony Freeman/PhotoEdit; **183t,** Russ Lappa; **183m,** Richard Haynes; **183b,** Russ Lappa; **184, 186,** Richard Haynes; **188,** Tanton Yachts; **189,** Richard Haynes; **191t,** Dorling Kinderlsey; **191b,** Richard Haynes; **193,** Image Stop/Phototake; **196, 203,** Richard Haynes.